D0040852

Table Talk

—from—

The Threepenny Review

Table Talk

—from—

The Threepenny Review

~

[EDITED BY]

Wendy Lesser, Jennifer Zahrt, and Mimi Chubb

COUNTERPOINT | BERKELEY, CALIFORNIA

Library of Congress Cataloging-in-Publication Data Is Available

ISBN 978-1-61902-457-1

Cover design by Emma Cofod
Interior Design by E.J. Strongin, Neuwirth & Associates, Inc.

COUNTERPOINT
2560 Ninth Street, Suite 318
Berkeley, CA 94710
www.counterpointpress.com

Printed in the United States of America
Distributed by Publishers Group West

10 9 8 7 6 5 4 3 2 1

CONTENTS

INTRODUCTIONS

The idea for Table Talk came from Leonard Michaels. Lenny, who had been closely involved with *The Threepenny Review* since its inception in 1980, was always coming up with new plans for the magazine, and most of them were horribly impractical. One that I particularly remember, for instance, was his suggestion that we expand into book publishing. "We could bring out novels that no one else wants to publish, sell them for one dollar each, and make a million dollars," he said in his extravagant, vowel-lengthening manner. I gently informed him that this business strategy would cause us to lose our shirts, and he backed off.

But Table Talk, which he came up with about ten years into *Threepenny*'s existence, was an excellent idea, and it has lasted. I don't know whether Lenny took the title from Hazlitt, who used it for several editions of his essays, or from Coleridge, whose literal table talk—that is, his dining-room conversation—was championed by his friends and acquaintances as better than anything he ever put on paper. Whichever. We were both happy to have an allusion to the nineteenth century in our late-twentieth-century magazine.

In their first incarnation, the Table Talk entries were anonymous, or signed just with initials, but we soon decided that was too coy and moved on to fully signed pieces. The only firm rules were that they had to be short (the offical upper limit was a thousand words, though some people have been allowed to exceed it) and that they would appear at the front of the magazine. We never insisted that the material be strictly conversational in mode: *Threepenny* editors know the difference between writing and speech. On the other hand, we always hoped that the tone would be a bit looser and quirkier in these pieces than in the longer *Threepenny* essays.

Some people took to the form with great panache, and these Table Talk reliables duly make more than one appearance in this anthology. Lenny himself, Bert Keizer, and W. S. Di Piero have all been given three selections each because they were all great Table Talkers who racked up many entries over the years. August Kleinzahler, Thomas Laqueur, Arthur Lubow, Irene Oppenheim, Nick Papandreou, and Michael Ryan are also well represented, with two entries each. If I have more than one entry (and I do), it is because my Table Talk count is more than twice as high as that of any other human being on the planet. When deadlines approach and we are short of Table Talks, I write one myself; or else I get my deputy editor to write one, which helps explain why five of these deputies—Mimi Chubb, Kathryn Crim, Francie Lin, Lisa Michaels, and Jennifer Zahrt—also appear here.

It's fun to look through this list of contents and see who shows up on it. Some are those you might expect, the writers who have made *Threepenny* what it is by writing for it frequently over the years. At least twenty of these beloved regulars are here, ranging alphabetically from John Berger to Dean Young. (That Dean Young piece, by the way, started its life as a paragraph in a casual letter he wrote me, and then got turned into a Table Talk piece because I wanted to share with everyone the typical delights of a Dean Young letter.) Others are admired authors whom I managed to snag for the magazine by offering them this one brief assignment; these unusual literary lights include (among others) the Russian-Canadian fiction writer David Bezmozgis, the critic and writing professor Susie Linfield, the novelist Claire Messud, the philosopher Alexander Nehamas, the former labor secretary Robert Reich, and the cultural historian Luc Sante. There are some close friends of mine—Charlie Haas, Tim Savinar—whose dinner-table conversation actually led me to say to them, "That would make a great Table Talk!" And there are people I'd never met or previously heard of, like Douglas Danoff, Mert Erogul, and Ben Merriman, whose pieces simply drifted in through the mail or, lately, the online submissions system. I always tell young writers that Table Talk is the easiest way to get into the magazine, and apparently this is true.

The collection starts in the winter of 1990 because that was when the first Table Talk appeared in the magazine; it stops in the summer of 2013 because we had to stop somewhere, though *Threepenny* has continued to bring out a dozen or more of these pieces every year. The anthology includes less than a third of all our Table Talks to date, with the selections chosen in part for their individual piquance, in part for their variety, and in part for their serendipitous overlaps. This kind of writing represents only one small section of the magazine, not the whole thing, and yet I think it is true to something essential about *The Threepenny Review*. But whether that essential thing is tone, or subject matter, or style, or topicality, or *lack* of topicality, or some inscrutable combination of all those is more than I could say.

For obvious reasons—at least, I hope they will become obvious as you read through—Jennifer Zahrt, Mimi Chubb, and I decided to arrange these pieces chronologically. The selections can be read in any order you choose, but something additional accrues if you read them in the order in which they first came out. We made only one exception to this rule, and that is the final essay: one of Leonard Michaels's early pieces, a favorite of mine.

If he had lived, he would still be trying out ideas in this form he invented, and I thought it only fair to give him the last word as well as the first.

—Wendy Lesser

~

Stacks of every back issue of *The Threepenny Review* can be found resting together on purpose-built shelves in a single room at the *Threepenny* offices. I was born around the same time Wendy Lesser founded the magazine, so this archive of issues effectively compartmentalizes my life into quarterly segments. When given the task of reading every Table Talk ever written for our pages, I began to relive my youth, beginning with the winter of 1990.

For two months, I sat at a glass table with a pile of twenty-three years of *Threepenny* before me. I read each piece in sequence, a total of nearly three hundred Table Talks, with the goal of selecting the most representative and interesting half. (Before we finished, Wendy would further narrow my choices to the ninety-nine found here.) As I encountered each Table Talk for the first time, I was treated to a crash course not only in the history of *Threepenny* as a publication, but also the history of the end of the twentieth century and—most surprising to me—my own perceptions of growing up in America during those years. The references to current affairs of the early Nineties reminded me of what I was doing then, and how *Threepenny* had been thriving throughout my youth, while I was still far too young to know about it.

As I worked through the Table Talks, I was treated to contemporary perspectives on movies I hadn't been allowed to watch as a kid, like Craig Seligman's on *The Silence of the Lambs*. A few issues later, I was flooded with an involuntary and slightly revolting nostalgia for my high school days, brought on by Luc Sante's views on *Pulp Fiction* and Beck's song "Loser." So this, I mused, is what the grown-ups were thinking and writing about while I was busy growing up.

Greater historical events also pierced through, such as the race riots in South Central LA or the coup d'état in Haiti in the early Nineties. I read W. S. Di Piero's haunting words on shootings in movie theaters and thought to myself that not much has changed. As the Table Talks progressed through my college and graduate school years, I found myself comparing my own perceptions with those of the authors, but the shock was less intense than with those written during the early years of my development.

I'm guessing that many of the Table Talks in this volume will resonate with readers of any age in similar unexpected ways. Every text carries traces of the time in which it was composed, but *Threepenny*'s Table Talks by nature foreground this temporal trace. What appears topical at the moment, what the authors think they are writing about, always seems to contain another element, some unexpected observation or point that juts out from the text as we encounter it years later. Reading these Table Talks now sharpens our view of the world in ways the authors could never have anticipated.

The prevalence of technology throughout these selections serves to highlight this. As time passes, it can be charming to read about our old relationships to things like the answering machine or CDs. Some authors overtly champion outmoded but still useful technology, like the typewriter, or even clotheslines. Perhaps the most entertaining moments come when authors reveal their earnest reactions to technology that no longer applies to our lives today. But some observations remain true. Over fifteen years have passed since Arthur Lubow's 1997 lament about the digitization of modern life, and yet his words seem as pertinent as ever to what we're experiencing now. We are reminded that these concerns have been with us for longer than we're used to remembering.

To borrow an idea Michael Gorra evokes here: as we read these Table Talks, it's as if they are also reading us. They mirror back to us who and where we were during the transition from the Nineties into the Aughts and now the Teens. They show us, whether explicitly or by omission, all the historical and technological and lyrical shifts we've made along the way. I'm sure this sensation is more acute for younger readers like me, who are only as old as the magazine itself or perhaps even younger; but longtime readers will also notice how the quarterly reflections on life and letters contained in the Table Talks record more than just philosophical musings on quotidian matters. Those observations contain windows that let us glimpse entire decades unfolding, reminding us how aspects of history and literature still resonate with us, at levels both personal and global.

—JENNIFER ZAHRT

~

I was first exposed to Table Talk—and to *The Threepenny Review*—through an undergraduate course Wendy Lesser taught at Princeton University, titled "Autobiography and Criticism." Our first class assignment was to write a short piece about something that had happened to us. We were to write about it in as interesting a way as possible.

In other words, we were to take a crack at producing Table Talk essays of our own.

I wrote an essay I felt proud of, about the drug-addled downfall of one of my father's old friends. I emailed my draft to Wendy a week or so before the deadline. She wrote me back almost immediately to say that the piece wasn't working. It was sentimental and fell into cliché, she said, and I probably shouldn't attempt the subject I'd chosen before I was about forty years old. She suggested that I try writing about something else, and added that as I wrote I might think simply of trying to write one true sentence after another.

I re-read my essay, and when I did I saw at once what Wendy meant. It had a wide-eyed, breathless falsity, relying on pseudo-innocence for cheap effect. It might sound strange, but before then it had never occurred to me to try for truth on the page—tonal, stylistic, and narrative truth, as well as mere factual truth—just as it hadn't occurred to me that what I'd first written had been fundamentally dishonest. I was electrified by the idea that written truth could (and did) take place sentence by sentence, accrue paragraph by paragraph, deepen page by page.

I tried again. This time I wrote about the summer before I left for college, when I'd spent days retraining an ex-racehorse and nights reading *Anna Karenina*. Once again, I emailed my work to Wendy and once again she got back to me right away with comments. This time she was more positive. She pointed out several places in the essay that needed expansion or clarification, and once again I set to work. When she returned my final draft to me in class a few weeks later, hidden between the pages was a note on *Threepenny*'s cream and gold stationery inviting me to publish my essay in its pages, as a Table Talk. I was astonished—and thrilled. It was my first publication. I had no clue then that nearly nine years later I would have the opportunity to become *Threepenny*'s deputy editor.

I've gone into all this because I think it illustrates something of the pleasurable democracy of Table Talk, where a young, unknown writer might appear alongside an older, famous writer—and where, unless you glanced ahead, you might not necessarily guess which was which until you reached the italicized name at the end. I remember getting a funny shiver of delight from the asterisk that followed my essay, separating it from the essay that came next, when I first saw it in the magazine. That asterisk felt to me like a lovely textual translation of the beats that sometimes take place in the best conversations, where listening and speaking verge into each other seamlessly. I liked that it belonged equally to my essay and the next, binding them together as much as separating them. I know that as you read this selection of entries, you'll find evocative juxtapositions to be one of the great joys of Table Talk.

You'll also find my writerly lesson borne out: in each of these pieces, truth unfurls itself sentence by sentence. One true sentence follows another, faithful to their writers' endlessly various voices, subjects, and aims. Whether those true sentences meander, in praise of digression, from Flaubert to the untidiness of lived experience (Claire Messud), or wind and bristle wittily through a childhood apartment cluttered with books and paintings (Javier Marías), or quest windmill-tiltingly for the lost arm of a Soviet statuette of Don Quixote (Julia Zarankin), all are voyages that begin somewhere unusual and bring you, the reader, somewhere unexpected. You will find idiosyncrasy here. What you *won't* ever find is the kind of laziness of voice that Wendy uncovered for me in that first failed class essay.

With that in mind, I think you will be hard-pressed to find a better, more wide-ranging primer for what it might mean to write as yourself—using that declarative, private, testifying, slippery, loose, prickly, vast, and tiny word "I" as your jumping-off point. I say this in spite of the fact that in several of these pieces the word "I" never actually, literally appears: I expect that as you read you'll agree with me that even in these cases it's hovering close by, implicit, just out of sight.

—Mimi Chubb

Table Talks

A movie imprisons your eyes. It acts on you, not you on it. Hence, you don't "see" or "look at" a movie. You *watch* it the way a cat watches a bird, until the cat strikes, kills, eats. Movie criticism often exhibits an aggressive, personal, killing response. In a famous attack on the famous movie critic Pauline Kael, much was made of her visceral response to movies, as if these were inappropriate. In fact, they are most appropriate, since you watch a movie—a predatory watching—with the primordial intention of eating and killing. It figures that the basic form of movies, literally and figuratively, is the chase, and that people would love to eat during movies, subconsciously anticipating the kill, the meal of blood. For the same reason, movie actors are more threatened by their audience than any other performers. No performer is more masochistic or suicidal. Marilyn Monroe, known for these qualities in her life and art, was "loved" to an extraordinary degree by the camera, the cannibal eye of her watchers, hordes gathered in the darkness, eating, eating. Too much was made of her sex appeal; too little of her edipeal. In a recent movie called *Chocolat*, which flows through eating scenes, the brilliant director Claire Denis conflates the erotic with the gustatory. The effect is as powerful as it is subtle, very like *chocolat*. Compare the rich metaphoric implications of the eating scenes of *Chocolat* with the stupidity, the gross unreflectiveness, of the eating scenes in *Tom Jones*.

—LEONARD MICHAELS
WINTER 1990

~

"I may say that only three times in my life have I met a genius and each time a bell within me rang and I was not mistaken . . . ," Gertrude Stein has Alice say in *The Autobiography of Alice B. Toklas*. The fact that this remark is devious self-flattery (Gertrude Stein being one of the three listed geniuses) does not make it one whit less memorable. The comment sprang to mind during Merce Cunningham's brief remarks, delivered after the screening of his dance videotapes at UC Berkeley in September. Cunningham is one of the century's geniuses—as a dancer, as a choreographer, and as an articulator of what he's doing in that choreography. And he brings back the root meaning of the word, in terms of *place of origin* (as in the genius, the spirit, of a place). For what Cunningham has done is to invent a dance language of which he is the only native speaker.

Watching *Story* (a rare 1964 film of Cunningham performing with his dancers in Finland) and *Blue Studio* (a somewhat later video in which he dances with up to five versions of himself), one couldn't help sensing that here, at last, was the essential meaning behind Cunningham's technique. What seems pure abstraction in other bodies is concreteness itself in his. At the root of his performance as a dancer is the notion of *articulation*—each muscle moved individually and expressively, each gesture full of speech. Yet the speech that Cunningham has invented does not refer outward to anything else; the gesture *is* the meaning, articulating itself.

Cunningham has taught generations of dancers to perform his works, and many of his company members move beautifully and with great precision. But, compared to him, they are a little like actors speaking a foreign language they don't fully understand, or even (at times) like perfectly guided automatons expressing someone else's ideas. Merce Cunningham has managed to create a "private language"—that so-called impossibility which the philosopher Gilbert Ryle subsumed under the notion of "the ghost in the machine." Such philosophical sneers can be answered with the quite unsneering observation that Cunningham's dancers are the machines for which he himself is the motivating ghost, the presiding spirit, the genius. He admits as much in the 1987 piece *Fabrications* (also presented at Berkeley this fall); here Cunningham performs the role of an aging Prospero figure, while his company members are his "fabrications"—a word simultaneously suggesting machines, lies, and the delicate tissues of art.

—Wendy Lesser
WINTER 1990

~

I remember climbing the long steep flight of stairs from Broadway to the ballroom of the Palladium, climbing quickly in my eagerness and yearning for the music and what I'd see, and then I'd stand in shadows along the edge of the dance floor, and I'd listen to Machito or Tito Puente all night. I did nothing but listen and watch the dancers, and it seemed good enough, or almost good enough. There were others like me who never danced, just loved the scene, and were much awed by the women in their tight skirts and ferocious high heels, which made their legs look good flashing on the dance floor. This was in the late Forties, at the corner of Broadway and 53rd Street in Manhattan. Next door was Birdland, the most famous jazz club in America, celebrated in a song that was beautifully rendered by Billy Eckstine: "Lullaby of Birdland . . . ."

Dances come and go—lindy hop, twist, jerk, L.A. hustle—but the dancing you see in Latin clubs has remained much the same. It's true the musicians now use electronic instruments, and they make you suffer amplification, something you expect only from rock bands, where nuance is nonexistent, rhythms simplistic, and lyrics best unheard. But, according to aficionados, a far more serious concession to American popular culture is that dancers now start on the first beat, on one—as if mambo were a kind of waltz—rather than on the second beat, closer to the heart of Afro-Cuban feeling.

Antonio Benítez Rojo, contrasting Caribbean and European culture, describes the waltz as the dance of imperialism, covering ground, conquering territory, and he finds it irreconcilable with Afro-Cuban rhythm, which goes nowhere except to pleasure, or joy in being. He's probably right, and so are the aficionados who detest the waltzing mambo; but I love the scene no less than when I was a kid. I go to see it Tuesday nights at Kimball's in Emeryville, or I drive into San Francisco, on weekends, to Cesar's

Latin Palace. The dancing still looks sensuous, passionate, and formal. The music still seems to seize the dancers and make itself visible in their hips and legs. I suppose there can never be a Fred Astaire of salsa—though there are some sublimely graceful *salseros*—because there is really no "dancing to" this music. It is a music of possession. It enters the dancers' bellies, quickened by the congas' abdominal slap. The rhythms derive from the religious rituals of the Yoruba people. They are part of a language addressed to their ancestors and the gods.

Without rhythm there is nothing. You couldn't walk, let alone make a sentence or write a poem, without rhythm. Even the worst sentence requires it to go from beginning to end. Nothing happens without it. The deep vehicle of meaning is rhythm. It is prior to words.

—LEONARD MICHAELS
SUMMER 1990

~

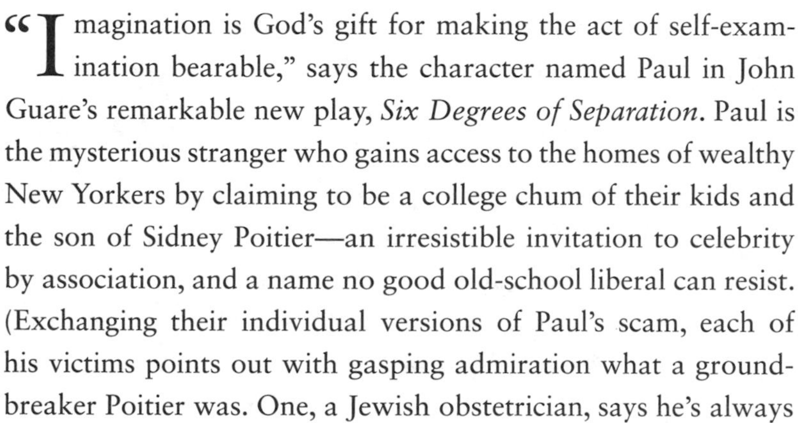

"Imagination is God's gift for making the act of self-examination bearable," says the character named Paul in John Guare's remarkable new play, *Six Degrees of Separation*. Paul is the mysterious stranger who gains access to the homes of wealthy New Yorkers by claiming to be a college chum of their kids and the son of Sidney Poitier—an irresistible invitation to celebrity by association, and a name no good old-school liberal can resist. (Exchanging their individual versions of Paul's scam, each of his victims points out with gasping admiration what a groundbreaker Poitier was. One, a Jewish obstetrician, says he's always identified with the black actor's triumph.) Paul brings each person whose life he invades a weird mixture of fantasy and reality. For Trent, who picks him up on the street, and whose high-school yearbook and treasure trove of information about his classmates grease Paul's forays into the aristocratic world Trent grew up in, he's a dream lover who shares his bed for three months and then disappears with all Trent's electronic equipment. For Rick, who's tumbled into the city with his wife Elizabeth (both are aspiring actors from Utah), he's the embodiment of Manhattan romance. Rick squanders the household savings on an evening he and Paul spend on the town, which culminates in a midnight carriage ride and a thrilling seduction, leading in turn to Rick's guilt-ridden suicide. For the New York socialites—parents of Trent's private-school acquaintances—whose doors Paul knocks on with fabricated tales about being mugged on the street, he combines the articulate, cultivated veneer they find comfortably familiar with an appreciative sweetness (he engages in conversation with them, he cooks them dinner, he entertains their guests) that their own angry, rebellious children never exhibit. "He wanted to be us—everything we are," one of them explains with wonder.

Paul isn't the protagonist of Guare's play (which was suggested by a true incident that occurred in the early Eighties to friends of his); profoundly mysterious, his own peculiar balance of shrewdness and delusion left largely unexplained, he's its catalyst, the way the Nick Nolte character is in Paul Mazursky's *Down and Out in Beverly Hills*. *Six Degrees*' central character is Ouisa (short for Louisa) Kittredge. When Paul shows up on their doorstep, she and her art-dealer husband Flan are preparing to host a rich South American friend whose backing they're hoping to gain for a deal to snag a coveted Matisse. Paul's charm casts a spell on the evening; the deal goes through, and Ouisa and Flan drift off to bed in the happy expectation of making cameo appearances in the film of *Cats*, which Paul says his dad will begin filming in New York the next day. Entering his room early the next morning, however, Ouisa finds a hustler fellating him and—over Paul's eloquently pleaded explanations—she and Flan throw him out. The next thing they know, their friends are coming around with similar stories. And he's not out of Ouisa and Flan's life, either: he tells his new friends from Utah he's Flan's bastard son ("the son of his hippie days, his freedom rider days"), so when Elizabeth loses Rick and her savings, it's Flan she comes to, demanding retribution.

Guare has conceived Ouisa as a revamped version of a Philip Barry heroine—Linda Seton in *Holiday* or Tracy Lord in *The Philadelphia Story*—who learns the necessity of wrestling with the accepted wisdom of her upbringing and holding onto whatever she can find in her life that's of genuine value. She also learns, like Tracy, that she's chosen the wrong husband, a man who—to use Ouisa's terms—is all form and no color, while she's all brush strokes, color without structure. Paul is a somewhat abstracted version of the outsider (i.e., outside of the upper crust) who effects that confrontation, like Johnny Case or Macaulay Connor. It's amazing to see Guare's lunatic lyricism and his free-ranging stylistic vocabulary (direct address to the audience, manipulation of time, footnoting of famous names, dreams and imagined conversations interwoven with traditional dialogues, as well as gleeful puns and promiscuous meanderings through the glittering corridors of language and literature, drama and painting and politics) swirling on top of the rock-solid high-comedy conventions that form the foundation of his play. You'd never guess the elements would fuse so brilliantly—but then, you never do with Guare, whose glorious (stated) experiment to wed Feydeau and Strindberg in his first major play, *The House of Blue Leaves*, led to such improbable mergings as Noel Coward and sci-fi (*Marco*

Polo Sings a Solo), or Ibsen, Shakespeare, Poe, and the Transcendentalists (the *Lydie Breeze* plays). While most American playwrights choose to work within narrower and narrower confines, Guare stretches out; an Elizabethan in his soul, he's in love with the endless *variety* of theater. Even the title *Six Degrees of Separation* is rich with possibilities. Referring to the notion (voiced by Ouisa) that each of us is separated from everyone else by six people, it evokes the play's take on the seductiveness of celebrity as well as its suggestion that the imagination of others can lead you back into yourself.

The problem with Jerry Zaks's production at Lincoln Center is that, bustling and attractive as it is, it's not staged as a Barry-like comedy of manners. The performers need to sparkle; only Stockard Channing does, as Ouisa (and Paul McCrane is superbly touching in the small role of Rick). Without the cast it deserves and a director who truly comprehends everything Guare's up to here, what remains are the play and Stockard Channing's depth and intelligence and confident high style. They're more than adequate: I walked away thinking that nothing I'd seen in the New York theater in several years had stirred so many different kinds of emotional and intellectual responses.

—STEVE VINEBERG
FALL 1990

~

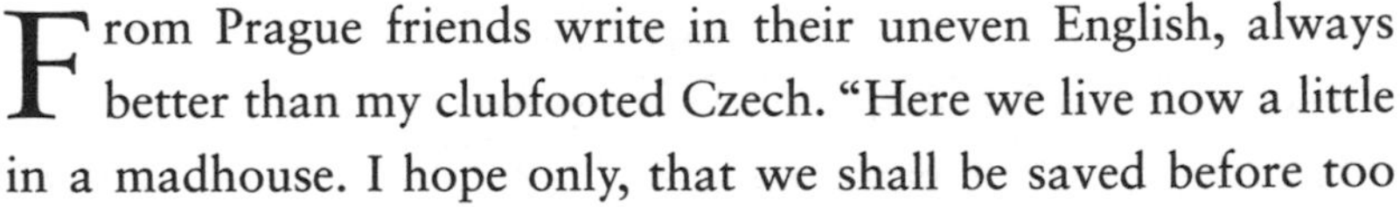

From Prague friends write in their uneven English, always better than my clubfooted Czech. "Here we live now a little in a madhouse. I hope only, that we shall be saved before too great idiocy. To teach and to learn the democracy is the most hard work in the world," reports one, a professor who was purged from Charles University twenty years ago. Later she joined the Magic Lantern Theater, long before it became the headquarters of the revolution.

Toward the beginning of last summer I was standing in the third courtyard of Prague Castle, watching Havel on the ceremonial balcony, a wet wind stirring his pale unpresidential curls as he surveyed the fond crowd. Havel's appearance was the centerpiece of a post-election "Carnival of Democracy." Giant witches and harlequins loped about on stilts, not one tendentiously identified with clownish old-regime ogres, and opposite the cathedral a military orchestra rendered, not too strenuously, Czech folk melodies. None of the citizens of the Velvet Revolution shoved for position, and strangers shared umbrellas in the intermittent drizzle: natives claim that Czechoslovakia's climate is changing as quickly as the politics.

There followed another month of moody Prague weather, from a heat wave of Mediterranean intensity to storm clouds piling in a Baltic chill. Every day new hordes of tourists beat the canonical cobbles from the Clock Tower over Charles Bridge and up to the Castle. At the base of the long slope of Wenceslas Square, a horse market before it was a political forum, tourists were mixed with punk flâneurs and black-market moneychangers. Across from the Powder Tower, the Czech history exhibit, which had spilled from a huge hall onto streetside kiosks, had been dismantled. Praguers had been effectively reminded of people and events long suppressed—starting with philosopher Tomás Masaryk, founder of the First Czech Republic, a non-person under the Communists, and including full accounts of the brutal Stalinist show trials and the 1968 invasion. At the back of the dark exhibition hall, near a film of the recent revolution, a row of the transparent plastic armors of Husák's riot police had an eerie immanence.

But already in July controversies were piling around the new government—Havel's freighted encounter with Kurt Waldheim, and the ever-present Slovak nationalism, embodied in a new memorial plaque at the birthplace of World War II Slovakian fascist leader Josef Tiso. Grumbling was general about price rises, a pre-Kuwait gasoline shortage, and the slow pace of legal and economic reform. For example, how were the courts, still operating in the old legal frame with many of the old personnel, to deal with thousands of petitions for return of private property? Meanwhile, some wondered aloud or in print whether secret police operations had truly been suspended. Obviously the carnival was over and the hard part beginning.

Maybe we wish Havel well not just because of his singular displays of wisdom and humor, courage and humility—qualities now rare among western leaders—but because of our fantasies fulfilled in his cabinet of writers and professors, architects and artists. These are people we can, so to speak, identify with, and they know each other as well as, say, the faculty of a small American college. But after losing twenty or more years of their productive lives under Communism, they now have not just personal and artistic freedom, but the heavy weight of making democracy and free enterprise work beyond that first revolutionary exhilaration. Limp in a plush wing chair in a huge empty salon in Prague Castle, one of Havel's closest advisors, a writer I had met at a PEN meeting in Berkeley, gave me a wan smile. "Exciting, yes," she said. "*Too* exciting." Of course she has no time for her own work, not even for the biography of Havel that she has contracted to finish by the end of the year. And she has to live with the hourly awareness that, as she succinctly put it, "Everything could fall apart at any time."

Still, as the summer passed, crowds were clustering happily around sidewalk tables set up as ad hoc markets for fresh piles of novels and essays by formerly banned writers like Josef Skvorecky and Havel himself. Despite an ongoing paper shortage, they were usually priced at less than a dollar. One noon I walked, loading my bag en route with new books, to meet a friend for lunch at U Zlaty Had. The Golden Serpent is where coffee was first introduced in Prague, and the booths are probably more uncomfortable than they were in the eighteenth century, but they give a certain illusion of privacy. Yet because in Prague everyone seems to know everybody, one tends to lower one's voice when talking politics, even these days. Ironically enough, after examining my booty my friend went on to confirm something I'd heard: that Czech publishers without government subsidies will be printing mainly moneymaking bestsellers, native and foreign, along with the technical books now in demand for the retooling of antiquated Czech industry. The latest publishers' lists, especially of scholarly books, poetry, and serious fiction, were already showing drastic cuts. Moreover, artists were complaining about inflated rents for work space. Even theaters, Prague's particular pride, were in trouble without government subsidies. "What if," my friend said roguishly, "the Golden Age of Czech arts turns out to have been under the Communists?"

After the initial honeymoon of Czech democracy—Masaryk's enlightened First Republic, squeezed between the Hapsburgs and the Nazis—the Communists took over in 1948. Then came forty years of the most completely nationalized economy in Eastern Europe. And although totalitarianism killed personal freedom, polluted the environment, and destroyed Czech craftsmanship and individualism in countless ways, there was full employment and enough beer, pork, and dumplings to go around. Everyone had a job, whether or not everyone worked. Often I saw half-a-dozen silver-haired women supervising a matinee movie audience of four or five. But the bankruptcies and layoffs of a free market economy were beginning. Already there were homeless in parks and at the railroad stations.

"Our revolution has not failed," said Havel to the crowd in Wenceslas Square marking the August anniversary of the 1968 Warsaw Pact invasion. "*Proste*, simply, it is not finished."

—FRANCES STARN
WINTER 1991

~

For textual maniacs, the crucial table has to be the one that has been evicted from *Henry V*. The Hostess tells of the death of Falstaff:

> Nay sure, hee's not in Hell: hee's in *Arthurs* Bosome, if euer man went to *Arthurs* Bosome: a made a finer end, and went away and it had beene any Christome Child: a parted eu'n just betweene Twelue and One, eu'n at the turning o'th' Tyde: for after I saw him fumble with the Sheets, and play with Flowers, and smile vpon his fingers end, I knew there was but one way: for his Nose was as sharpe as a Pen, and a Table of greene fields.

Must we take the First Folio's word for it? The paltry Quarto keeps mum here, ending at "one way."

People have tortured this Table to get it to explain itself. Racked brains have envisaged a table covered with the green cloth usual in counting houses; a memorial tablet pointed in Gothic fashion in the green fields of a cemetery; and an engraving of Sir Richard Grenville. But, famously, most editors now accept the inspired emendation of Pope's Dunce, Lewis Theobald: "and a' babbled of green fields." The handwriting people can tell you how the presumed "babld" could have been misread as "Table." Anyway, the interrogators have ways of making Falstaff talk. Of making Table talk.

Table talk, then. Thiselton suggested "Tatld," as a slightly likelier piece of penmanship than "babld" (sharp as a pen, this Thiselton). And F. W. Bateson put in some good words for the good word suggested to Theobald by a "Gentleman sometime deceas'd": the plain word "talkd." Bateson pointed out that when the Quarto rendered down this speech, it substituted for the Folio's "and play with Flowers" the words "And talk of flowers." So perhaps Theobald was a touch too inspired, and we should settle for "and a' talk'd of green fields."

But then is it just a coincidence that there should indeed be such a thing as Table Talk, given that the Hostess's Table finds itself emended either to "talk'd" or to a word—"babbled"—that means talked? As soon as "Table" is replaced by a word that means, or is, "talk'd," you might wonder whether what originally went wrong was not that something got misread but that something got left out. For "Table" read "talk'd"? Or: After "Table," *add* "talk'd"? "And a' table talk'd of green fields."

The Hostess spends her life among tables and among table talk. Falstaff had spent much of his life likewise, and in dying he rounded on his great drink and "cried out of sack." And "table talk" cries out to be made a verb, the verb "talk" being so acceptable. By the nineteenth century, there is no problem about saying "table talkers."

Shakespeare liked making play with "table talk." In *The Merchant of Venice*, Lorenzo and Jessica banter each other.

> LORENZO: I will anone, first let us goe to dinner?
> JESSICA: Nay, let me praise you whle I have a stomacke?
> LORENZO: No pray thee, let it serve for table talk, Then how some ere thou speakst 'mong other things I shall digest it.

The *Oxford English Dictionary* ("talk at table; familiar conversation at meals") cites it from 1569 and 1608; in the transferred sense ("a subject for table-talk; a theme for general conversation"), the dictionary has an example from one of Shakespeare's favorite books, North's translation of Plutarch:

> Antonius commanded him at the Table to tell him what wind brought him thither, he answered, That it was no Table-talk, and that he would tell him to morrow morning fasting.

But the instance which is actually starting to make the whimsical floater of this notion believe that there may be something in it is the occurrence in Sir Philip Sidney's *Apology for Poetry* (1595). Sidney praises poets for

> not speaking (table talke fashion or like men in a dreame) words as they chanceably fall from the mouth, but peyzing each sillable of each worde by iust proportion according to the dignitie of the subiect.

The delirious dying Falstaff is like a man in a dream, words falling from the mouth; he is, moreover, a soldier, and six lines earlier Sidney has spoken of a soldier. And immediately following this about table talk, Sidney has a sequence of which the first sentence musters words which are colored with death ("Anatomies" and "condemnable" and "sentence") and where the run of thirty lines depends for its momentum on one reiterated word:

> to what immediat end soeuer . . . the final end . . . priuate end . . . the highest end . . . the end of well doing . . . next end . . . his farther end . . .

—and as the last of all "the ending end."

What Sidney does grandly, the Hostess was to do modestly, within the space of five lines:

> a made a finer end . . . vpon his fingers end . . .

The conversational move from "a finer end" to "his fingers end" is casually corporeal, dextrous; and "finer end," of which the main sense is simply that Falstaff will have done better than end in Hell, is touched in this death-scene with finality too and may have been prompted by the thought of "final" in relation to "end." In which case, it might have been prompted by Sidney's very words "the final end," in the immediate vicinity of that touching parenthesis of his about inconsequential utterance, "(table talke fashion or like men in a dreame)."

I have a dream, that future editions of *Henry V* will have a note:

> [*babbl'd*] *Theobald*; Table *Folio*; talk'd *Gentleman sometime deceas'd*; table talk'd *Ricks*.

—Christopher Ricks
spring 1991

~

The buzz you get from a movie with a grisly subject is a kind of reward: the more a shocker exhilarates, the less it disturbs. We leave the poetic masterpieces of horror—a *Vampyr*, a *Vertigo*—exalted by the gruesome poetry; on a grungier level, we cackle at the excesses of a *Dawn of the Dead*, a *Texas Chainsaw Massacre*. Beauty on the one hand, evil fun on the other.

But a deeper, meaner horror bubbles up out of some movies. In such cheap productions as the original *Night of the Living Dead*, the horror grows out of a fundamental ugliness that grows, in part, out of the cheapness. Production values—or, more generally, aesthetic values—distance us and thus comfort us. Flatness is creepier. Flatness was the striking novelty in *Henry: Portrait of a Serial Killer*, though *Henry* had expressionistic elements (like its music and its consciously artful camera set-ups) that came straight out of the chiller tradition. The recent Franco-Dutch production *The Vanishing* is so determinedly flat that you're hardly even aware that it's a chiller—until too late. *The Vanishing* is malignant and upsetting, and you walk out sick at heart; next to it, *The Silence of the Lambs*—a funhouse you exit feeling happily spooked—seems almost innocuous. Films like *Henry* and *The Vanishing* achieve their clunky, disquieting horror not by stylizing or poeticizing evil but by throwing it at you, like mud; a viewer may end up feeling soiled, violated.

The peculiar theme of *The Vanishing* is the terrible need to know. A vacationing woman (Johanna Ter Steege) disappears, without a trace, from a highway rest stop; her companion (Gene Bervoets) searches for her, and goes on searching, and on and on, growing so blistered with curiosity that when, after three years, her abductor finally shows up at his door, he voluntarily puts himself in the psychopath's hands. Anything, he tells himself, is better than not knowing—and at the end, horribly, he knows.

On a metaphorical level, the movie is grimly nihilistic. (It recalls the nightmare about God in *Through a Glass Darkly*, in which the dreamer waits and waits to be admitted to God's presence and then finally, when she is ushered through a door, finds herself face to face with a giant spider.) But *The Vanishing* never pushes its metaphors; they, like everything in this poisonously efficient movie, have been scaled down to an apparently modest level. The director, George Sluizer (who collaborated with Tim Krabbé on adapting Krabbé's novel *The Golden Egg*), keeps you mildly intrigued, mildly interested—curious, but never really scared—right up until the inexorable, inescapable, awful end.

As a work of art, *The Vanishing* is shapely, elegantly wrought, almost seamless, and certainly effective. But is it successful?—which is to say, is it any good? It has garnered plenty of admiration. Terrence Rafferty, for example, writing in *The New Yorker*, credited it with "the elusive but unshakable poetry of nightmare." Poetry, though, is precisely what *The Vanishing* lacks. (Unshakability it has.) If it offered some poetry, just a little beauty or warmth, you might be able to hold it at a distance and admire it as an object of art. But the aesthetic is mundane and understylized—unexceptional—and the flatness gives it a this-world credibility that allows it to sneak up on you. What marks *The Vanishing* is its singlemindedness, which was characteristic of *Henry*, too, but it's flatter than *Henry*, in which the mangled corpses pile up rather baroquely. *The Vanishing* sacrifices all the satisfactions of horror movies—the dark beauty, the electric charge—in order to gain its single point, and it gains it with a vengeance. But as you lie awake later, wishing you could get it out of your head, possibly wishing you hadn't gone at all, you may wonder what, exactly, the point really is.

The Silence of the Lambs—directed by Jonathan Demme and closely based on Thomas Harris's novel—belongs, on the other hand, right in the pounding Hollywood Guignol tradition; its psychos are so flamboyant that you want as much of them as you can get. Anthony Hopkins, as the witty and murderous Dr. Hannibal Lecter—evil incarnate—has about as much fun as an actor can have overacting. In *Henry*, by contrast, Michael Rooker plays the killer as a man committed to a harsh, distasteful job, as though killing were his responsibility, his cross to bear. And though Raymond Lemorne (Bernard-Pierre Donnadieu), the teacher who executes the scheme at the heart of *The Vanishing*, complacently informs one of his victims that he's a sociopath, he's a stodgy one, planning out his crime, over months, so methodically that he might as well be doing his taxes. Maybe that's what makes his sadism so unbearable: its lack of imagination, its creative torpor. It has no spontaneity, no vigor, and certainly no poetry; and it gives Lemorne (a grating presence on the screen) nothing like the mad high that Hannibal the Cannibal derives from a dinner of fava beans and census-taker's liver, or that Jame Gumb (Ted Levine) gets from peeling the skin off his victims. The preposterousness of these Thomas Harris creatures defangs the horror. At least, it ought to. A lot of reviewers have treated the movie as a serious, even devastating psychological shocker, but it's too garishly imagined to be convincing; the serial killers who show up in the papers don't have anything like Jame Gumb's originality. On its highly stylized level—and Demme's mastery of style goes far beyond anything Harris approaches with his typewriter (Harris's forte, which is for morbid detail, is something the movie has to forfeit)—*The Silence of the Lambs* is rattling, but unless you have a low shock threshold you can laugh about it the minute the movie ends.

But can you laugh about Jame Gumb? Because his transexualism, or pseudo-transexualism, comes across as warped homosexuality, Demme's movie has been accused (sometimes bitterly) of homophobia. Yet the character is too grotesquely conceived to be taken all that seriously. The picture isn't credible on any level, and this lack of credibility is what allows the audience to relax—morally speaking, at least—and have a good time. (If Jame Gumb were as colorless as Henry or as Raymond Lemorne, he would be lethally offensive.)

The film's heroine, an FBI trainee named Clarice Starling (Jodie Foster), isn't very credible, either: Foster concentrates so fully on Clarice's nervous uncertainty that she makes her seem practically inept. Moviegoers who have been defending Demme's intentions on the ground that he has created a feminist hero don't seem to care that Clarice is no match for Lecter, or that when she finally confronts Gumb, her finesse—which Harris demonstrates on the page—looks, in Demme's version, like beginner's luck. But even if Clarice doesn't know what she's doing, she does have good impulses, and you can't help liking her for them. Jonathan Demme has good impulses too; his good impulses are his claim to fame. He handles Clarice with dignity (he has even spoken of *The Silence of the Lambs* in terms of blows against the patriarchy), but he treats Lecter with dignity as well, even with awe, and his feelings for Jame Gumb come closer to fascination than to contempt. Which is a stroke of luck for the audience, since it allows you to enjoy these psychopaths in a way you can't enjoy Raymond Lemorne. It's impossible to believe that Demme could have malice toward gay people. He doesn't even have malice toward his serial killers.

—CRAIG SELIGMAN
SUMMER 1991

The world of *The Brothers Karamazov* which the dying Father Zosima enjoins Alyosha to sojourn in is characterized by unmediated rage of an intensity conducive to murder, with special emphasis on father-murder. Dmitri, at the Karamazov family gathering in Father Zosima's cell, has no sooner expressed his regret for his "brutal rage" in the Snegiryov incident than, promptly provoked by his father, he gives it unrestrained voice: "Why is such a man alive? Tell me, can he be allowed to go on defiling the earth?" Later that day, he breaks into his father's house, clutches the war-whooping old man by the hair, flings him to the ground, and kicks him "two or three times with his heel in the face." "Damn it all," brother Ivan whispers to Alyosha afterwards, "if I hadn't pulled him away, perhaps he'd have murdered him."

It is from its pronounced contrast to this patricidal rage of the grown men that the nine-year-old Ilyusha's "mighty anger" in defense of his father against his schoolfellows' daily contumely takes on, in Alyosha's eyes, its great moral significance—great then, and all the greater in light of the events transpiring in the adult world in the remaining two months or so of Ilyusha's life. The murder of old Karamazov has been accomplished. Dmitri and Ivan, both desiring their father's death, have brought it to pass; the father-hatred which permeates the world of the novel has brought it to pass. Ivan, at Dmitri's trial, naming Smerdyakov and himself as the joint murderers of his father, turns upon the court: "Who doesn't desire his father's death? . . . They all desire the deaths of their fathers." The fifteen-year-old Lise has already observed this. "Everybody loves his [Dmitri's] having killed his father," she tells Alyosha, who agrees, "There is some truth in what you say about everyone." Fetyukovich, Dmitri's defense attorney, is himself so delighted by the idea that, though he actually makes a convincing case for Smerdyakov as the murderer, he cannot resist going on to argue in justification of his client's alleged patricide: "Such a father as the murdered old Karamazov cannot be called a father and does not deserve to be. Filial love for an unworthy father is an absurdity, an impossibility." For this, the vindication of a son's right—failing his father's ability to show proof of deserving filial love—to look upon his father "as a stranger, and even as an enemy," Fetyukovich reserves his greatest eloquence; and for this he receives from "a good half" of the audience—including the honored elders of the town ("old men with stars on their breasts"), and, even more ominously, the prescriptive custodians of the young, "the fathers and mothers present"—the most thunderous applause.

Who, then, is to defend the children, to arm the rising generation against the perils besetting them in this world so avid to champion father-hate, father-murder, to jettison the old life-and-soul-saving pieties? The author, in his foreword, foresees the reader's asking such "unavoidable questions" about his hero as "What has he accomplished?" If Alyosha's influence on the adult world is arguable (though he affects everyone he associates with), what he has indubitably accomplished, as we witness in its most dramatic and concentrated form in the scene with which the novel concludes, is the amendment of the boys—an ongoing process epitomized in the person of the manifestly endangered and dangerous Kolya Krasotkin, their acclaimed leader. Only now, with the introduction of Kolya into the narrative, and face-to-face with this thirteen-year-old eminence, does Alyosha—whom we have heard nothing of since his leaving the monastery for good, three days after Father Zosima's death—reappear on the scene, the "one man in the world who can command Nikolay

Krasotkin." In Alyosha Kolya finds his authentic measure of manhood.

Manhood, wherein it resides, what signalizes it in the child, what best sustains and safeguards it in the man, is the core theme of Alyosha's farewell address to the boys ("about twelve of them") at Ilyusha's stone, just after the funeral. The impulse from Alyosha's soul that moves him to make his speech is prompted by his total recall of a certain scene at that stone, described to him there in private by Snegiryov some two months earlier, of how Ilyusha, inconsolable, weeping and hugging his disgraced father, had cried, "Daddy, Daddy, how he insulted you." But this is not for the boys' ears. The image he evokes of Ilyusha for the boys to lay to their hearts forever is one of heroic proportions. "He was a fine boy, a kind-hearted, brave boy, he felt for his father's honor and resented the cruel insult to him, and stood up for him." This, he intimates, with perhaps a glance at Kolya's self-serving feats of daring, is what courage, what manliness, is. "And so in the first place, we will remember him, boys, all our lives." Character monumentalized by a deed. It is this deed of Ilyusha's—how boldly the diminutive ragamuffin stood up for his father, "his unhappy, sinful father," alone, against the whole school (not to mention that world beyond school that sanctions Fetyukovich's new-fangled conditions for filial devotion)—and, in its redemptive wake, the feeling he inspired in his schoolfellows here in his last days, the "good and kind feeling" uniting them all, to which Alyosha returns full-circle at the end of his speech.

He returns to it by way of a short homily on the moral power (intimated to him by his own early recollection of his mother, and conclusively affirmed by Father Zosima in his last conversations) of "some good, sacred memory preserved from childhood." It is just such a memory, "good for life in the future," that Alyosha is fore-arming the boys with here; one which, he predicts, will prevent "the cruelest and most mocking of us" from ridiculing in adulthood his feeling young self, will keep that young self alive in the grown man and save him perhaps from great evil. Out of the raw material of their experience of Ilyusha ("at whom we once threw stones, do you remember, by the bridge?") in all its phases ("how we buried Ilyusha, how we loved him in his last days, and how we have been talking like friends all together, at this stone") he is fashioning that sacred memory and implanting it in them as a permanent moral touchstone. Similarly, in the process of calling their attention to the loving feeling ("which we shall remember and intend to remember all our lives"), he is refining and developing the feeling and reinforcing their unity. "Just now," he says, in reference to Kolya's crushing put-down of Kartashov (who, for all his bashfulness, has lately had the temerity to challenge comparison with his chief), "Kolya said to Kartashov that we do not care to know whether he exists or not. But I cannot forget that Kartashov exists and that . . . he is looking at me now with his jolly, kind, happy little eyes." And next to Ilyusha's exemplary courage and generosity, it is not only Kolya's special virtues but Kartashov's too that Alyosha holds up for the boys' emulation. Thus, as Alyosha's speech draws to its close and the boys take up their antiphonal chorus, the voice that cries out "Karamazov, we love you!" is "probably Kartashov's"; but their hearts are so harmonized by now ("'We love you, we love you!' they all caught it up") that any one of their voices speaks for them all.

Still, as Alyosha, having made the memory of Ilyusha safe for as long as these boys live, now commits it to eternity, it is none other than Kolya, the erstwhile atheist ("Of course, God is only a hypothesis"), who raises the subject of man's immortality: "Karamazov, can it be true what's taught us in religion, that we shall all rise again from the dead and shall live and see each other again, all, Ilyushechka too?" Thus prompted, putting the finishing touch to the memory, Alyosha opens the heavens: "Certainly we shall rise again, certainly we shall see each other and shall tell each other with joy and gladness all that has happened!" Certainly, certainly. Upon this belief depends the very survival of humankind. Scrap the belief in immortality, and virtue would have no cause to exist, iniquity would know no restraint, everything would be lawful. So Ivan wishfully argues, and so he effectively demonstrates. He says there is no God, no immortality, "none at all. Absolute nothingness"; and directly out of that ("It was following your words I did it," Smerdyakov tells him at last), riding on Dmitri's opportune fury, comes the murder of their father.

By no manner of means could Alyosha, for all the dying Father Zosima's desperate urging, have prevented that catastrophe. Only when they have wrecked themselves are his brothers accessible to his ministrations. The murder is actually taking place while the risen Father Zosima, in Alyosha's beatific vision, is bidding him, joyfully and without haste, "Begin your work, dear one, begin it, gentle one!" But it is with the boys, not his brothers, though they are made of the same Karamazov clay and heir to the same Karamazov passions, that Alyosha is at work the next time we see him; and with them, completing that piece of work, the last time we see him, in this sublime scene with which the author completes the novel barely three months before his death.

—Deirdre Levinson

FALL 1991

~

"Let's go slumming," sang the Ritz Brothers in the 1937 movie *On the Avenue*. The Avenue was the Bowery, the southern reach of Third Avenue in New York, where the composer of the song's music, Irving Berlin, had got his start quite a few years before as a singing waiter, Izzy Baline; and when the smart set wanted to go slumming in the 1930s that was apparently where they went. I wandered through it by chance on my first unescorted exploration of Manhattan in 1954, but by then it was just a wide dirty street with a lot of poor drunks passed out on the sidewalks, still roofed by the El in its last year. Fifty years earlier Henry James had gingerly paid it a visit, guided by a live Jew. He records his adventure in *The American Scene*, an exasperating description of his visit to the United States in 1904. By this point of his career his great gift is for the suggestive abstraction (he says of New York City that its "real appeal . . . is in that note of vehemence" sounded by its sheer unstoppable activity), and his weakness is in a lack of specification: though he is fond of saying that something or other "fairly bristles" with life, he seldom emerges from his cloud of preliminaries long enough to observe the nature, let alone the detail, of the bristling. His genteel distaste for the Lower East Side and for Jews in general is pronounced, but we'll never find out from him what it felt like to be walking on those streets.

As an antidote to James's lofty evasions, a friend recommended Luc Sante's recent book *Low Life* (Farrar, Straus, and Giroux, 1991, $27.50), and it was as good as a tonic. Indeed, Sante could be referring to James when he says that during the last century "it became the fashion to visit New York's lower depths, which usually meant a rapid escorted stroll on the Bowery, to be followed by diary jottings of the appalling mix of races and the lack of fastidiousness in dress to be found there." His account of the poor in Manhattan 1840–1920, which reverts again and again to the Bowery as its natural center of activity, certainly provides bristle, for it consists almost entirely of historical, statistical, anecdotal, and mythological particularization. A chronicler who loves gossip, Sante tells me all the things I have wanted to know about the city my feet have studied in every subsequent visit, and I begin to understand what it might have felt like to live there in the times of Melville or Stephen Crane. In that most discontinuous of cities he yet believes in continuity, showing you how the past and the present interpenetrate, describing himself at night alone on a deserted street, where "the past can be seen as if through a smeared window," pointing out the old uses of existing structures.

On the Bowery just off Houston Street, for example, a building still stands which was once McGurk's Suicide Hall, a bar so famous for its suicides *in situ*, committed mainly by prostitutes at the end of the line, that tourists visited it in the morbid hope of witnessing one in progress. The bar welcomed the reputation but found the event itself an embarrassment: "suicide attempts were so common that the waiters, upon getting an indication of same, would form a flying wedge and hustle the party out before she (or occasionally he) succumbed." These are the same waiters who would "line up in their aprons and harmonize to 'The Curse of an Aching Heart'." Such stories accumulate into a fascinating and beautifully assembled record of the gusto and misery that made up eighty years of a great city.

Of course, I am not alone in being a sucker for this kind of thing. However recent city-romanticism may be, its appeal is now as obvious as that of nature-romanticism (which is not that old itself). It too is largely literary in origin. I first felt it for London not just because I lived there but because I lived there and read *Bleak House* when I was fifteen. I recognized the city I lived in—it still had its pea-soup fogs then, smog so dense that once or twice I couldn't see more than a yard or two in front of me when coming home from school—but Dickens also made me realize that I lived in a place where anything could happen. The city is cruel and monstrous; my pulse quickens when I think about it. In Baudelaire I could read of evening approaching in Paris, when

> La prostitution s'allume dans les rues,

and though I had never been there, I knew I loved Paris—it too was the City. And New York!—New York in a sense tops London and Paris at their own game; it is, says Sante, "an attraction-repulsion mechanism so extreme no one could have made it up." Absurdly seductive in its bruised glamour, the City offers a promise of promiscuous excitement that is equally an appetite for life and a contempt for it. Short of the death-wish, it is the ultimate romanticism. James too had been susceptible to it once, when he set down the unrefined and grimy London of *The Princess Casamassima*.

—THOM GUNN
WINTER 1992

~

I recently moved from Los Angeles to a hillside in California's Napa Valley. Here, my nearest neighbor lives across the road. And perhaps because it's a dead-end road two miles from the nearest grocery, or simply because we do not live wall to wall, there's a lot of interchange between us about mail, or about who needs milk, or about the fickle collection of vehicles we depend on to get anywhere.

This neighbor's first name is Sarah Kate, but she prefers the unadorned initials SK, so that's what we all call her. Though SK is good at doing lots of different things, her talents tend to be of the sort that don't bring in much money, so she is always looking for work. Usually this means walking up to the counter of someplace like the video store in St. Helena with a standard, "You need any help?" They never do.

"I'm too weird," SK says. And it is true that, with her denim jacket with an "Impeach Bush" button on the lapel and her home-cropped hair topped with a baseball cap, she might seem like a risky prospect to the local tradesfolk.

A few weeks ago, however, SK appeared at my door waving the classified section of *The Napa Valley Register*. "Got an interview," she announced as she triumphantly pointed out an ad. "DELIVERY," it read. "We need you to deliver telephone directories in your local community." SK slapped the paper down on my table. "Right," she said. "Now that's something I can do."

The interview was set for ten-thirty the next morning. At around ten, I watched SK climb into her orange Chevrolet pickup truck (from a now-defunct line Chevrolet blunderingly dubbed "LUV") and head out for the thirteen-mile drive to the stipulated Napa fairground location. I didn't see her again until it was about six PM and already dark. She phoned from across the road to tell me I must have put hot ashes on the ash pile because it was on fire. By the time I got over, she'd already hosed the pile down to a smolder.

"Lousy day," she said. "I did great on the test. But then they say I'll get paid about fifteen cents a book for this route that they claim should take three hours. Well, I've been at it more than four hours now and I'm maybe a third of the way through." I suggested she just bring the rest of the books back and get paid for what she'd done. She shook her head, saying that she'd contracted for the route and if it wasn't completed she didn't think she'd get anything at all.

There's no arguing with SK about legal fine points, so I said, "Two has got to be faster. What about if tomorrow I go along?"

"Yeah," she agreed. "That might work."

The next day we set off at nine-thirty, just late enough to let the heavy morning fog turn misty. SK's route was near where we live in the Oakville–Rutherford area; she's lived up here for eighteen years and knows the area well. Still, it was hard going. The route sheets, which I now held, listed each residence by number. This being a rural place, however, many of the houses don't have numbers, or there are houses behind houses, which means that even if there are numbered mail boxes on the road, matching them to structures can be tricky. Also, because this is wine country, a lot of rich people live around here, and we'd often be delivering four or five books (one for each phone line) to enormous, eerily empty mansions a mile into the vineyards, or hidden among the trees and twisting roads of the hills. Or we'd find ourselves among the low barrack-like buildings that, when there was work, housed the grape-pickers and pruners. These too tended to be strangely empty. The only sign that people lived there might be some clothes hanging on a back line, or a few children's toys in front of one of the cabins. Usually the whole place had only one phone line. Since our route sheet would stipulate that the single phone book due them be left at "Building A," we'd poke around, finally choosing a doorway where we hoped the book would eventually meet up with the phone.

There is an art and etiquette to delivering phone books. On a rural route such as ours, one of the more artful aspects was dealing with dogs. Now, the Hazard Evaluation Form SK had been given prominently listed dog bites as a "Potential Occupational Safety/Health Hazard," and advised us not to "go into any area where there is a dog that is not fenced or tied up." Inasmuch as there were dogs at virtually every place we were supposed to deliver books, we developed our own technique to deal with this problem. When confronted by a barking dog, SK would tentatively put her hand out of the truck window. If the dog lunged, we'd move on. If the animal stayed put, SK would soothe it with remarks like "Good dog" while I leapt out the other side and tried to get the book to the door. This worked pretty well, though at one house where we thought there were only a couple of dogs to be pacified, others kept appearing, until I found myself surrounded by four large, noisy dogs, all of whom were comfortingly overweight (they couldn't be too hungry) but were threatening and persistent nonetheless.

When confronted by all that barking and fur—I mean, these were big Shepherd-type dogs—I had virtually thrown the book toward the house, but in more pastoral circumstances I'd carefully prop the book against the hinge side of the door. SK said they'd been shown a video about that; it was so people wouldn't trip over the books when they came out their doors and sue the phone company. I also tried to leave the books where they couldn't get rained on and, if I was unable to get to an actual door, I'd put a book in a yellow plastic phone-company bag and hook it to a gateway or one of those punch-in-the-number boxes at the entrance of many of the big houses. At one of the fancier places, the security box was located in a real red English phone booth, so I left the books—they had a lot of phone lines—right there.

By the time we made it to the English phone booth, it was mid-afternoon. We'd backlooped once. SK had noticed a field where the grapevines were still unpruned and we went back so she could ask if they needed help on their pruning crew. They didn't. That was okay. SK expected it. It was when we stopped for coffee and she bought a copy of the *San Francisco Chronicle* that she really blew up. She read me part of a sports-section article about some Australian doctor saying that if Magic Johnson played on the Olympic All-Star team he'd advise the Australian players to stay home. SK threw the paper in my direction, slammed her fist on the dashboard, and started off. She said "Idiots!" a lot of times, with each time punctuated by a *thwap* on the gas pedal, until I thought we were going to end our delivery careers by slamming into a tree. But we didn't. She calmed down.

By four-thirty, when it was turning dusk, we were on Walnut Drive with around fifteen names still on our list. By this time we'd seen just about every kind of house: mobile homes with plastic windmills decorating a front patch of grass; one ramshackle place that might once have been a farm but was now surrounded by fields full of the rusting carcasses of every vehicle or appliance the household had ever owned; a gate that said "Llama House," where SK said they had planned to raise llamas but never got any; and a Buddhist retreat way up in the hills, where we delivered the phone book to a white-domed yurt.

We stopped when it got too dark to see whatever numbers there were. We still had three names to go on Walnut Drive (SK did them the next morning) and three people we couldn't find. That evening SK grimly calculated that counting the two days, she'd spent twelve hours total on the route (I'd been volunteering), driven over 150 miles, and used up a full tank of gas. For this she was contracted to receive $39.42 for 318 books delivered to 248 addresses. There was no gas or mileage allowance.

When I pointed out that what they were going to give her came to less than the required minimum wage, SK brightened right up. So I wrote a letter for her to hand in, stating that she was entitled to receive twelve hours pay at the minimum wage of $4.25 per hour. This didn't come to much more than she'd originally been promised, but she felt better about it and they didn't argue. In fact, they said they were having a distribution of business phone books the next month and offered her a route. She said she'd think about it.

—IRENE OPPENHEIM
SUMMER 1992

~

Alice is my student. She's white, twenty-three, married with one child, and pregnant with her second. Her father's a famous Caltech physicist; her husband, also a student, comes from a well-to-do family. By her own description, Alice has never had to think about money. It has always been there and it always will be. She is part of the American aristocracy.

I've taught many children of the American aristocracy—at Southern Methodist University, at Princeton, at the University of Virginia. What's unusual about Alice is her character. She works in nursing homes and treatment centers for abused children and regards this as a privilege, a way to enrich her life. The night of the Rodney King verdicts, after Reginald Denny's skull was smashed with a brick on live television on the corner of Florence and Normandie, Alice went down to a nursing home in South Central to get the old people out of the area. She went because, besides the threat of fire, their lungs can't stand the smoke. Three old people with emphysema died. Her husband went with her with a gun tucked into his pants. He managed to talk a few of his friends, Marines with burr cuts, into going along. Alice says there is really only one reason they weren't harmed. One of the

Crips happened to have a grandfather in the nursing home, and had recruited members of the gang to help get everybody out. Alice said it was pretty strange to see the burly white Marines working side by side with the Crips. She lives in Irvine, where I teach and she goes to school, a "planned community" physically untouched by the riots; she was in South Central from Wednesday to Sunday, her child at her parents' house, and when she got back to Irvine she slept for thirty hours. She's still six-and-a-half months pregnant, at the stage where her navel enters the room a few minutes before she does. When I asked her how she felt, she said, "I feel lucky not to have had to stay home and watch it on TV."

What makes Alice Alice? I don't mean to idealize her. She has been my student in four courses (she wants to be a poet), but I really don't know her. Some people would say what she did was irresponsible. She risked not only her own life but her unborn baby's. The child she already has could very easily be an orphan right now. All this for a bunch of old poor people with a few years left in a neighborhood where crack addicts urinate and throw bags of shit out third-story windows? Alice would say no. Alice would say she did it for herself.

I have been trying to understand this. Does Alice value other people's lives as much as her own? "Of course not," she said. "The only person who did that was Jesus." From her point of view, what she did wasn't heroic. When I asked her why she did it, she said, "I had no choice." You may have had a choice, I may have had a choice, but Alice had no choice.

She's not starry-eyed or mawkish or evangelical (Auden is her favorite poet; she's a bit of an Anglophile and loves elegant ironies). She said it was a lot easier to go to South Central for four days than to do something hard over a longer time, to always be loving to the people she loves.

Her idea of giving is not a new idea, but it was moving to hear of it enacted so dramatically, and in this town. Nothing could be more unlike Tinseltown, whose animating principle has always been Me Me Me and, when possible, more Me. A few days after I heard Alice's story, I heard another story, about an actor who was filming in South America during the week of the riots. Besides his seven-figure salary, he demanded first-class airplane tickets for his wife and children and maid and nanny and secretary and personal assistant and girlfriend, and two apartments—one for his family and one for himself so he could be "alone."

I'm sure he is alone, all the time. It's easy to see how bewildered someone else is. And it's easy to blame someone else for the riots, especially since we have a president who doesn't know what a bar code is—which indicates a little difference between his experience of money and that of people in South Central, the difference between having so much money other people do your shopping (cooking, cleaning, washing) and having so little money your stomach clenches as your groceries flash across the scanner. If you can't buy what you need to live, the lack of money is slow murder, and soul-murder.

That's reality in South Central, but it's also an anxiety for most Americans. We act out of the fear of deprivation, which is cultivated in us. We earn a living. We have to take care of ourselves and our families. We vote our pocketbooks. We confuse self-interest with selfishness.

Instead of we, I should say I. I'm just beginning to understand the depths to which I am still an all-American boy. Alice said, "I almost called you. We needed big guys to help." I'm a big guy, all right, but I also saw on TV the windshields being smashed, the white people being pulled from their cars and beaten. I'm not that big. I was scared enough behind my locked door in Santa Monica. I saw the pictures of the police watching the looting because they couldn't stop it. The iron curtain between the two distinct societies had been ripped, and it was frightening.

My experience of money is different from Alice's. My parents went through the Depression; fear of the lack of money tormented my father during my childhood. He hated his job but was terrified of losing it. I didn't feel poor but I always felt strapped, as if a tidal wave could hit our house at any moment and sweep us into poverty. It's as difficult for me to give without expectation of reward as it is to feel I have value because I'm alive, because I'm a human being, not because I've "earned" it, not because of anything I've accomplished, not because of the way other people respond to me in these terms.

Alice has this ability and a strong faith. I asked her if she had been scared. "Scared to death," she said. "But I knew God wasn't going to let me die." Famous last words. Then the Crips were there. You can call it luck or you can call it Providence. It matters very much what you call it, but it doesn't matter for the point I'm trying to make. Which is this, from Chekhov: "There's only one method: compassion down to your fingertips." Chekhov meant method of writing, but he knew that to write it you have to feel it, for yourself and for others, and that you can't feel it for yourself unless you feel it for others.

I don't know if my compassion will ever reach my fingertips. I hope so, for my own sake. I do know that we must do something right now about South Central, forty-five percent of children living below the poverty line, half the men unemployed, the stacked deck, the degradation and hopelessness. And that it's not for their sake we should do it, but for our own. We have been divided from ourselves for too long, and it shows itself in the most intimate ways: not just in the way the rich treat the poor but in the way adults treat children; not just in the way different races feel about each other but in the way men and women feel about each other. Our communal life pervades our private life, and vice-versa, and they are both rooted in the same cultural assumptions that are exploding in our faces. No one is responsible for causing our problems. They are too old and too deep for that. But we are all responsible for dealing with them, in whatever way we can. For Chekhov, this meant squeezing the serf's blood out of his veins, and his public acts—the schools, the free medical care, and the writing—were his transfusions. What he did didn't change Russia and didn't change the world, but it changed him, and it gave a few people life and still does.

—MICHAEL RYAN
FALL 1992

~

Two days before I met him, Pedro had purchased his first suit—a cheap navy one—in Lima. Shortly after he arrived at our home in Minneapolis, he showed me a worrisome wrinkle in the sleeve.

"Is there anything we can do about this?" he asked.

Grateful to have been presented with a small and manageable problem, I (who despise ironing) ironed with a sense of accomplishment and solidarity.

Pedro was born in Belgium and his given name is Pierre Ruquoy. He is a missionary priest who runs Radio Enriquillo, a radio station in the Dominican Republic.

The Dominican Republic shares the island of Hispaniola with its neighbor, Haiti. Although the inhabitants of both countries are of largely African descent, the languages of the two countries differ.

The official language of the D.R. is Spanish. In Haiti, although French is the official language, most Haitians speak Creole. (Creole appears to be a mixture of French and Spanish and African dialects, a secret language of resistance created by African slaves.)

After the September 30, 1991 coup d'état, in which President Aristide was physically removed from his office and homeland, one of the first acts of the Haitian military was to muzzle the press. Radio stations that provided information about the army's repression, the people's resistance, or international solidarity were shut down or destroyed. Since eighty-five percent of the Haitian population is unable to read, radio is Haiti's major means of communication.

"Our radio waves covered a large portion of Haitian territory," explained Pedro, "so we began broadcasting the news to Haiti in Creole."

Shortly after Pedro began his Creole broadcasts, the Dominican government, under pressure from the Haitian military, informed Pedro of a law that prohibits foreign language news broadcasts.

"I understand," said Pedro. "Would it be okay to broadcast musical programs in a foreign language?"

The answer was, "Yes, of course."

And so, during the last five months, for one hour every morning and one hour every afternoon, Pedro has *sung* the news in Creole to the people of Haiti. His listeners call Radio Enriquillo "a ray of sunshine in the middle of a storm."

This was, and still is, risky business. Local sugar-cane cutters and other community members frequently gather to protect the station from attack. Several Haitians have been shot just for listening to Radio Enriquillo's news.

Pedro played a tape of one of his Creole broadcasts for me. It began with a greeting song so sweetly assuring, it could have been Mr. Rogers' invocation, "It's a beautiful day in the neighborhood." The next portion of the broadcast, still sung in Pedro's gentle tenor and with guitar accompaniment, was a reading from Exodus and a reflection on the liberation of God's people. The song then flowed into an announcement about a political rally to be held outside the National Palace that afternoon at 3:00 PM.

I ironed the wrinkle out of Pedro's suit, and he wore it the next night when he received a human rights award. President Aristide, who was a guest speaker at the event, invited Pedro to his hotel room afterwards to catch up on the news. The next morning Pedro's eyes were still sparkling. As we hugged and said goodbye, he invited our family to come and visit him. He reminded us that there would be no running water, but that we would be welcome in his neighborhood anytime.

—RICKI THOMPSON
WINTER 1993

[Editor's Note: Since the writing of this article, President Joaquin Balaguer of the Dominican Republic has banned all radio broadcasts into Haiti.]

~

As a spiritual exercise, listening to an oldies station in the car is not especially healthy—though of course neither is aging. (Frequently I've got these two little boys riding with me, six and three, oblivious to the drama and the dulling this music is subjecting their middle-aged father to.) Lately on the air you could have heard Aretha Franklin sing "Deliver Me" for Pizza Hut. It is a straight "cover" (as they say in the music industry; or "knock-off," as my garment-center relatives would say) of Fontella Bass's quite exhilarating "Rescue Me" of 1965—which itself sounds cousinly to Aretha's classic 1967 version of Otis Redding's 1966 "Respect."

This either casts you down or lifts you up—the repeatability of value. It buoys me, somehow. Aretha's songs, and Fontella's hit, I'll take them in almost any guise. Fontella's voice was not quite Aretha's but what is? Yet the style of singing was the same: reaching, digging, drum-dirty and horn-dirty, toe-curlingly frank. Entreaty never sounded so menacingly rhetorical. If you didn't give either singer the respect or rescue she wanted, she was in one minute certainly going to just snatch it away from you, bozo, the way someone wet-handed snatches away the dishcloth uselessly riding someone else's shoulder.

It buoys me because I think, unconsciously and innocently, Sixties innocently, we loved Fontella's song for being simply *more Aretha*, and vice versa. To hear current young white singers cover Atlantic or Motown records is to feel more queasy—the greed underlining the ersatz, its hem shows. And, to me, that Aretha—even for Pizza Hut, even for its lucre—sings Fontella's song seems merely to close a wonderful circle.

This all got seated more firmly if oddly in mind the other day when, in the mail, from New York, came a gallery announcement of a show of new paintings by the interestingly mystical painter Vija Celmins. Celmins paints photo-like pictures of the night sky or of waves or of two yards of parched desert floor—she squares-off the infinite. She's even taken desert and ocean stones, used them to make bronze casts, and then upon the duplicates painted the very colors and patterns the stones wore originally. Her work is remarkably disturbing—the way she seems to be trying less to get at and *under* the truths of natural creation than simply to lay its own pattern back *over* it. It's not an art of representation, it's one of transposition and restitution—of giving back what's not even for the taking. How to frame waves, stars, earthen cracks? The greatest glories of reality seem those that shrug off not only our stamp but even their own.

—Ross Feld
WINTER 1993

~

A Tom Stoppard play does not habitually produce in its audience the reaction, "How lifelike! How well he's captured reality!" So it was with some surprise that I noticed the extraordinary parallels between Stoppard's most recent play, *Arcadia*, and the even more recent solution of Fermat's Last Theorem.

Stoppard's play has been in repertory at London's National Theatre since it premiered in April of this year, and I saw it there in June. I enjoyed every moment of the evening—I did not, that is, agree with the somewhat deaf old gentleman two rows back who muttered loudly to his companion, just before the mathematical explication began, "This is where it starts to get boring." But it was an enjoyment similar to that which might have been produced by an evening of particularly elaborate fireworks. The scientific and technical know-how were impressive, and impressively translated into accessible form; the high points were brilliant and striking; and the careful timing of the whole affair, its extremely competent execution, allowed the experience to build toward a satisfying crescendo. But, like even the most beautiful fireworks display, *Arcadia* was quick to dispel itself in the mind. It was hard to remember, as little as a few hours later, what it had all been about.

I was forcibly reminded of that content, though, by the news of the solution to Fermat's Last Theorem, which first came out in *The New York Times* on June 24th and was elaborated in an article on June 29th. You don't need to understand higher mathematics, or even know the formulation of the theorem itself, in order to appreciate the story. Suffice to say that in 1637 a French mathematician named Fermat wrote a deceptively simple equation in the margin of a book and then added, "I have proved this theorem for all numbers, but I don't have room in this margin to show how" (or words to that effect). Then he died, proof still unexplained, and for the intervening 350 years mathematicians of all kinds vainly sought to reproduce his solution. You can see why this idea would appeal to Stoppard—the romance of the Last and the Lost—and in fact he refers to Fermat explicitly in *Arcadia*.

Like many Stoppard plays, *Arcadia* intertwines two plots: an early-nineteenth-century plot about a girl genius named Thomasina Coverly and her Byronically handsome tutor, Septimus Hodge, both of whom inhabit a grand house called Sidley Park that is in the process of being re-landscaped; and a late-twentieth-century plot in which two literary biographers and the Coverly descendants sort through the documents still remaining at Sidley Park in order to solve the mystery of what happened there during Thomasina's time. In one of Thomasina's mathematics lessons, Septimus (charmingly played by Rufus Sewell) assigns her Fermat's Last Theorem to keep her indefinitely occupied. She concludes that Fermat was just teasing people; but she then goes on, at the age of thirteen, to propose the idea of equations that could map, not just regular geometric shapes, but the irregular curves of natural forms. (This is where all the emphasis on landscaping comes in: the classical grounds versus the romantically gothic garden, the geometric versus the wildly irregular, the artificial versus the natural—though the "natural," in Stoppard's version, takes enormous artifice to produce.)

All that remains of Thomasina's discovery, 180 years later, are some obscure notes and numerous pages of "iterated," increasingly amplified drawings. But one of her family's descendants—not incidentally, a mathematician—gradually realizes that Thomasina has solved the very problem he is now addressing himself. What Thomasina's notes and drawings convey is that she was working on mathematical problems that did not even come into existence, in a public form, until centuries after her death—and that she used for her solutions certain principles and techniques which did not get developed until the age of computers. The heartening news behind Stoppard's play is that what is lost can be found again, that the old landscape is not obliterated by the new, and that secret discoveries made in the past can o'erleap time and reappear in the present.

This is also the news behind the June 24th and 29th issues of *The New York Times*. Not only did Andrew Wiles manage to solve (or re-solve, if we believe Fermat's marginal notes) a centuries-old problem in mathematics; but he did so in a way that used late-twentieth-century techniques. The two-hundred-page proof, which has yet to be published and verified, depends heavily on discoveries from another realm of math entirely: a realm developed to map the shapes of irregular curves. The parallel to Stoppard's play is so remarkable as to suggest that 1) Stoppard was tapping Wiles's telephone over the past seven years—or rather, was tapping his brain, since Wiles was notoriously close-mouthed even with his colleagues; *or* 2) Stoppard himself is a mathematical genius with an instinctive sense of how such discoveries come about; *or* 3) Stoppard's plays are right, and we *do* occupy a Many-Worlds universe in which different times and places intermingle and co-exist in ways beyond our capacity to perceive.

All three of these alternatives seem to me to be highly unlikely, but the third strikes me as the least impossible. (Wasn't it Sherlock Holmes who suggested that if we eliminate the impossible, we are left with the unlikely truth?) And if Stoppard's play is right, then Wiles's solution should indeed make us happy, even those who are not mathematicians. We can all be cheered at the finding of the lost, the Lazarus-like resuscitation of a once-dead solution, the confirmation of the past's secret intimacy with the present.

But Stoppard's play contains an additional element as well: the Byronic sense of romantic melancholy. (Lord Byron is a character in *Arcadia*, though he never comes onstage.) And this too appears in Wiles's story, or in the newspaper version of Wiles's story. For at the end of the June 29th article, the reporter quotes Wiles on the "sadness" entailed in reaching this conclusion:

> "All number theorists, deep down, feel that," he said. "For many of us, his problem drew us in and we always considered it something you dream about but never actually do." Now, he said, "There is a sense of loss, actually."

—WENDY LESSER
FALL 1993

~

One of my favorite movie scenes occurs in Hitchcock's *Sabotage*, his adaptation of Conrad's *The Secret Agent*. A Scotland Yard inspector, investigating a cell of conspirators in wartime London, walks down the side aisle of the Bijou Cinema, owned by Mr. Verloc, who lives with his family on the premises. We track the agent as he moves, catching his slant view of the screen, its twitchy shadows and lights, the audience rapt and laughing. He then sneaks behind the screen to eavesdrop on the saboteurs meeting in Verloc's lodgings. When he inserts himself behind the illusion, the image we saw moments ago projected on the front of the screen we now see looming on the verso, gross and tissuey and hyperbolic. Its power to control group emotion seems all the more grotesque and scary when we see the massive wafered image close up, depthless and wraithlike. We hear what the inspector hears. On one side, the vivid social life of image fiction—the projector's throaty roll, the audience's rustling amazement; on the other, voices which have power to bring death to innocents. (Later, the young brother of Verloc's wife, unknowingly transporting a terrorist bomb to Piccadilly Circus along with film reels of *Bartholomew the Strangler*, is killed when the bomb goes off in a crowded, slow-moving bus.) The cozy preserve of the moviehouse rumbles happily just a few steps from the kind of terrorist intent that can turn a Bijou into a shambles.

From when I was a kid, spending weekends at double features, I've loved moviehouses for their shared secrecy, anonymous company, and unmenacing spookiness. Even now, in my overlit suburban multiplex, I feel the same queasy anticipation before the big screen that awaits its images. When I've moved from place to place, I always pay an early visit to the local moviehouse, to eavesdrop on the conversation up there on screen. Testifying to big manipulative moving images in a big dark room feels like the first stage of local citizenship. My ritual is, I suppose, an example of the way the drama of moviegoing is inseparable from our sense of "the movies." We wrap narratives of our presence or involvement or stage of our lives around the narrative of the picture itself. We *contain* moviegoing in a candid, social, often urgent, always intimate but shareable way.

In the early 1970s, at the old Telegraph Repertory in Berkeley, a showing of Sam Peckinpah's *The Wild Bunch* (the most complete version of which I had seen at the old Embassy in San Francisco, an exquisitely decrepit and now defunct Market Street movie palace that doubled as a relatively safe flophouse for winos, druggies, and transients like me, and where we all got to participate in the "Big Wheel!" contest spin that interrupted evening shows) was followed by riotous cries of "Fascist bullshit!" countered by equally vehement shouts of "This is real American art!" A few nights later, while I waited to squeeze into a small auditorium to see a clandestine print of the then-sequestered *Titicut Follies*, a young man behind me talked thrillingly about finally seeing that excruciating and legendary documentary about conditions in a state-operated insane asylum, but along with that he speed-babbled some anecdote about Callas singing *Tosca*, bits of which he explosively sang (in beautiful Italian) even while nattering about the forbidden document we were all about to see.

Social unrest was different then from what we see around us now, more anarchic, voluble, and historically informed, and was not defined or contained by social and economic class. Around that same time, multiplex cinemas were coming into vogue. Ironically, they began when art houses carved themselves into multiple viewing chambers to accommodate more independent and foreign pictures, or to show mainstream movies that would offset the expense of showing less conventional work. Culture atrophies if it doesn't change, and change brings the pangs or pains of the unfamiliar displacing what's known and rosy. I try not to get cranky at my local multiplex when the feature is projected on a curved screen designed to accommodate the satellite-pod viewing rooms spoked around a huge central lobby that functions as a combined mess hall and video arcade. This particular multiplex, constructed on a strip of land between a freeway and marshy bay-shore, was built to serve communities, my own working-class suburb among them, on the mid-Peninsula south of San Francisco. Mushroomed there at land's end, in an enormous parking lot, along a row of car dealerships and unfinished furniture outlets, my multiplex lies nearly two miles from our small downtown and is called an "Entertainment Center," though it's not the center of anything. While its ambiance and offerings have adapted to (and helped mold) suburban habits, it has kept at least one traditional social function. It's a place where you know you can always find people. And so last summer when angry teenagers from one of our neighborhoods wanted to find the boy they felt had "dissed" them, they drove by the multiplex at one PM of a sunny day and fired into the available teenage crowd. One adaptation of the suburban multiplex is to have made itself, by virtue of its physical isolation, a good shooting gallery. Inside the center are video games imaging mock firepower of very imaginative kinds, and beyond these are the cinemas themselves. On their screens, behind which lie no spaces for investigators or saboteurs, firearms of the most ingenious designs are being gleefully fired at all shapes and sizes of human beings, and at mock humans, too, at holographic and androidal and virtually real human beings, and at molten humanoids that can revivify themselves so that they may be shot again. What kind of nostalgia will someday make this memory's favorite home place?

—W. S. Di Piero

SPRING 1994

A straight line is the shortest distance between two points.

—Euclid

This statement bears all the seeds of epigram. How well it flourishes in English, with the alliteration between "straight" and "shortest," the concealed rhyme of "is" and "distance." When I was fourteen, and encountered this sentence in the first pages of the First Book of Euclid, I was amazed. No one had told me that Geometry is witty, but this sentence gave the game away. It also opens the door to the world of Pure Reason, where nothing is as it is in the Real World, though everything reflects on that Real World. Geometry means "world-measuring," but we can measure our world only by getting away from it, into the land of glorious abstraction.

A straight line is *the* straight line, for it exists in humble superlative. It is always shortest, and can never put up with being anything less, that is with being more. Oh, that I could travel on that perfect path, the straight line! But I shall never walk that way, for on earth itself (physically), and in the world (metaphorically), there are so many bumps, lumps, hills, declivities, gradients, distractions, street signs, advertisements, friends, primroses, dog turds, potholes, gas stations, thunderstorms, turbulences, downdrafts, and states of mind—No, it is not on the cards that I shall ever walk, drive, or even fly on the straight line. Even police officers catching drunk drivers, the most Euclidean of *gensdarmes*, speak with loose pragmatism when they ask a driver to walk in a straight line. Come to think of it, can a biped, a two-footed creature (with or without feathers), ever walk in that perfection? For the biped (Adam, Eve, Cock Robin or Kanga) needs two tracks, whereas the Line is unitary. No, I shall never be on the straight, not really, not even if I take counsel and find out how to get to a destination "as the crow flies." For my direction-giver too knows that we are not crows, and the crow-path is always given as a contrast to our own. (No one asks the crow to fly it, or takes a breathalyzer from a beak.) Nay, though I walk the straight and narrow—or try to—I shall not be on the Euclidean straight, for that is narrower. It goes to the point, which, as the next page of Euclid wittily informs us, "has position without magnitude."

A straight line is the shortest distance between two points. What elegant economy is here displayed: there could not be a word less, and should not be a word more. The formation of the Euclidean sentence is the model of epigram—La Rochefoucauld and Oscar Wilde were descendants of Euclidean culture. They are Euclid's children, geometry's tots, though not like the child Pascal, that epigrammatist in his own branch, who was able to reinvent Euclid on his own. Euclid's line is a puzzle, a tease, a contrast and a paradox. It translates the "line" which we think of as a human sign, a mark scratched by the human hand, into "distance." Distance is thought of as existing in Nature—even though the word noticeably reflects our perception of that nature. Distance is space measured by the human mind. "Line" is artifact altogether. Yet here we see that Artificial Sign = Nature—or rather, that is the first impression. The sentence has already begun its reverse action by the time we have traveled the distance to "distance." Nature then becomes Artifice. The business of the sentence is to transform Nature into Artifice, to complete the work begun in a hidden way with the very existence of the word "distance." The business of the sentence is to super-load the artificial which we take for granted. The Line starts out as the hero of this sentence, but is quickly deposed. Deprived of the apparent position as subject offered by its initial position, it is subordinated in the predicate. The line becomes involved in a new and humbling quality, which is its distinguishing quality, that is, in its in-between-ness. The Line is merely a means to an end—or rather to beginning and end, which are not expressed in temporal terms, nor (by the end of the sentence) in truly spatial terms either. The two glittering "points" may be anywhere and nowhere. They are not the Line, but they are what gives meaning to the Line. They cannot be fixed in Nature. The major relation is between these mysterious "two points." The straight, the truly straight, scratch or signifier is merely the invisible and unattainable perfect road between them. The "straight line" rules nothing but is the humble servant of Necessity.

The sentence supplies the basic model for the epigram, relying on the simple formula of definition, X = Y. To tell us that X = Y must always be to express the known.

If you know X you really know Y also. Definitions are always partly comic in their redundancy, and this comedy of surplus is something that can be played with. Y is always an extra, either a gift or an intrusion. It is a superfluity if one already knows X. But of course one wasn't aware that knowing X entailed knowing Y too, and to see Y is to come back to X with a discomfitingly revised vision. We thought we knew, perhaps, what a "straight line" was—now we see it in its hyperbolical unnatural demanding perfection. It will never be realizable in the pencilled line I draw on a piece of wood with the help of a ruler. To make the acquaintance of Y is, in short—and of what are we thinking but shortness, the shortest?—to undergo change, to adventure into the predicate. After that adventure we cannot go home again to an earlier subject. An epigram might itself be partly defined as a sentence which makes this process explicit, even with some violence, if only the violence of abruptness. An epigram completes one cultural operation by making that operation visible, even as it begins another cultural work. Euclid makes the assumptions behind the idea "distance" visible and jerks us towards a theoretical realm where we part with Distance's natural space. The jerk or yank is playful; the epigram delights us with surprise, as its definition sensibly reorients us—plays with our sense of things. Surprise and reversal are the standard components of epigram, e.g. "Work is the curse of the drinking classes." But Wilde's epigram is a trifle, a frivol with a bromide, compared to the depth and awfulness of Euclid's epigram as he sets out to map for us the unreal world.

—MARGARET DOODY
FALL 1994

One night in 1949 the chemist Burgess Collins, who worked on the processing of plutonium at the Hanford Atomic Project in Washington, had an apocalyptic dream. It was, he has said, "a strong and convincing dream that the world was going to completely destruct by the year 1975." Soon after, he left his job at Hanford and went south to San Francisco, where he began to paint fulltime.

Last spring, forty-five years after the appearance of that dream, the San Francisco Museum of Modern Art showed a retrospective exhibit, "A Grand Collage 1951–1993," of the art of the painter Collins, now known simply as "Jess." The exhibit comprised four distinct sections of images—an anteroom with a few examples of the artist's earliest works, entitled "Nonobjective and Romantic Paintings"; and the main room divided into three parts: "Translations" (reproductions in color of found images in old photographs or engravings); "Paste-Ups" (montages of images from books, magazines, comics, jigsaw puzzles, etc.); and "Salvages" (repaintings on the original surface of early paintings of the artist's or of paintings by other artists found in thrift shops). Seen as a whole, the exhibit created an effect both surprising and disturbing, with its continuous obscuring of surface and its reclaiming of old images.

Obviously Jess's work was infused with many influences after 1948, particularly that of the poet Robert Duncan, with whom Jess had an intimate relationship from 1951 until Duncan's death in 1988. Both men, throughout their years together, were intensely involved in a study of myths, quests, romances, and allegories, which they integrated into their daily life as well as their work.

But many if not all of Jess's works still carried traces of that apocalyptic dream, dreamed when Jess was still Burgess Collins. To walk through the exhibit was like wandering through a landscape in which everything—image, medium, surface, even light itself—was in the process of transmutation. Often I thought of the word "alchemy," with its emphasis on the changing of base metals to gold and its concomitant emphasis on the mystical. (Indeed, Jess used the words of the alchemist Thomas Vaughan as a supplemental text to the last painting in the exhibition.)

Going through the exhibit a second time, moving through the dizzying piling-up of images, I found it difficult to find any resting place before these extremely skillful but somehow desperate-seeming works. Then I came to one particular "Translation" that held me still. Entitled *Mind's I: Translation #12, 1965*, it is a reproduction in color of an engraving, *Concave Mirror*, from a *Scientific American* of 1887. In the upper-left-hand corner of the painting is an eye; on the right edge is a concave mirror. Against a background randomly splotched with thick dabs of paint, a line of sight goes from the eye to the mirror to a flower, lit from below by two candles. When I saw *Mind's I* as *Mind's Eye*, I suddenly realized that in this artist there was something radically different in the connection between hand and eye, in the effect of mind on both hand and eye, in the way the mind intruded between hand and eye, acting as both catalyst and impediment.

On the wall next to the painting was a quotation, selected by the artist to supplement the work. A paragraph from the scientist Charles Sherrington's *Man on His Nature*, it read:

> The sun's energy is part of the closed energy-cycle. What leverage can it have on my mind? Yet through my retina and brain it is able to act on my mind. The theoretically impossible happens. In fine, I assert that it does act on my mind . . . Physics tells me that my arm cannot be bent without disturbing the sun. Physics tells me that unless my mind is energy it cannot disturb the sun . . . Let me prefer to think the theoretically impossible does happen . . . I take it my mind *does* bend my arm, and that it disturbs the sun.

Reading this text, I felt a nudge of memory. In early 1947, a year and a half after the end of World War II, I went to work in Oak Ridge as a low-level physicist on the NEPA project. (NEPA was an acronym for Nuclear Energy for the Propulsion of Aircraft. Neither during the short term I was in Oak Ridge, nor in the few years that the project continued, was any headway made on this bizarre intention.) According to the exhibition catalogue, Jess—or Burgess Collins—had also worked in Oak Ridge as a draftee in the army, from 1944 until early 1946, when he was discharged six months after the War's end. While in Oak Ridge, he had worked at Clinton Labs, monitoring the processing of plutonium for use in atomic weapons.

Surrounded by Jess's paintings, I recalled the strangeness of Oak Ridge, cut off in secrecy from the surrounding world. Even after the war, there hung over that constructed community in rural Tennessee an aura of what had been released over Hiroshima and Nagasaki—and what might now be released by others elsewhere. A few of the scientists talked of World Government. Some spoke of the necessity of educating people to the fact that there was no "secret" of the atomic bomb. Some were desperate to make up for what had happened; others were fearful of a new threat to come. But most of the scientists went to work each day and thought about the technical questions of the production of plutonium or U-235 (this production in itself a form of alchemy, one might say), and then at night came home to their families and tried to live their ordinary lives, not thinking about what the scientific mind they so venerated had brought about in the real world. (Was the sun disturbed?)

Looking at the painting *Mind's I: Translation #12, 1965*, it occurred to me that perhaps there were many in Oak Ridge—as well as Hanford—who dreamed apocalyptic dreams.

Only Jess has told us of his.

—MILLICENT DILLON
WINTER 1995

Seventy-five-hundred dollars in pennies, spread luxuriantly across a warehouse floor, a honey-lush expanse. Two live sheep in a pen. Fragrant eucalyptus leaves embedded one atop the next in walls of beeswax. A table overbrimming with hundreds of white, starched, singed, and gilded men's dress shirts. Dozens of snails slowly munching their way through a pair of halved cabbage heads in an otherwise empty glass terrarium. One hundred and fifty plain kitchen glasses lined on shelves along a wall, each containing a mysteriously spinning liquid, a humming waterspout. Another floor, this one covered over with ten tons of old-fashioned linotype, a bed of words. Another table, this one made of iron oxide and covered over with tens of thousands of discretely spaced, individual teeth, animal and human (the table dripping red paint from below). Two turkey carcasses being methodically picked clean by swarms of crickets. Another floor, another vast warehouse space, this one carpeted in a pelt-sea of meticulously layered horsetail tufts.

With a bit over a decade's worth of offerings such as these, who knew what Ann Hamilton was going to be having up her capacious sleeve for her recent installation in the Projects Room, off to the right as you enter the Museum of Modern Art. Actually, those who'd been following her most recent work might have expected something around the theme of textual erasure or narrative obliteration. Last year, at the Dia Foundation downtown, that vast space with the horsehair sea had included, off in the distance, a simple table at which a seated figure (either Hamilton herself or one of her surrogates) spent hour after hour, systematically poring over antique hardcover books and burning out each successive line of text as it was read, with the aid of a hot-tipped electric stylus (smoky tendrils wafted up from the table, a delicious acrid smell pervaded the room). More recently, at the Ruth Bloom Gallery in Santa Monica, Hamilton herself sat silently for hours at a time at the end of a long table, systematically extracting the precut lines of text from specially prepared books—a vermicelli of words—and winding the strands of text into progressively larger balls which, once they'd achieved the heft, say, of a nice, ripe cantaloupe, she pushed through a gap in an intervening scrim screen, allowing them to roll out onto the table beyond . . .

And, sure enough, a similar motif had initially animated Hamilton's thinking as she approached the MOMA space, or so she commented one day last November as she supervised the final phases of its installation. The centerpiece of Hamilton's Project was a vast glass triptych—about the size of some of the Pollocks upstairs—onto which a single video loop was being projected from behind. "Originally," she said, "with regard to that image, I'd been thinking of scrawling an almost indecipherable text, with water-soluble blue ink, across a transparent pane of glass, and then videotaping it close-up from below as a water-tipped finger smearingly erased the writing, leaving only the fingertrace. But as I experimented with that image at the Wexner Center" (ever since unexpectedly receiving a five-year MacArthur Fellowship, two years ago, the bicoastal Hamilton has transplanted herself back to her Midwestern roots, and she's currently living with her husband in Columbus, Ohio, where she's been conducting various sorts of research at OSU's Wexner Center for the Visual Arts) "I began to think it too literal-minded, so instead I came up with this." The screen was projecting a sumptuously mysterious rosy image, a huge spheroid pad languidly moving through fields of golden viscosity: a fingertip navigating through honey.

Hamilton is in her late thirties. Her face is broad, open, an unaffected full moon beneath a thick thatch of short salt-and-pepper hair. And she was quite pregnant. "Seven months," she acknowledged with a smile. "I found out in the middle of doing that last piece in Santa Monica. I was sitting there, slowly, intently winding those spools of text into those neat little balls and then pushing them out through that little scrim opening and into the world, and then one day, realizing what I was doing, I almost blushed crimson with recognition."

Gazing upon the video screen, Hamilton explained, "I'm interested in the intersection of seeing and feeling, of sight and texture." Meanwhile, she was ripping open seam after seam from a pell-mell pile of used red clothing for another part of the installation—two long benches in the foreground of the space, in front of the video screen, onto which she and her assistants were plying the flat flanks of deconstructed red clothing into two neat, chest-high mounds ("They're red," she noted, when asked, "just red, and *real* real. It's flesh, I suppose, a further trace of the body, but at the same time, with that color, quite edgy, so much so that a dog won't even lie in it.") "Wasn't it McLuhan," she continued, returning to the video image, "who said the mission of the artist is to retactilize the world? And Ashley Montagu who points out in his book *Touching*, with its marvelous subtitle, 'The Significance of Human Skin,' that fingertips are among the first things to firm in the human embryo, already with individually distinct prints, even in identical twins? I'm trying to evoke an image that, while flat like that against the wall, will nevertheless still seem to press out upon the viewer, so that you can't help but see it feelingly."

And the effect was quite wonderful. Talk about action painting! At one level, Hamilton's installation instantaneously entered into a marvelous dialogue with all the other artwork upstairs: five minutes mesmerized before Hamilton's huge, lazily pressing finger ("The moving finger writes . . . "), and the Twombly show upstairs, for example, was completely transformed. But standing there beside the busily cheerful Hamilton, one couldn't help but free-associate to other, less specifically artworldly referents. For the marvelously amorphous globular form, moving pulsingly in its rosy glow, momentarily resembled nothing so much as a giant blow-up of a sonogram.

—LAWRENCE WESCHLER
SPRING 1995

~

About nine years ago, somewhere in lower Manhattan, a graffito caught my eye. Hastily scrawled in black marker on a wall, it read CHEW MAIL POUCH. My immediate thought was that this had to be the most recherché piece of illegal public expression I'd seen yet. But there was something a little eerie about it, too. It reminded me of the story I had read as a child in one of those Frank Edwards bizarre-phenomena compendiums, about how REMEMBER PEARL HARBOR! was found painted on a sidewalk in Owensville, Indiana—in December 1939! This bulletin might have come from the past. When I got home, though, I entered it in my notebook as a singular example of "post-modern" graffiti. I never saw the scrawl again, and didn't think about it until just recently, when I found the entry while looking for something else.

Now it strikes me that the phrase, on that wall, exemplifies postmodernism as concisely as anyone would wish. First of all, there are its three distinct aspects, which hinge on different levels of knowingness of the graffito's beholders. The first camp would be made of those who know that Mail Pouch is a brand of chewing tobacco. For them the sight of a gratuitous advertisement for the product might just inspire a chuckle—a slightly outré pop-culture joke, it would seem, with a trace of that double-edged acceptance of merchandising that's come down to us from Warhol. The second party would comprise those who have seen the fading slogan on old barns in increasingly remote parts of the country. They might also give the artist points for cleverness, but at the same time feel a shiver of melancholy, of nostalgia. They might think about those old barns, these old tenements, all of them listing a bit; or they might feel a sudden yearning for the countryside, the seeming opposite of the Lower East Side, which will in turn appear crummier and smellier than it had a minute earlier. The third element would consist of those who have no idea that Mail Pouch is a brand of chewing tobacco or anything else—as well as those who do but consciously choose to disregard their knowledge. For them CHEW MAIL POUCH will be a cryptic mantra, the expression of a disgruntled postal worker, a stage direction by Tristan Tzara, or just a poem, sufficient unto itself.

Those three aspects—consumer-culture irony, nostalgic wistfulness, ambiguous formal brio—are all present in the work, of course, regardless of the graffitist's intention. But they cannot have presented themselves simultaneously to even the most astute of passersby. At full intensity, they operate in sequence. They do not cancel each other out, but neither do they enhance each other; the work is tripartite but not what you'd call dialectical. Rather it is like a three-pronged version of one of those puzzle pictures in which you can make out the vase and the profiles, but only in succession. The effect is distinct from that of, say, Duchamp's *Fountain*, which is a public outrage, an authorship claim, and an exhibit of pure sculptural form, all at once, with each quality boosting the others. CHEW MAIL POUCH, then, is postmodern both in its specific aspects and in the way it unfolds them to varyingly attuned viewers.

I find a similar business occurring in my two favorite certifiably pomo works of the past year, *Pulp Fiction* and Beck's song "Loser." The former is variously a B-movie pastiche, a depiction of the fantasy lives of minutiae-obsessed cultural consumers, and a narrative Moebius strip. The latter fricassees such earlier macedoines as "Memo from Turner" and "Subterranean Homesick Blues," spotlights the homeboy in his roach-encrusted kitchen playing country slide guitar, and performs a virtuoso act, in both composition and execution, of constantly verging on muddle without ever falling in. In both cases each facet is perceptible, again, one at a time. This means, among other things, that even audience members who don't get all the references can appreciate the work. The hipsters, meanwhile, may feel as though they've been admitted to the VIP lounge, but their appreciation is really only quantitatively enhanced. You can deconstruct these texts for all you're worth, but the exercise is optional. *Fountain* without the benefit of interpretation, on the other hand, is just a urinal. So maybe postmodernism, in its fullest expression, is a truly democratic model, able to embrace all three brow sizes without giving preference to any of them. Despite the claims that postmodernism consists of nothing but recycled cultural fodder, this seems genuinely new.

—LUC SANTE
SPRING 1995

~

The enemies of the National Endowment for the Arts claim that government has no business subsidizing art. They also argue that, if it does, the subsidized art has no business offending the American people. They are wrong on both counts. Historically, governments have always subsidized art, and some of that art has always been offensive.

Many critics of the NEA present themselves as defenders of traditional culture and values. It is therefore particularly ironic that their attack shows how ignorant they are of the traditions they profess to champion. William Bennett, for example, has called for the elimination of both the NEA and its sister organization, the National Endowment for the Humanities, because they support works that "undermine American values." His view betrays the shallow understanding of the values he praises and the virtues he advocates in his current bestseller, *The Book of Virtues*. For the tradition he celebrates has consistently valued state support of the arts, and is itself partly constituted of works that offended their original audiences.

Pericles, the ancient Athenian statesman, used fully ten percent of the tax revenues generated by the Athenian Empire to enact one of the most ambitious artistic programs in western history. His program resulted directly in the building of the Parthenon and many of the monuments through which we remember Athens' "Golden Age." Indirectly, it provided the impetus for the writing of the great Greek tragedies, which were presented in state-constructed theaters during state-sponsored festivals; the state often compensated the working members of the audience for their lost wages.

Yet these state-supported artworks were far from uncontroversial. Pericles met with heavy opposition for his lavish expenditures, while the works he brought about were strongly criticized. Plato, for instance, mounted a vicious attack against all tragic drama, accusing it of confusing the authentic with the fake, of being suited for representing only vulgar and violent subjects, and of inducing even good people to act in shameful ways. (Critics of television, take note.) And when Pheidias's monumental sculpture of Athena was discovered to contain the artist's self-portrait on the goddess's shield, Pheidias was tried for impiety. Blasphemy and immorality—the accusations which shook the NEA in connection with the Serrano and Mapplethorpe cases a few years ago—are actually among the most ancient charges the arts have faced.

The fact is that government has sponsored most of the great art in the world; it has also financed vast amounts of inferior art. The danger is endemic in the enterprise: you have to have a lot of a bad thing if you want a bit of good as well.

Art and government have always had complex relations, and the state has not always cut off the artists who defied it. Michelangelo, in a fit of rage, abandoned Rome and wrote Pope Julius II that if he wanted him, he could go look for him; instead of persecuting him, Julius arranged a reconciliation and commissioned Michelangelo to complete the decoration of the Sistine Chapel. Velasquez, the quintessential establishment artist, was a painter to the Spanish Court, but scholars still do not agree about whether his paintings are objective, flattering, or deeply critical and insulting portraits of his noble patrons. Mozart submitted an incomplete libretto of *Don Giovanni* to the censors, and delayed completing the opera, which was to open in Prague, until the Archduchess Maria Theresa, who would have been scandalized by the work, had left the city.

Most of the states that have supported the arts, like most states in the world so far, have been authoritarian. That can lead to great abuses. But though many government-supported works in the past have celebrated the systems that sponsored them, others, even in authoritarian states, have attacked them—and artists have been masters at disguising their defiance. Unlike authoritarian states, however, democracies supposedly tolerate the criticism of their values and encourage dissenting voices. Democracies do not need to force artists to subterfuge and hypocrisy. A truly democratic state does not put its principles aside when it comes to the arts.

Senator John Ashcroft opposes the NEA because it sponsors controversial works. "If the definition of art means that it has to challenge and be offensive," he has said, then the Endowment's existence "is in serious jeopardy." But though it is certainly not part of the definition of art that it must always challenge and be offensive, that is just what it will sometimes do. And some challenging and offensive works will inevitably survive their present—and, as history testifies, become the building blocks of the tradition of the future.

Mindful of the traditions they claim to defend and aware of the virtues of the democracy they champion, the enemies of the NEA should combine historical knowledge with political wisdom, and come to their senses and the agency's support.

—Alexander Nehamas
SUMMER 1995

~

On one of my recent visits to New York, my Grandma Libby, the archivist of the family, produced a pristine copy of *Life* magazine, dated November 21, 1969: the day I turned three. Johnny Cash is on the cover, playing acoustic guitar in front of the massive wheels of a freight train, steam gusting up around his waist. He has one pointy boot poised on the edge of a railroad tie, a silver lamé scarf glitters at his neck, and his black hair is slicked back into a perfect helmet: "The Rough-Cut King of Country Music," the headline reads. Inside is an article on Jesse Jackson—"black hope, white hope"—and photographs of Dr. Elisabeth Kübler-Ross's first seminar on death and dying, in which a beautiful twenty-two-year-old woman talks about her diagnosis of leukemia while health care workers weep behind a two-way mirror. It is a sampling of the times, but that wasn't why my grandmother saved it for twenty-five years.

On the last page of the issue, under the heading "Parting Shots," is a picture of me just shy of three, carrying an unfurled Vietcong flag easily three times my size across a patch of trampled grass. At the top of the frame, the flag bisects the body of a man, leaving a diagonal of rumpled coat, one arm stuffed into a pocket. Long, bottle-nosed cars are parked on the street behind him, bleached white by the glare. What looks to be cold New England light shines through the flag—two silky panels with a star in the center—and lifts a white corona around the edges of my head. I look highly serious, hunched over to counter the weight of the long pole, wearing a short dress and little brown work boots. Pint-size Bolshevik, trudging along, head down, my chin slung forward slightly in concentration.

The editors at *Life* wrote a poem to go with the picture, which they called "The Burden of Protest":

> Is toting a Vietcong flag
> In a war demonstration the bag
> Of a child or a parent?
> We'd say someone's errant—
> This kid should be off playing tag.

It is a smarmy piece of copy; only prigs take moral potshots in a limerick. Notably, it took a potshot at my mother, who to the editor's mind was conspicuously absent, having loaded me up with my ideological burden and disappeared.

But my mother says she was there that day, and the picture lied: I had picked up the flag on my own. She can almost recite the doggerel from memory. "That poem was a criticism of my parenting," she says, with a little laugh. "Some of the mothers were real worried about stuff going on at those rallies, but me, nice girl from the suburbs, I was a trusting soul. I came to pick you up from your dad and there you were dancing around with that flag. Your dress—you can't see this from the picture because it's black and white—was red velvet, a real thick velvet, and some part of the flag was red and you looked gorgeous. And while in that one moment you looked driven, burdened, really you were having a blast. And the photographer knew it. You were swinging that flag around, twirling it. The whole crowd was watching you."

The first time I saw this picture was in my father's house in Berkeley. I must have been eight or so. He had trimmed away the offending poem, framed the photo in mat board, and typed his own caption. I can't reconstruct his text entire, because the picture was lost in some move, but his final line sticks in my head: "Could it be that at three you caught the spirit of the worldwide movement for Socialism, and shouted, 'Hey, everybody, wait for me!'"

Whether I knew anything of a worldwide movement for socialism at three is doubtful. At eight, when I looked at my father's handiwork, hung in the living room, the site of many a strategy meeting and leaflet-folding session, I knew that what he saw in the picture had little to do with me. That caption says much about what my father needed me to be: a comrade, a willing enthusiast for the work that needed to be done.

Amazing now, that my father and all those who passed through the doors of that house in 1974 could read those words without irony. I remember a little girl I played with around that time who had Marxist coloring books—the fat factory bosses wore three-piece suits with watch chains, the workers were lean and muscled and wore overalls. She told me I was only allowed to use red and blue crayons for the "proletariat," with an eight-year-old's mock-adult adamance. She might have been telling me the correct way to eat an Oreo. The Capitalist Running Dogs were to be filled in with heavy black strokes.

But caption or no caption, looking at that picture now takes my breath away. November 21, 1969. Two months earlier, my father had carried that same flag into the Harvard Center for International Affairs and, along with twenty or so of his fellow Weathermen, had run screaming through the building, dumping over filing cabinets, smashing windows, punching professors and staff. And two months after the picture was snapped he would be in prison. When I danced carefree across the Boston Commons (if I can take my mother at her word), I swung that flag in pure ignorance. It was a swath of fabric to me, nothing more. I waved it over the sunlit grass in the calm between emergencies, one sock up, one down, oblivious to what was to come.

I tell my mother the story of my father's caption, twenty-six years after their divorce, and she laughs with a rueful note of recognition. Still, I am surprised when she doesn't leap at the chance to peg him. Instead, her laughter winds down to a sigh: "Well, I suppose my reading is just as suspect. So Pollyannaish: the sun was shining; you were the perfect child." And it's true, out of the tangle of the past my mother preserves mostly primary colors, the quality of the light, my power and exuberance. Even though she knew in those months that my father was preparing for his trial, that she was planning to pack up and head for Mexico, that our lives were about to fly apart.

It wasn't until I was at UCLA in the early Eighties that I came to that photograph again. Surrounded by neo-Republican coeds, I made friends with a left-wing activist. Tim spent a summer building houses in Nicaragua, listened to the Carter Family and other vintage folk bands, and was an ardent student of Marxism. He was the butt of his own running joke: in which our young socialist shows up late for the demonstration and can't even get arrested for jaywalking, and so on. He loved the idea that I was a red diaper baby. He would call my answering machine and quote passages from books about SDS which referred to my father, who was usually up on some stage making strident remarks.

For the first time, my family life seemed glamorous. My father and stepmother's jobs at the auto plants, their union organizing, the threats of tapped phones, my father's prison time: all the things I tried to hide from my small-town friends, tried to whitewash or bury, were now prized.

One day, studying in the reference room at Powell Library, a huge domed room with sooty windows, I led Tim over to the bound volumes of *Life*. Even I was surprised to find the picture there, pressed between leather covers on a dusty back shelf.

"That's you?" he said, peering closer. "What the hell were you doing?"

—LISA MICHAELS
SUMMER 1995

~

How long is it since I noticed one of those discreet corsetry shops on a leafy side street off the main boulevards, small show-window lined with dull-toned grosgrain drapes against which the sole identifying object on display was the plaster figure, half or quarter life-sized, of a female torso topped by a modestly pretty head and face whose demure vacuous gaze evaded every admirer? The surprisingly full and shapely body would be clasped by an elaborate girdle: boned, hooked, bound, and strapped—all the skills of corsetiere-proprietor exhibited like a sampler stitched by an eighteenth-century girl as evidence of her skill, and the truncated lower parts veiled by a frill of faded ecru lace. How delightful to have a little lady like that at home, for my very own. Preferably alive.

My mother would laugh indulgently as I elaborated on the fantasy. But later, older, arm in arm with some uncertain young suitor, if I stopped entranced before such an illuminated display, I sensed a certain uneasiness, even alarm, at hearing this wish expressed.

By the time I came to appreciate their miniature allure, these figures were anachronisms. Their worn appearance testified that no replacements existed. Chips and knocks inflicted while being moved in and out of the window for trappings to be adjusted or changed revealed dead-white (or crumbling, porous, dirty) plaster under the painted surface. Through the slow effects of time and dust, their painted features darkened into a curdled puce and mottled ochre that evoked the complexions of those plaster heads with antique coiffures and missing noses—like saints in post-Reformation churches—which still survived in occasional hairdressing salons of the outlying suburbs, or the powdered faces of their increasingly short-winded clientele.

Sometimes, between glowing globes of green and purple liquids in shabby pharmacies, I would sight the plaster figure of a man—proportions similar to those of the corset lady, but usually with all limbs and parts intact—garlanded by bandages, trusses, and splints. The two of them seemed to form a pair: a devoted couple maimed and cruelly separated by the exigencies of survival. The appurtenances for which their bodies served as mannequins were tangible evidence of the fellow-workers who had manufactured them, as victimized as themselves.

More than other associations their nakedness and small size might suggest, they served as proletarian ikons. But I do not recall any urge to reunite them, nor ever wanting to take the little man home with me.

—RUTH FAINLIGHT
SPRING 1996

~

I currently teach a class in Humanities at LA Trade-Tech, a large vocation-oriented community college in downtown Los Angeles. It's a night class, and the students are mostly adults with jobs and families. A few of them plan to go on to four-year colleges, but the majority are working toward certification in areas such as nursing, contracting, waste management, or auto mechanics. Humanities is one of the few academic classes required for graduation.

Since the school catalogue states that my course—which surveys Western culture from Mesopotamia to the Middle Ages—is supposed to have a "perspective as revealed in the arts," I decided those revelations might productively include exposure to a theatrical performance. So, on the last weekend of February, the class convened in front of a small theater in Hollywood to communally ingest a production of Peter Shaffer's *Equus*.

I thought my choice was a good one. Admittedly, *Equus*' simplistic psychology and touted theatricality owe more to calculation than inspiration. But given the dreary realism that dominates Los Angeles theater, the bits of dramatic iconography that appear in the Shaffer play stand as high creative virtues. Also, for my purposes, the *Equus* Greek connection had its appeal. At that point, we were studying Hellenic culture, so I hoped my students would find Dr. Dysart's wistful references to Mycenaean acrobats and the red soil of Argos vaguely familiar. And I hoped, too, that flicker of recognition would make this disparate group—whose backgrounds range from Nigeria to Belize—feel slightly more at home among the detritus of Western civilization.

I warned them about the nudity in *Equus*. I additionally gave warning that this production, at the Deaf West Theatre, was exceptional. Most of the major players were deaf and would use sign language, while speaking actors, either on stage or via earphones, would simultaneously offer voice translations. In that only a few of my students had any prior live-theater experience, confronting them with a dual language performance did seem risky. But as it turned out, comprehension was no problem at all.

At Deaf West, as is typical in *Equus* productions, the entire cast remained on stage throughout the play. In this case, that included the speaking actors. Casually dressed in black, they sat in long benches that flanked either side of the playing area and synchronized their speech and sometimes intense physical responses so exactly to their deaf counterparts that it seemed as if they had eerily become the characters' inner voices or alter-egos. In Deaf West's version, directed by Andrew Shea, the psychiatrist was female (and was played by the wonderfully expressive deaf actress Phyllis Frelich). This change subtly altered the doctor's relationship with the boy (the lanky, poignantly young deaf actor

Aaron Kubey), muting the plays noted homoerotic undercurrent. Whether male or female, actors playing Dr. Dysart must still confront in Alan Strang their actual and spiritual sterility. But as played by Frelich, a new jealous tension was apparent in the scenes between her and the boy's mother, Dora. Though damaged and wrongheaded, Dora Strang has at least given birth to this boy. He stands as her creative act, and in this production Dr. Dysart painfully acknowledges that triumph.

In Deaf West's *Equus*, the horses (reduced to five on the cramped stage) pranced in their metal sculpted heads; the good doctor agonized; the boy was at first defiant, then longed for relief from his muse-daemons—all as usual with *Equus*. And yet the performance was particularly shocking. Perhaps this was due to the constant motion, the almost primal gestures of the signing actors, or to the doppelganger quality of characters represented by both speakers and signers. Perhaps it could be accounted for by the famous, generally dimly lit horse-blinding nude scene being played here in the full-out white glare of a hospital office. As this scene progressed, I felt the student sitting next to me shiver. Later she would say it was all "okay." She just wished, she said, the nude boy "hadn't jumped around so much." But when the class gathered again there were other things said too—about parents and children; about passion and repression; about theater and imagination; and at one point, about the relation of all this to things Greek.

—IRENE OPPENHEIM
SUMMER 1996

~

In his now-classic essay "Unpacking My Library," the critic Walter Benjamin strikes an easy, elegiac tone as he fusses among crates, cartons, and torn paper to gingerly unearth his beloved books, "piles of volumes that are seeing daylight again after two years of darkness." The general mood is that of a wine tasting.

It's the more chaotic essay Benjamin *didn't* write, however—the one he might have titled "Packing (and Lugging) My Library"—that I've always wanted to read. There would be the same "disorder of crates" that Benjamin mentions, the same "air saturated with wood." But instead of the Bergmanesque sighs and murmurs, there would be this: twisted ankles and damaged knees; sweaty introverts hurling invective at one another (if two book owners are moving together); and quick-but-long-remembered spats over who really owns that funky edition of Faulkner's *Pylon*. (Such spats are resolved via legal maneuvering on the order of, "Look, that's *my* red wine stain on page 67.") Here is what Walter Benjamin knew but didn't say: One way or another, books take their toll on us.

People who own enough books to stock two or three small-town used bookshops (we do) don't tend to uproot themselves very often (we don't). But my wife and I decided to flee our old neighborhood, Park Slope in Brooklyn, at what seemed like a perfect moment. A trend-sniffing *New York Times* reporter had recently anointed Park Slope a "hip" new literary playground—Paul Auster's *Smoke* was filming nearby—and frappuccino bars were crowding in while rents were spiking up. Over hash browns at the local diner, goateed guys with cell phones could suddenly be heard noodling on about their screenplay options.

Happy as we were to be leaving, it can be easy to forget, if you're a book person who hasn't moved for a few years, how pulverizingly awful an adventure this can be. (There's a similar delusion involved when a mother convinces herself that birthing that second child will be no sweat.) And generally you have to march along this heavy trail alone; close friends—some still stooped from your last move—mysteriously quit returning your phone calls. If reading is a solitary activity, so too is lugging the aftermath around.

Cree and I were pretty certain we'd survive the move to Greenwich Village with our relationship intact—if only because of our ironclad prenuptial agreement regarding all matters textual. ("Whoever leaves this marriage first shall forfeit to the other all books, paperback, cloth, or otherwise.") But the move managed to be fairly ugly anyway.

To lighten the burden somewhat, and because our new Village apartment is approximately the size of three Honda Civics parked side-by-side, we decided to sell some less vital books at the Strand ("Eight Miles of Books"), the venerable used bookstore. In some respects, the Strand is the Dirty Little Secret of New York's literary community. On any given moment on any given afternoon, you'll find a handful of critics, editors, and publicists at the store's downstairs purchasing desk, hawking the new hardcover review copies they've received lately. No questions asked, no tax income declared. Our sale of used goods, happily, brought us a few hundred dollars—enough to rent the Hertz moving van.

As it happens, our Strand earnings were also enough to rent an extra pair of hands from a Brooklyn company called Amazon Movers, the city's only all-woman moving company. Our personal Amazon, Chris, turned out to be a short (maybe 5'5") and none-too-brawny undergrad at Columbia. But Chris didn't wince when she saw the dozens of thirty-pound book boxes stacked toward the ceiling. Instead, she strapped on some sturdy gloves and began carrying, at a rapid clip, two boxes at a time down the several flights of brownstone stairs. This was disconcerting, not merely because I could only breathlessly manage one box at a time, but because Chris could descant knowledgeably on American literature while she heaved. My responses were Harry Crews–style (I hoped) grunts.

That night, we slept in our now-empty apartment, the groaningly loaded van parked just outside. At two AM, we heard someone smash a window and arose to see a man sprint from our van toward a waiting car and screech off down the block, leaving rubber. Cree—certain he'd made off with her prized, pulpy collection of Forties-era paperbacks—chased the car barefoot, in her nightgown. When the police finally arrived, we learned the (almost as annoying) truth: the thief had stolen the van's computer control circuit. Street value: $400.

Five sleepless hours later, the control circuit and broken window finally replaced after a long tow to New Jersey, it was time to meet our sweet Amazon in Manhattan to carry the books up another two flights of stairs, into our new apartment. Stunned and woozy as we were, the steamy July morning seemed to fly past. There wasn't even any bickering until, hours later, I tried to persuade Cree that her filing system (novels here, essay collections there) paled in comparison to my own tried-and-true method (alphabetical all the way). "Just keep your books away from mine," she spat, finally.

That night, shelves stocked, the ancient apartment building seemed to sink and sigh slightly under the weight. We were too content, however, to be alarmed. As Flaubert, who must have moved more than a few times himself, once put it, "Me and my books in the same apartment: like a gherkin in its vinegar."

—DWIGHT GARNER

WINTER 1997

~

Before you rush out and buy your pieces of split rail fence I recommend you talk with someone who knows something about what will be required. I mean the pieces themselves seem very simple, this slot into this notch and how complicated can an eighteen-inch posthole be? I'm here to tell you that there is indeed something very complicated about it and even if the fence is conceived of solely as a support for roses, envisioned as rough-hewn or honed or whatever, crooked turns out to be an exceeding likelihood, so much so that even the squirrel that sits upon it looks like a woolly question mark knocked all the hell out of shape. But there nonetheless the fence stands, for at least the moment under its own power. I cannot look at it without the vague sense that perhaps I've been drinking too much.

—Dean Young
SPRING 1997

~

This Christmas, I made my own small rebellion against the Zeitgeist. I took my LPs out of cartons in the storage room and alphabetized them. I dragged out my old turntable and the traditional revolutions resumed.

People say that we are living through a Communications Revolution, by which they mean that all information is being converted into bytes. As the happy result, you will not only be able to read a customized version of the *The Wall Street Journal* on your computer screen in the morning, but you will also be able to eat a bagel that the computer instructed your toaster to warm at seven. In practice, if not in principle, I am in favor of innovations that reduce the need to leave the house. What I am beginning to worry about, however, is not the interactivity but the digitalization that permits it. I am remembering why it is that I am not writing in Esperanto.

Let me say quickly that I never noticed any artificiality or harshness or whatever it is that audiophiles bemoan in CDs. Compared to the sound that my decrepit turntable produces, CDs seemed an improvement. But even if my ears are too crude to hear it, I am troubled by the thought of what happens when you convert a wave into a series of dots. If I understand Zeno's paradox, something is getting left out.

And more and more I am realizing that leaving something out is at the heart of modern life. In the supermarket, when I try to buy chocolate chips, I find that every brand includes vanillin, not vanilla. I feel about vanillin the way audiophiles feel about CDs. (Even more strongly, perhaps. CDs don't leave an aftertaste.) Vanillin is a chemist's attempt to isolate and reproduce the essential elements of a substance that is extracted from the seedpod of a climbing orchid. It is a chemical that tastes like vanilla. Pernicious as it is, though, it doesn't belong on the menu of the ninth circle of hell, where they are all munching on Florida winter tomatoes. Crafted to ripen and ship under adverse conditions, the Florida tomato is an interesting product. It exists only as an allusion to ripe summer tomatoes. If a Florida tomato didn't remind you of something else, you couldn't even imagine buying it. You would have no idea what to do with it.

The world is starting to resemble a Florida tomato. Everything is being reproduced in an "improved" form: cheaper, cleaner, safer. I don't mind change—well, I do mind change, but

I know better than to think it can be stopped. What I dislike is that what's new is a thinned-out version of what was old. If you want to flavor chocolate with a chemical, why not come up with something original? If you require a fruit that can be sliced on a sandwich in December, does it have to be round and red?

There is much talk in New York about the "new Times Square." The old Times Square offended many people (not least among them, the owners of the newspaper based there) with its irredeemable scuzziness. Although tourists thought of it as the Great White Way, the locals knew it as a place where you pushed your way past whores and pimps and three-card-monte hustlers. Now, I have no sentimental fondness for any of these social categories. However, it is a peculiar fact that, in any of the cities I know—New York, Boston, London—the theater district and the vice district grew up side by side. Why is that? I don't know, I'm not a social historian. What I do know is what you get when you try to retain the excitement of Times Square without the scuzz. You get the new Times Square: a hodge-podge of electronic signs that to my eyes don't appear to be advertising anything, really. What they are doing—pathetically—is attempting to recapture the thrill evoked by the old Camel sign. Which, by the way, was not only blowing smoke—it was mainly selling cigarettes.

When an architect begins working in a novel medium, he naturally recreates the forms of the past. That's why the barrel-shaped rock temples at Mamallapuram have staves carved into their granite domes, and why the columns in the cast-iron buildings of New York mimic their Corinthian marble ancestors. But the aping that we see around us isn't a toddler's first step toward understanding a new world. It's an old man's attempt to take everything he liked in the messy, uncontrollable universe and transpose it to a gated community. No list, no matter how many sharpened pencils labor over it, can contain all that has evolved with no master plan. The best the list-makers can do is compose a simulacrum. You may not be able to specify what has been lost, just as you might not consciously recall what was going on in a corner of the movie frame. But you feel the loss.

What I think of as the digital revolution is making it ever more pointless to leave our homes. For one thing, as its cheerleaders constantly remind us, we can get almost everything we want without opening the door. For another thing, it hardly seems worth the bother to venture past the door when the outside world, like a petrifying forest, has less and less life to offer.

So I'm glad to have my LPs back. I don't really have anything against CDs. The main argument against them (that they distort) is something I can't detect aurally and I know, logically, is also true of LPs. But, Schrodinger notwithstanding, I prefer waves to dots. For that matter, I like analogies. In a digitalizing world, I play my LPs in hopeless affirmation of the analog.

—ARTHUR LUBOW
SPRING 1997

~

In October of this year, barring divine intervention, the vast circular Reading Room of the British Museum will shut down, to be reopened, if at all, as a sort of museum of itself, a place where people can come and see what the famous Reading Room of the British Museum once looked like. Whereas it is now open only to ticket-holders (not that it's so very difficult to get a ticket), it will soon be made accessible to all the six million people who visit the Museum itself every year. They will have the chance to admire its soaring painted-and-gilded dome, through which light streams down on the battered blue-leather desktops below. They can see for themselves how much it resembles a huge, shabby cathedral, and will be told, presumably, that not only Karl Marx—its most famous denizen—but Matthew Arnold, Yeats, Ruskin, Swinburne, Gissing, and all sorts of other writers virtually lived here for long periods of their lives. (The historian S. R. Gardner spent just about every weekday in the Reading Room for almost fifty years, and read all 23,000 pamphlets from the English Civil War. George Bernard Shaw, who also put in his time here, made it one of the three residual beneficiaries of his will: imagine how many books were bought with the profits from *My Fair Lady*.)

Nobody in England seems pleased with the decision to abandon the Reading Room in favor of the giant new British Library, half a mile away. The new building has been variously likened in the British press to a dog food factory, an oversized public lavatory, and a "Babylonian ziggurat seen through a funfair distorting mirror." The most expensive public construction project ever undertaken in the British Isles, it has been denounced in the House of Commons as "a colossal waste of taxpayers' money" and "one of the ugliest buildings in the world." Committees have been formed to look into the disaster—originally due to open in 1980, the building is still not ready for use; a recent inspection showed up over 230,000 defects in its construction; despite being immensely scaled down from its original plans, it has already gone wildly over budget, and the end is not yet in sight.

Nor is the need to have shut down the Reading Room entirely clear. True, it was no longer possible to store the entire collection on the premises, which meant some books were warehoused miles away, and could not be "accessed" for several days. But this problem could have been handled by keeping the Reading

Room for the humanities, and building a separate facility for the other disciplines. Alternatively, it might have been solved by amending an antiquated law under which the Reading Room was awarded the Crown's privilege of receiving a copy of every publication issued in the British Isles: this has made it necessary to find room not only for countless vanity press books but for knitting magazines, parish newsletters, and local council reports on public toilet facilities in Northwest Wales.

Those few defenders of the new library try to justify its existence on the grounds of superior efficiency, yet it is already clear that it is not after all as efficient as they want to pretend. Its electronic shelving system, its computer system, its fire alarm system have all been shown to be defective. Even its storage space is rumored to be inadequate. The real question would seem to be, is it actually necessary for a library to be so very efficient? How quickly do most of us need access to what we now choose to call information rather than knowledge? How disastrous is it if we can't get hold of a particular book for two whole days? Nobody any longer seems willing to admit that whatever he or she is doing is not terribly urgent, that it really doesn't matter if the book or the letter or the proposal arrives today or three days from now. Because we can get things to each other in two seconds via fax or email, we are suddenly persuaded that it is absolutely necessary to do so. Or we are persuaded that the very fact of feeling under pressure, and feeling frantic about it, is proof of our own importance.

In fact, there is something very salutary about the leisurely process of ordering a book in the Reading Room, of trotting around to the various windows where the various bits of paper have to be handed in and then waiting two hours or two days for a book to arrive on one's desk. It restores the old sense of time, a contemplative rather than harried awareness of its passing. It makes the arrival of the awaited volume into a significant and pleasurable event. It can even confer serenity: to sit under that dome, reading a paperback to while away the time, and then to glance up and catch sight of a pink-and-white old man snoozing gently several seats down, is an oddly dignified experience. One feels sunken into deep time; one does not feel hurried or harassed or even normally impatient. That is what the tourists who will visit the restored Reading Room are not going to understand: the different sense of time, which, as much as the physical beauty of the place, was the great legacy of its Victorian past.

—EVELYN TOYNTON
SUMMER 1997

~

The debate over physician-assisted suicide is an expression of bewilderment about how to speak of death. It has become a technical problem. It manifestly is more, but the question of *what* more is deeply confounded. Consider the strange circumstances that make the most improbable of the rights claimed in the present court cases—the right to "a liberty in choosing the time and manner of one's death"—seem even *prima facie* plausible. On first hearing, it is ridiculous. Death is present where it might be thought absent; it is unpredictable (in the middle of life there is death), irresistible, unstoppable, autarchic, uncommunicative, and unsympathetic to pleas for just a little more time.

On the one hand, all this is not quite as true as it used to be. The mortality curve has become more of a box; now there is less death in life, at least in the first seven or eight decades. Death in the intensive care unit can—and is, in fact—scheduled with awesome precision: ninety percent of the people who die in the San Francisco General ICU are turned off at a specified time. In short, modern medicine has given us the capacity to alter radically the temporality of death, to stretch it out, to keep it at bay for various periods of time. Natural death, as it once existed, is a thing of the past.

We do not wait patiently for death to come, for nature to take her course. Resignation is thought prodigious and ennobling. Cardinal Bernardin and Jacqueline Kennedy Onassis did no more than what was ordinary a century ago, and were celebrated as models for us all. The death of a young girl whose mother refused (from the grave, actually, since she herself had previously died of AIDS) to have her treated aggressively for that same disorder was the subject of a full-page *New York Times* feature.

So "choosing the time and manner of one's death" may not be so wacky after all. In fact, it is a central tenet of modern medical thinking and action. But that said, the interim successes in our war against death and disease do not call into question the final result. And once this becomes clear, it must also be acknowledged that letting nature take her course is considerably less pleasant than it once was. The body, having been the venue for battles of Verdun-like intensity, is in far worse shape than it would have been when it gave up the ghost in the old temporal regime. In the struggle of the soul to leave the body, modern medicine has given the flesh unprecedented, powerful weapons.

Asking physicians for help in hastening death at this stage is asking a former ally not to forsake us, now that the war is over and we have lost. Since doctors have radically altered the temporality of death in one direction (expanded time), the request that it be altered in the other direction (contracted time) does not seem too implausible after all. I do not think it is a constitutional right. I do think that it is something of an ethical obligation, for those who have conspired with patients to fight so heroically over the landscapes of their bodies, not to abandon these bodies to their own fates once all is lost.

For people who are very far down the road of an expanded time of dying, hastening death at the end does not seem so problematic. And yet it is. We think relatively little about taking just one more technical step to keep death at bay, although managed care will undoubtedly make us think more. But it seems almost indecent and certainly odd to make demands for its imminent presence in such unabashedly technical terms. If death is the "distinguished one"—to use Henry James's form of salute as he sank from a stroke—then it is one thing to battle to keep him at bay, another to invite him with a Seconal overdose. A trivial move in a serious game: the furor over physician-assisted suicide is another sign that we do not quite know how to play it yet.

—THOMAS LAQUEUR
SUMMER 1997

Recently, upon rereading Flaubert's *Sentimental Education*, I realized that my favorite passage in it is a gross irrelevance. It is not set in the maelstrom of mid-century revolutionary Paris, which dominates the novel; it does not deal with Frédéric's consuming obsession with Madame Arnoux, the novel's central plot. It is, rather, a pastoral digression, a dainty episode in which Frédéric and his lover, Rosanette, flee the city for an idyllic outing near Fontainebleau. They wander in the woods, they dine at an inn. Flaubert describes their absorption in the countryside with passionate precision and tender patience. Then, lured by newspaper reports of fighting in Paris, the couple heads for home.

"There is a similarity of form between the novel and the dream," wrote Paul Valéry in his "Homage to Proust"—itself a curious document, given that Valéry, in his diaries, recorded only disdain for his contemporary, deeming him "spoiled on fine literature, acute nonsense," with "not a whit of intellectual force" (for the record, he despised Flaubert as well)—and that similarity lies in the fact that "*their deviations are an integral part of them.*" Reflecting on the novels that most excite and engross me, I recognize the vital truth of Valéry's assertion, one so obvious as to seem banal. Laurence Sterne, in *Tristram Shandy*—that testament to deviation, to the serious play of art—says much the same thing: "Digressions, incontestably, are the sunshine;—they are the life, the soul of reading;—take them out of this book for instance,—you might as well take the book along with them;—one cold eternal winter would reign in every page of it."

For Sterne, as for other eighteenth-century novelists, digression was crucial: their form was picaresque, and deviation gave invigorating pause to its relentless linearity. For Proust, in whose precocious literary modernity the linear had all but dissolved, deviation took the place of plot: for him, as for Henry James or Virginia Woolf, it was, far more than a narrative device, a route to essence. Doubtless, too, it reflected a social climate in which readers had, or aspired to, the leisure requisite for longer fictions, in which the prolaptic sentence (because digression can, of course, be manifest even in units of grammar) reflected not only the author's insistence on precision but presumed the reader's rigorous devotion to that insistence. The Surrealists championed meandering as the creative overspill of the unconscious (a link to Valéry of which he would doubtless have disapproved), and their descendants, the Paris intellectuals of '68, painted the city with slogans such as "Rêve + évolution = Révolution." American counterparts of the Sixties, Pynchon chief among them, penned novels afloat on unchartable streams. Digression, not so long ago, represented inspired, and inspiring, transgression.

But today, as I struggle with the novel I am writing—from which this little musing is itself a diversion—I recognize that our culture has lost its taste, or its patience, for digression. (Pynchon, it would seem, has addressed this shift by setting *Mason & Dixon* in the eighteenth century; his current bestseller cheats the present, appropriating that period most tolerant of his tendencies.) More than transgressive, it is becoming taboo—the last one, or a new one, perhaps, when incest and abuse, alcoholism and perversion are subjects common, in contemporary fiction (and memoir), to the point of cliché. Say whatever you like, reveal your most sordid inclinations by all means, we cheer, as readers—with this caveat: keep it concise, and to the point. We like our sentences short, our paragraphs a sentence or two long; we require that chapters should have clear little epiphanies and narratives big ones. We seek—we demand—closure, that contemporary buzzword, the tidy redemptive knot that will sum up a book and encapsulate its lessons. Conditioned, perhaps, by the rigid parameters of televisual and film narrative, critics applaud the most tightly woven novels, as if an impeccably detailed outline were the key to successful fiction, as if distilled messages were an artistic goal. In a recent *New Yorker* review, John Updike referred to a novel as "Joycean" with ambivalent condescension. After all, who can be bothered with long-winded efforts at exactness when approximation will suffice? Why trouble with the effort of exploratory invention, when the ending, or the message, is valued so far above extraneous, interruptive adventure? What are we sacrificing but artistic chaff? Would *Sentimental Education* not be much the same without Frédéric and Rosanette's poetic little expedition?

It would not. Granted, any filmmaker would give it a miss in adapting the screenplay, because it is a small event, and narratively messy. But the novel is a form unto itself, which still exists (I pray) as something more than fodder for screenplays. To continue to be relevant, the novel must do what film cannot—which is also what the novel does best. The passage in question, vibrantly textured, gives voice to Flaubert's most lyrical prose and, as the quiet at the eye of the storm, represents a moment of absolute human truth. It is art at its closest to life, simultaneously real and unreal, and supremely unpredictable. In deleting such idiosyncrasies, the sacrifice is art itself, the relevance of irrelevance, the sacred handling of invented life as something truer than life, which can speak to our mortal existence and alter it, however subtly.

Real life, for all we try to impose order upon it, is but an endless string of digressions (in which art itself is a digression); any life that wasn't would be exceedingly dull. In spite of this, we order our actual experiences increasingly according to the principles of story: what is memoir, after all, but the ultimate willed conflation of the two? And as we look for closure and containment in reality, so, too, we leach the truth of life from fiction.

—Claire Messud
FALL 1997

~

The typewriter I'm working at this morning is an Underwood manual of a vintage you may occasionally see on screen as a 1930s movie prop, or ensconced in a glass case at an arty stationer's, serving as a bit of nostalgic decor. Solid, square, and black, with an open metal frame that leaves its inner workings penetrable to curious eyes and to dust (I clean it regularly with an old toothbrush), it bears the stamp of NATIONAL TYPEWRITER EXCHANGE MONTREAL, and a sales-service phone number (MA 2147) whose six digits and letter-code exchange seem almost as antiquated as the article itself. On the back, a fading sticker attests that THIS TYPEWRITER WAS REBUILT ACCORDING TO THE SPECIFICATIONS CONTAINED IN ADMINISTRATOR'S ORDER A-394 OF THE WARTIME PRICES AND TRADE BOARD.

I did not acquire the Black Monster (aka Old Faithful) as a piece of antique treasure-trove. It has been with me almost as long as I can remember: in fact, I taught myself how to touch-type on it, at the age of eight or nine, out of an old stenographer's manual propped up on a bent coat hanger (progressing by slow taps from ASK A SAD LAD to the full-alphabet intricacies of THE QUICK BROWN FOX JUMPS OVER THE LAZY DOG and THE LAZY HORSES GAVE A QUICK JERK WHICH BROKE THE AXLE AND HURLED THE FARMER UPON HIS HEAD). The typewriter had been my mother's during her student years at McGill University. If I lift the front of the metal frame, resting the heavy beast on its hind feet, I can still read on the inside back frame, in white-painted lettering (nail polish, perhaps?), JULY 31 '44 and what looks like a T, my mother's initial. Recently she reminded me that she sold a jewel of a Heintzman upright piano (on which, as a teenager, she'd learned to play *Für Elise* and a handful of other perennials) to buy a typewriter for college. The piano, a quality musical instrument and fine specimen of cabinet-making, would now be worth thousands of dollars; the typewriter, an obsolete piece of technology, might fetch as much as fifty dollars on the curio market—and then again, might not. It's something she periodically gnashes her teeth over.

The Heintzman does give me some pause (I studied piano seriously for a decade, and still play), but I can't regret the Underwood. I love this old machine. I love it for its history: that it crossed the country with my parents when they eloped to Vancouver, where I was conceived—crossed it back again two years later for Columbia University and New York, where I was born; that most of my early poems and stories were tapped out on it, and some not so early ones. I did eventually "upgrade"—first to a later-model Underwood acquired at a police auction, then to a 1950s Royal, a portable, with the marvelous feature of Magic Margins—but both of these replacements eventually malfunctioned and could not be repaired. Technology caught up with me only in 1993, when I did a slow circle dance around my husband's new computer before zeroing in, with something like a sob of gratitude, on its usefulness for correspondence, "deadline" writing, and manuscript preparation. But I still prefer to do much of my early draftwork, especially for poetry and fiction, on a manual—and the Black Monster is now my one-and-only.

Old Faithful. I'd love it for its familiarity even were it not beautiful, but it is in fact, in the way of old machines, strangely beautiful. I love its keyboard: the round, glass-capped keys, ringed in raised metal to hug the fingertips; a simple alphabet of block capitals stamped in white (now mostly aged to tan) on a black ground. The glass caps mirror the light, the silver rings gleam beguilingly—to look at the typewriter is to feel the magic that resides in letters, to want to feel keys beneath fingers, ready to dance. I love the cheery ting of the carriage bell as a tiny arm flies up to strike its silver dish with a puck-like hammer. I love the intricacies of the visible innards, the precision of tooled metal parts cunningly hinged and interlocking: the toothed flywheel for reversing and rewinding the ribbon, its retractable handle perfectly molded to thumb and forefinger; the margin-sets, released by pincer grips, sliding smoothly along their steel bar.

All right, so it's true the margins are confusing to set—the left governing the right, and vice versa. And it's true that the manual tab-sets in back, with their tiny interlocking teeth, almost aren't worth the trouble, even when they aren't frozen in place for want of oiling. It's true that the heft of the carriage is hard on the shift-key pinky; that in general the machine is not for wimps—you've got to pack a whack to get it clacking. Quirks. But reliable? Who could ask for better? Half a century after my mother acquired it (and don't forget, she bought it *rebuilt*), it is a fully functional machine. It has been dropped in transit and survived with the mildest of denting; it bears no signs of rust. One of the rubber carriage handgrips is missing—rotted away in the damp of a single Vancouver Island winter—and two of the rubber feet, similarly eaten, have had to be bolstered with electrical tape. The letter Q sits slightly low in the keybed and is sluggish on the return, but it still types. Otherwise, not a thing wrong. My overhead on this piece of equipment over thirty years has been under two hundred dollars, total. (Three professional cleanings and a few boxes of carbon ribbons—I've begun to stockpile these, they're getting harder to find.) No reason to suppose, given moderate use, it shouldn't last another fifty years—longer than I will, in all likelihood.

Today I'm typing on the Black Monster not by preference but because my laptop computer, nearing the end of its three-year warranty, is in for repairs for the third time in as many weeks. I'm fond of my laptop, and it had given me little trouble until a month ago, when a single prong snapped off one of its electrical plugs. A defective piece of metal, I supposed; a simple matter of replacing the plug. Not so. The plug, explained the repairman, was integral to the board, and the whole board would have to be replaced. Back came the computer with a functional plug on its new board—and a battery of problems it never had before.

Back at the dealer's, I protested that a defective board must have been installed. The repairman conceded the "new" board might be a rebuilt one: "You're still under warranty, they might not provide brand-new parts." But when I asked if I could insist on a new board, he admitted, "Truth is, they might not make them for this model any more. Your computer's three years old." Stunned, I mumbled something about what the laptop had cost: surely it could be expected to last more than three years? Not necessarily, I was advised with a gentle smile—and, in fact, the newer models came with only a one-year guarantee.

The end of this story isn't in yet. (The dealers are still "working on it.") But my meantime has taken the form of a loving reacquaintance with an old friend. Remembered sensations: the weight and spring of a manual space-bar, the coolness of ringed glass keys, the clunk of the carriage shifting (my pinkies are getting stronger), and the *clackety-clack, tap-tap-tap, ping!* of a thought-rush spilling onto paper. The peaceful silence *between* thoughts: absence of flicker and hum. A slowed-down, ruminative rhythm, conducive to daydreams and digressions.

As if the very weight, the solidity and substance of the square black frame grounded me, somehow inviting a freer play of the mind. As if a meter had been shut off. As if there were time and to spare for a feast of remembering.

—Robyn Sarah

FALL 1997

~

I witnessed my first time capsule burial when I was eight years old. It took place on the grounds of Fort Wright College, a Catholic women's school in Spokane, the same summer as the first moon landing. As the only boy in our family, I got the privilege of accompanying my father, owner of the Inland Empire Coca-Cola Bottling Company, who had been invited to contribute. At a precisely choreographed moment in the ceremony, he deposited a pristine Coke bottle into the mini *faux* missile, which was to remain underground, untouched, for a hundred years.

My mind buzzed with questions I was too well-behaved to ask. How will anyone ever find it? Who'll remember the right spot to dig it up? What will they learn about us? And, most urgently, who'll get to drink the century-old soda pop? I remember little else about the time capsule but this: the keep-me-up-at-night impatience I felt for it to be unburied, just as soon as the missile hatch was shut.

Curiosity drove a boy to the brink of an existential crisis that would seem more hilarious now, twenty-eight years later, if its impact were not still reverberating. The Coke-bottle time capsule taught me an incisive lesson about mortality that the catechism nuns never did manage to clarify. The capsule's opening date was just far enough away to ensure that none of the original witnesses would be remaining. No matter how I added up the math, I knew that even an eight-year-old would not be alive in a hundred years. Our elaborate surprise was meant for a whole new world.

I've since discovered that it was some unsung genius at the Westinghouse Corporation who dreamed up this idea. The first time capsule was conceived as a promotional spectacle for the 1939 New York World's Fair. It shared exhibition space in an elaborate, omega-shaped building with the Singing Tower of Light and the Fair's star attraction, a giant performing robot named Elektro. Shaped, without irony, like a torpedo, the sleek, seven-and-a-half-foot-long bombshell bore peaceful greetings from "present-day America to the people of Earth of 6939 AD." Copper-bound, glass-lined, and nitrogen-filled, designed to survive war or natural disaster, it was enshrined fifty feet underground in a mysterious place called The Immortal Well.

As a staff member of the San Francisco AIDS Foundation in 1992, I finally got a chance to help create a time capsule for my own community. Across Civic Center Plaza, crowds cheered marchers as they passed beneath an enormous rainbow of helium balloons spanning Market Street. Yet the mood was somber within our humid vinyl tent. When I looked up from the table, I saw a steady flow of men waiting in a line that did not shorten until late in the day, when the Gay/Lesbian Pride Parade ended and the fog rolled in. They were waiting longer and more patiently in that line than they would to buy a bottle of beer. Single men, couples, and groups of friends, pumped-up, sun-burned, half-undressed, young men propped on canes and leather-daddies in sweat-drenched chaps: all waiting to send a note to the future.

They were asked to respond to two questions on a single sheet of paper: *How would your life be different without the threat of AIDS?* And, *What message would you send to people fifty years from now about your experience during the AIDS epidemic?* I handed out pencils and blank sheets of paper, and tossed completed responses in a cardboard box at my feet. At parade's end, the box was packed, taped shut, and unceremoniously left in a storage closet at the office, among cartons and cartons of accounting receipts.

If a community's faith in the future might be measured by the date set for a time capsule's opening, then it had lapsed considerably since 1939, when the World's Fair version was sealed for five thousand years. For the AIDS Time Capsule, we gave it just fifty. "Do not open until 2042," the box was labeled. Our time capsule was awfully pathetic-looking: it would hardly survive Recycling Day, much less the Armageddon. But I see now that its disposable appearance was irrelevant. Beneath the indestructible, whiz-bang trappings, the contents of the World's Fair time capsule were also touchingly prosaic: newspapers, a newsreel (but no newsreel projector), and thousands of pages on microfilm. The text of everyday life, America, 1939—carefully set aside for future reading.

The AIDS Time Capsule continued this custom, one that's linked in my imagination much farther back in history, to the messages found embedded in temple foundations in ancient Babylon. For in its purest conception, a time capsule need be no more complicated than words on paper, items hand-sewn, or images on film: evidence of a life, saved. In fact, it need not be enshrined or buried underground, but can be left in a scrapbook or hung on a museum wall. Creating a time capsule requires only the unshakable faith that the people of Earth will continue without you; the desire to invest an object with meaning; and the belief that at least one benevolent future being will find it, wishing simply to know: *What was your life like then?*

As I write this, in 1997, I see us poised on a delicate threshold: a glimpse of hopefulness and progress in the AIDS pandemic that we didn't envision when we made a time capsule five years ago. The new protease inhibitor drugs give us more life, yet more time to wait; these drugs may delay death, but have not stopped HIV. As it happens, too, the human race is at century's edge and, I think, we could fall either way: backwards or forwards in time, upon memory or imagination. We are standing at the lip of The Immortal Well with no idea what's going to happen next. This is what present tense is.

—Bill Hayes
winter 1998

~

It was the summer of 1977 and people were still hopeful about Jimmy Carter. In the Capitol Hill office where I was an unpaid intern I enjoyed the daily luxury of an IBM Selectric, and watched the specially-trained technician at the next desk fight with our single computer, a large clattering machine used to generate mass-mailings. I answered letters and wrote small speeches that were never given but which appeared in the Congressional Record as if they had been, and researched the possibility of generating hydroelectric power in New England. Two or three times a week I spent a couple of hours in an airless attic storeroom of the Cannon Office Building, producing a handwritten log of constituent mail for a purpose that was never explained to me.

I lived with three other boys from Amherst College in a high-rise overlooking a Virginia freeway; we were each in rotation supposed to produce dinner but didn't have a single cookbook among us. One night we went to the annual interns' reception at what was then called the Chinese Embassy. We stood sweating through our suits on the lawn and listened to the Taiwanese Ambassador's speech, his earnest wish that when, as adults, we returned to Washington in positions of power, we would remember what a good time we had had at his house when we were young. That summer I learned to parallel park and how to explain myself on the telephone. I ate Vietnamese food and drank Mexican beer and tried *tripes à la mode de Caen*. But the Potomac never made my temperature rise, and so all that I've just described counts as nothing in comparison to something that then seemed unimportant.

I read *Emma*. Most mornings I took the bus to work, forty-five minutes of apartment complexes and highway, and when after a few days I realized both that I wouldn't miss my stop and that nothing bad would happen to me if I did, I began to read. I read *What Maisie Knew* and *The Ordeal of Gilbert Pinfold* and *Great Expectations*. But *Emma* has stayed with me the most, and in looking back I now seem in that one summer to have been Jane Austen's perfect reader—perfect in my complete and credulous naiveté.

Because I trusted Emma Woodhouse. I didn't much care for her but I trusted her, this smug and meddlesome girl just my own age, nearly twenty-one. I believed that Emma's values were those that the novel held dear, and though I judged her, I never saw that Austen herself had shaped that judgment. I didn't like Emma, no. But I identified with her: I thought she was a reliable guide to her world. I know, now, that Austen enforces that identification by showing us almost everything from Emma's point of view, so that our perceptions come to us filtered through her limited consciousness. I know that what the other characters say about her can help us see through Emma's opinions even as the novel tempts us to share them; know too how Austen's choice of words—"clever," "seemed"—serves from the book's opening sentence to invite our skepticism.

Now I know how the trick was done. But I saw none of that then, and so I didn't pay much attention to Mr. Knightley, the one character to criticize Emma. I might agree with his calling her spoiled, but that was just between us, it didn't change how I saw the novel. I discounted his words when he told her that the fatuous clergyman Mr. Elton wasn't at all in love with her protégée Harriet Smith, and instead agreed with Emma that he didn't have "the skill of such an observer on such a question as herself." So I have never had a bigger shock as a reader than on the morning when, as my bus snaked its way through Fairfax County, I not only realized that Mr. Knightley was right but that Mr. Elton was in love with Emma herself. Her feelings when she receives his proposal were mine as I read it: "How could she have been so deceived! . . . Such an overthrow . . . Such a blow."

And the curious thing is that we neither of us learned from our mistakes. I continued to trust her, and we kept on being wrong together about the rest of the novel's characters, and about the state of her own heart. I believed the stories she spun about other people's love lives, about Harriet and Jane Fairfax and Frank Churchill and the always-offstage Mr. Dixon. I even believed her when she said that she herself had very little intention of ever marrying at all.

Perhaps it was the noise and the crowd of the bus that made the book so difficult, the starting and the stopping as I read a few chapters each day in my Modern Library Giant. Perhaps it was simply Austen's brilliance, the skill with which she'd gulled me. Yet I think my real problem had to do with my own lack of experience with the genre. I was a serious English major. In my classes I had read *War and Peace* and *Ulysses* and *Paradise Lost*. My earlier reading had, however, been the boys' hardboiled cocktail of Hemingway and Tarzan. I had never before opened a novel about courtship, a book that turned on a woman's choice of a husband. So I read without expectations—I didn't realize that *Emma* was a novel about growing up, and that it would have to end with her wedding, that somehow maturation and marriage were the same thing. And I never imagined, until she did herself, that she would have to marry Mr. Knightley, that in novels of courtship as in mysteries the suspect has to be present from the start.

For a long time I thought my own first encounter with *Emma* was typical, that most readers would react to it as I had. Yet after a dozen years of teaching the book to first-year students at a women's college, I've still never found one who did. Remembering my own sublime bewilderment, I ask my students to describe, as carefully as they can, their reactions to Mr. Elton's proposal; and almost without exception they tell me they expected it. I used to wonder why, and for years I felt a disappointment that I'm afraid I couldn't quite hide: in them, for not having the same reading experience that I did; and in myself, for not being able to give them that sense of confusion and delight.

But my students already know how to read this novel. They all know that Emma can't be trusted, and they can, most of them, pick out from the opening chapters the man whom she will marry. This isn't because these young women identify themselves with her. None of them sees Emma's story as a mirror for either her own life or her own process of reading. It's rather that they are prepared for the novel in a way that I wasn't. Maybe they have read *Pride and Prejudice* or *Jane Eyre*, maybe it's that they can see the connection between *Emma* and any number of film comedies, from *Bringing Up Baby* to *Clueless*. No matter how, they already understand the conventions that structure this book, the conventions that in lesser hands still shape so many bestselling romances. And my finally recognizing this—recognizing the role that an awareness of genre can play in our reading, and of the way that such an awareness can even now depend upon gender—has given my class more to talk about, not less.

I taught *Emma* badly for years precisely because it was so crucial a part of my own formation as a reader. My experience of it had been so powerful that I couldn't separate those days on a D.C. bus from the book itself, and maybe the fact that I now can marks a kind of maturation, not as a reader this time, but as a teacher. I'm not sorry I was so naïve when I met this book, that I made such exhilarating mistakes when I was on my own for the first time in a great city; and at times I still wish that some of my students were unformed enough to do so as well. But they will have that experience with other novels, perhaps, and in the meantime how wonderfully disconcerting it feels to find that after twenty years, *Emma* still defines me: that it has gone on reading me, telling me who I am and how I've changed, and how much I will always have to learn.

—Michael Gorra
summer 1998

~

In 1945, while my dad was overseas, I lived with my mother at her father's beach house on the strand at Hermosa Beach, California. I was three. Part of the daily ritual in that sunny, sandy cottage was listening to a broadcast of the horse races from Santa Anita. My grandfather, a rotund cherub with a cigar and a worn beret, sat in a wicker armchair, and I squatted on the floor directly in front of the Philco's speaker.

I had a tiny green-and-gold jewel box which held the pennies I won betting with my grandfather on the races. It was a good deal: he would bet a penny on one horse, and I would bet one on all the others in the race. (Many years later, when he got in a little hot water over some gambling debts, I figured out why he picked that particular horse when he bet with me, and why he cheered that horse on so loudly when only a penny seemed to be at stake.)

After each race, I would examine the date and mint stamp on each penny I won, and if I already had a duplicate, I would put it aside to accumulate and change into nickels. The ones with date and mint stamps that weren't duplicates, I would keep in the jewel box—each one unique. No, this is not "how I got rich"; this is how my penny collection began.

My collection has its rules: no buying, no trading, only finding. These are the laws a True Collector obeys, and there is, therefore, no reason for the True Collector to go to coin shops. In fact, such things as complete mint sets or a 1909 S-VDB only depress or sadden the T. C.

But after a lifetime of diligent inspection of each penny that came my way, and careful cataloguing, this year I gave in to curiosity and, for the first time, went to a coin shop with my three blue cardboard folders containing my hundred and thirty or so pennies (a collection with many gaps). I didn't really care what the collection was worth—but who could resist asking, using an oblique and apologetic tone? I just wondered, theoretically, if it would be difficult or expensive to complete the collection by buying the pennies I was missing.

What I found out was at first humbling: the entire collection, a lifetime's labor, was worth about eleven dollars, and, with the exception of four coins (costing $250, $100, $35, and $35), the collection could be completed for another fifteen. As I said, the news was humbling; but it was also wonderfully liberating and satisfying. Confirmed were my laws of collecting, that the collection was of value to me only, no one else, and that the effort put into it could only give me the joy and satisfaction of the pursuit, the chase—the ostensible goal would never be achieved. And this is joy and satisfaction enough.

—TIM SAVINAR
FALL 1998

~

"The maid, averting her frozen, wanton eyes, carried in breakfast on a tray."

There is nothing particularly remarkable about this sentence, at least as it is translated into English. I do not know Russian, so I cannot tell you what rhythmic, syntactic, or phonemic textures, movements, and balances are at work. Babel is too great a writer, and Russian too musical a language, not to have some sort of phono-textual action working hand in hand with the image and literal meaning. Nor can I identify the modulations and associations generated by individual words or combinations.

Even as it stands, though, it is the beautiful cap to one of the extraordinary short sequences in prose literature.

> "How did you do it?"
>
> I spoke of style then, of the army of words, an army using all types of weapons. No steel can pierce a heart so icily as a period placed in the right place. She listened, her head down, her painted lips parted. A black light played in her neatly parted, smooth, lacquered hair. Her legs, with their powerful, gently curving calves encased in tight, fine stockings, were planted wide apart on the carpet.
>
> The maid . . .

In the context of the story, an impoverished young writer has been invited to a wealthy St. Petersburg home ("A red carpet covered the stairs. Plush bears stood erect on the landings with crystal lamps sparkling between their bared teeth") to assist the matron of the house with her hopeless translations of de Maupassant's stories. We are first introduced to the maid in this fashion:

> The high-bosomed maid sailed solemnly across the room. She was straight, short-sighted, and arrogant. Debauchery was frozen in her gray, wide-open eyes. She moved slowly. I felt that when making love she would move with uncanny agility.

The martial language and ardor of the young writer explaining *style*, and the posture of the older woman *receiving* the explanation are obvious enough that the sexual analogy need not be belabored. In fact, the entire story is permeated by the analogy between sex and writing.

A few sentences before the charmingly corrupt mise-en-scène, the narrator comments:

> A sentence is born both good and bad at the same time. The whole secret lies in a hardly perceptible twist. The control handle must be warm in your hand. You must turn it only once, never twice.

Babel telegraphs his move with this sentence before the admiring Mrs. Bendersky asks the young writer, who had improved her translation, "How did you do it?"

> The piece of lace between her compressed breasts slipped sideways and fluttered.

Then, having told us what he is going to do and how he is going to do it, Babel very meticulously sets us up and, with "a hardly perceptible twist," takes our breath away with the entrance of the maid.

—AUGUST KLEINZAHLER
SUMMER 1999

~

I decided to learn how to drive an eighteen-wheel truck on the streets of Manhattan largely because, when I was little, my parents drove an enormous four-wheeler—a Cadillac sedan about eighteen feet long. I recall it managed to squeeze out double-digit gas mileage only on the highway. New York City, where I grew up, always struck me as a strange place for such a mammoth vehicle as our Cadillac to live. It seemed to belong on open runs of roadway where it could stretch itself out a bit. At the same time, there was something refreshing about the laughable incongruity of driving around in a car that probably had no business being anywhere but in the suburbs. On the city streets, we routinely held up traffic and pushed the limits of our allotted lane. Every time we drove past a particular building with reflective street-side windows on Twenty-Third Street, it took a full second for me to comprehend that the black behemoth moving slowly across the mirrored glass was the car in whose back seat

I was buckled. As a boy, being in that huge vehicle—sheltered from the world by its reinforced-steel carapace—gave me a sense of security nearly equal to and as essential as my mother's embrace. Still, at an early age, I realized the responsibility that came with driving an automobile—particularly one that size. I would see fear flash in the eyes of compact-car drivers forced to share Lexington Avenue on our terms. Even when our car was stationary at a red light, pedestrians would cross its bow cautiously, as if apprehensive that its dormant power alone might deal them a deadly blow.

My own apprehension prevented me from getting a basic driver's license until I was twenty-five. (Fortunately, by then my parents had traded in their old whale for a newer, abbreviated machine. Even so, I drove it seldom.) Others in my family have shown a similar reluctance. My Grandma Syd lived to eighty-seven and never got a license. And my sister is approaching her twenty-eighth year without so much as a learner's permit. (Once, when she was twenty-one, my sister went down to the D.M.V., but only to get a nondriver's ID card to show bartenders.) Partly to establish a new chapter in my family's brief driving history, partly to challenge my fears—and partly because of the ridiculous image of an enormous vehicle driven around an already congested metropolis by a novice with barely any experience operating basic four-wheelers—I recently decided to drive an eighteen-wheeler in Manhattan.

At the D.M.V., I couldn't resist obtaining, in addition to the basic permit to operate a big rig, endorsements to haul unwieldy and hazardous cargo and to drive vehicles even more specialized than a standard tractor-trailer. So, ultimately, I had the blessing of New York State to do the following: pull double and triple trailers the length of half a football field; drive gasoline and milk tankers; transport hanging meat in refrigerated trucks;

haul livestock (not to be confused with hanging meat, and usually moved in unrefrigerated trucks); and transport ammunition, blasting agents, and explosive devices, flammable and nonflammable gases, flammable liquids and solids, combustible liquids and spontaneously combustible solids, and oxidizers, organic peroxides, corrosives, and most poisons. Grandma Syd must have been looking down on me in disbelief.

Permit in hand, I enrolled in a driving school whose motto was "Think big . . . Earn big. Learn to drive tractor-trailers, trucks, or buses." (Regrettably, operating gasoline tankers and transporting either hanging meat, blasting agents, or spontaneously combustible solids were not part of the curriculum. The school also lacked for triple trailers.) Right away, I was lent a tractor-trailer—just a single—and a driving instructor. Almost as quickly, Angel, a sixty-something Puerto Rican with a pointy, distinguished face, threatened me with relegation to a lower form of automobile. "You're going to have to start in a car until you learn how to use the stick shift." No way, Angel. "Well, you got to remember it's like a dance—one two, one two," he said, tapping his ring against the window to at once mark the beat and get the attention of a shapely woman crossing Fourteenth Street. Part of the problem was that before my first afternoon in the eighteen-wheeler (which not only had a manual transmission but required double-clutching), I had never driven a stick-shift vehicle of any kind. I also had some difficulty distinguishing between Angel's directions of "No clutch" and "Now clutch," twice nearly stripping the gears by "no-ing" when I should have been "now-ing." I stalled too often to count—three times on one particular block alone. Once, I conked out on Seventh Avenue in front of a policeman, who glared first at the huge truck's "Student Driver" bumper sticker, then at me through the windshield. But, downshifting smoothly for the first time somewhere along

Essex Street on the Lower East Side, I felt a satisfying, anxiety-clearing swoosh, like a safecracker who had just gotten the final tumbler of a Mosler to slip into place.

When you sit in the cab of a big truck, with your head ten feet above the pavement, your perspective on New York changes measurably. In a city dominated by tall things, mounting yourself on the driver's seat of an eighteen-wheeler makes you a tall thing, too. And, although not to the same extent as when you look down from atop the Empire State Building, things around you seem fractionally slower—just enough to lull you into a sense that driving isn't dangerous. But then you come within inches of flattening a bicycle messenger who has emerged from a blind spot and whipped off a left turn in front of you, and you quickly reacquire your measure of the parlous reality.

I suppose what I loved most about driving that tractor-trailer around Manhattan was the truck's out-of-placeness; like our old Cadillac, it was a vehicle so clearly belonging somewhere else that I couldn't help operating it here. So, on my last day of lessons, when Angel asked me where I wanted to go for my final spin, I smiled and, without hesitation, coaxed the big machine towards Twenty-Third Street. The building with reflective street-side windows was still there, exactly where I'd left it. Although I probably shouldn't have, I removed my eyes from the road and glanced right. And I immediately knew that the silver behemoth moving slowly across the mirrored glass was the truck in whose driver's seat I was buckled.

—Douglas Danoff
SUMMER 1999

~

A friend tells me that for men in America, watches are the only really accepted sartorial indulgence. That and shoes. We are allowed to fuss over our timepieces and the shine of our boots. We have to be on our feet and on time, and it's this smoke-screen of practicality that makes our drag dignified, so acceptably masculine. A man isn't supposed to need much. My boots anchor me, my sneakers make me fly. I have five watches on my dresser, waiting to determine my day.

They are all somewhat different. Only one of the five is digital, with time announced in LED numbers. The strap, cheap blue plastic, resists water, as does the watch itself. When I resumed wearing watches in the mid-Eighties, when I began having to be in particular places at particular times to avoid general poverty, this is the kind of watch I chose. I have had several since, none of them distinguishable from each other. They are designed to be useful, and discarded when they are no longer. Modern time. I buy them on Canal Street in Chinatown, usually from small electronics shops peddling impermanence. This watch reminds me of schedules and deadlines, its alarm useful for calling me back to the laundromat when the load is done (twenty-four minutes), or waking me up in the hotel bed for the flight home, or enabling me to catch the bus back from the teaching job. It can be used to gauge fish broiled in the Canadian method (ten minutes per inch), the length of a series of student recitals, the allotted time for a funeral oration. It means nothing to me, yet it is the most useful of all of my watches. Its grey face shows no character, and no memory is encased in the scratch-resistant plastic.

Another, a pocket watch with a gold chain, is seldom attached to me. It was a gift from my mother, who thought I would like its elegance, yet her interpretations of my desire for "elegance" were dated and somewhat worn; like my desire for art deco and black clothing, phases I passed through years ago, but more recent than my brief desire for a watch chain dangling out of a smoking jacket. As with many of my mother's gestures toward luxury or elegance, it is not the real article, but a knock-off whose imitation is sadly self-conscious. In a brushed gold case, it is diminutive, one could say ladylike, and electronic, although the legend SWISS MADE is lettered on its face. This is not a watch that made the Swiss reputation for efficiency and precision measurements of time, having ceased keeping time a year after she gave it to me. I retain the watch, afraid of hurting my mother's feelings if I abandon it. She would have to discard a younger image of me, and that would mean a loss far more significant to her than my own feelings regarding the original gift. Like myself at an early age, the watch tries to be something it is not, with false labeling and inadequate finish. Perhaps that is why I cannot part with it; it reminds me that I once wanted something like it, and this is what I got. This is what I was at one time and do not want to be again. Like the watch, I wanted to hide behind clothing, snuggled in a pocket, not necessarily mine.

Two other watches are recent additions, left to me by my father. I like wearing things that belonged to him: the suede jacket Mother "splurged" on, the cashmere sweater from a Neiman Marcus sale. I am surprised and pleased that his things fit me, as he was always bigger, more massive. I think of him when I wear these things; his arms wrap around me and I am his son. But it is the watches that feel ceremonial, significant.

When he was dying, on Election Day, he was not wearing either watch. My attention was on his wedding ring, which my mother, in a gesture of finality that still haunts me, removed from his hand: the hand she had placed it on, so many years ago, the hand she had guided to sign that last absentee ballot. He was alive, but she knew he would not be much longer. For my father, the lapsed Catholic, this was as close to extreme unction as he would get. What I interpreted through my confused grief as an overly practical and almost acquisitive act was instead a realistic, final acknowledgment by my mother that her husband was leaving her life, permanently: "There's no reason to have this burn up." She wanted to save this one thing, this thing she had originally given him. The next day my father died, and I will never know if removing that ring was permission or a push. My mother has kept the ring, offering it to me abstractly, unsure if she wants to part with it. I don't wear rings, and neither does my partner. So I am offered my father's watches.

The first one, the larger and cheaper of the two, my mother says has no real value, sentimental or monetary. It was one of a series of "practical everyday" watches he owned, with durable spand-o-flex metal bands. I splay open the links of the band, crusted with dirt, Dad's dirt. Is it dirt from our avocado grove that we worked together for so many years, dirt from the tomatoes he bragged about, or from the roses he took to in his later years? Or is it residue from the lab, toxic chemicals from his career as a chemist, the particles that possibly shortened his life? We have burned his body, but this dirt remains. It's not the watch I want, but the father I loved who wore it.

His other watch, a present my mother bought early in their marriage, is more formal. It is a watch more in keeping with her delicate frame, a bit small for my father. His name, Walter Michael McMahon, is engraved across the 14k gold case. The "genuine lizard" band is new; did Dad ever wear this? My mother tells me that he was far too casual with it: "You know how your father is about taking care of things" (she still speaks of him, often disapprovingly, in the present tense). After she had to replace the crystal several times, cracked against lab beakers, tennis rackets, and rusted water pipes, she regulated its use; this watch would be for special occasions only. My entire family operated on this principle, the "Sunday-best" approach to dressing. God forbid you should wear out your nice clothes on everyday use. We buy nice things but don't wear them, afraid of being profligate. Some recessive WASP gene, suspicious of show, but wanting to be ready just in case, shops with us. This watch, this indulgence, which I do not recall seeing my father wear, is the heirloom, pedigreed and retrograde, waiting to be wound. It is the real thing, and demands attention, attention to the monitoring of time passing. And the passing of those who wear it.

And finally there is my everyday watch, the watch I purchased four years ago after deciding my plastic ones were just too cheap. I had been attracted to another watch, on the wrist of a friend I had a brief affair with. What I really wanted was his watch; something about a deep blue face, ringed by gold. I found its poorer cousin at Macy's, looking more elegant than the cost would indicate, yet having some whimsy about it. Made by a Japanese firm clearly out to give Swatch some competition, it has the endearingly pointless displays of English that Asian companies like to use as design elements: "Official Time," "Registered Style," "Authentic," all in small type on the blue face. It has a fake-antique look that manages to be charming yet casual, as I try to be. I was initially quite taken by it, but now its status has declined, pushed out by Dad's Girard-Perregaux, which makes it look shabby, with no history. When I put this watch on my wrist, nothing accompanies it, and all that it gives is the time. With such a watch, I move forward, not backward, in the time that it so practically and objectively measures. It records time but does not contain it.

—Jeff McMahon
SPRING 2000

~

I went to see the Kirov Ballet when they played the Met a while back.

I saw a fabulous ballet show.

The show was *The Sleeping Beauty*.

This new production was, they tell me, a deeply researched reconstruction of the ur-show: 1890, Maryinsky Theater, St. Petersburg, Russia. Let's be proud of the people who kill themselves trying to reconstruct in minute exactitude the original symptoms of a historic production.

Although I am generally a big fan of things like the Early Music movement, I am skeptical. Are you sure about all of this? Really? Did Tchaikovsky hear it this way? Is that what Petipa meant? Did they like it? Was it performed beautifully? Was the show thrown together? At the last minute? Was it a hit? Was the dancing any good? Did anybody get it?

I don't much care.

Here's what I want to know: How was it the other night?

Great.

Four hours long. Three intermissions. The opposite of boring. The costumes were bizarre, wildly varicolored, a little bit Danny Kaye. Perfect. The sets were heavy and detailed; gobs of fake draperies, blankets of cobwebs, flocks of plumes.

The dancing was thrillingly all-over-the-place. Never less than interesting. Good mime.

Aurora (Irma Nioradze) was a real beauty—regal, shy, tentative. She resembled the original. The omnipotent Lilac Fairy (Daria Pavlenko), the real boss of the ballet, ruled with grace, strict kindness, and a bunch of flowers. The fairy dances were a fascinating mess of styles. The National and Fairytale divertissements were aggressive, distinct, a little bit violent.

My favorite character was King Florestan XIV (Vladimir Ponomarev). It was so exciting and fun to hear the King music and, at the same time, watch the tender, grand, romantic storytelling of this wonderful artist.

The music was astonishing. For the first time ever, I understood that *The Sleeping Beauty* might be Tchaikovsky's best ballet score. The florid violin concertino as entr'acte, historically justified or not, was heaven. The band played extravagantly well under Gianandrea Noseda. He swings.

If the band plays so well, we have only Valery Gergiev to blame. Over the past few years I have seen him conduct the Kirov Opera and Orchestra. The music is consistently vibrant, passionate, big. I welcome the occasional mistake as proof of the players' mortality. As chief music director of the Kirov Ballet, the Opera, and the Orchestra, Gergiev has rediscovered and exposed the miracles of Russian music played Russianly.

What a rush. What a *Beauty*.

—Mark Morris
SPRING 2000

~

He looked ghastly, my perp, sunken-eyed, pale, and sweaty, staring straight ahead beneath the glaring lights of the police lineup. I knew that most of those five men must be undercover cops, but they appeared just as queasy and tense as he did, seated and holding large numbered cardboard squares. For sheer elation, nothing quite equals fingering a felon at your local precinct, especially when he can't see you. Peering through the two-way mirror, I told the detective that my choice was Number 4, although he'd been standing up and smiling when I last saw him, only six days before. The handsome detective chuckled. "I can make them stand up," he said gleefully, "I can make them smile." If I wished, each man would rise to his feet and say, "I am Marvin Westover." I flashed on "I am Spartacus," but I was late for the theater and had to pass up that beguiling spectacle.

The con game had begun on the telephone—as it had for a series of my Manhattan neighbors for nearly a year. A rasping, cozy older man's voice had said, "Nora, do you know who this is?" Ordinarily I don't take no-name calls, but I was absorbed in correcting proofs and thought I recognized the inflections of a retired Dartmouth professor who'd contributed several plums to the research for my last book. Assuming that he was in town, I asked, "Is that Conrad?" Yes, the caller said, and then described the plight of a friend of his who had been in a car crash near my home. The friend (Marvin Westover) was bruised though not injured, but his girlfriend was badly hurt and she was in New York Hospital, two blocks from me. Westover needed $300: could I loan it to him? I never keep that much cash on hand, but—remembering how helpful Conrad had been to me—I offered $90.

"Conrad" said he would soon visit the woman in the hospital, then he would drop by and reimburse me. He explained that Westover would phone and arrange to collect the money—which he did, in a totally different voice: deeper and crisper. (In court he had a nasal twang.) On my doorstep he looked respectable: a balding man with a hawk nose, a neat dark-blue sweater. He thanked me and walked quickly away. But instead of heading for the hospital and the wounded girlfriend, he strode off in the opposite direction. My inner alarm bells went off at once. Fearing that I'd been duped, I rang the real Conrad in New Hampshire and his housekeeper said he was giving a lecture in North Carolina.

Stunned that I'd been so deftly conned, I was mildly consoled at the police station less than a week afterward. There I found four agitated people who had also been summoned to identify Joseph Calli, aka Tom Usher, Marvin (Westover to me but often Rosen), Frank Rizzo (he must admire the late mayor of Philadelphia), and Frank Cerone. It seemed that Calli chose surnames that sounded Italian, Jewish, or Anglo-Saxon, to match the names of those he called. Exchanging our stories, we sputtered with laughter and outrage. He'd anxiously asked each of us, "Is it a good hospital?" as though he were from out of town. Of course we were furious at ourselves for having been taken. Perhaps that's the essence of being conned: disgust with yourself expands your anger at the miscreant.

I met two more of Calli's prey when we testified before the Grand Jury. What staggered all of us was that in each case we ourselves had supplied the name and character of someone we trusted: one woman thought the voice belonged to her accountant, a man assumed it was his son-in-law, another victim thought she was talking to her husband's good friend. Yet another was certain that Calli was an attorney she knew well. A gifted actor, he had used a variety of voices as he played the roles we assigned to him. And at times he was a "business associate" who'd last seen his quarry at "the reunion." Now age fifty, he'd clearly missed his calling: I was disappointed to learn that he'd worked "sporadically" as a repairman for Electrolux.

New Yorkers pride themselves on their city wits—we don't walk naked and alone into Riverside Park at midnight—and after two small burglaries I kept my amethysts in the oven on the advice of the police. Yet our urban overconfidence can make us easy targets for unfamiliar scams. We know about the wallet on the sidewalk near your bank: the person who "finds" it at your feet volunteers to split the contents if you'll match the $800 inside it with $400 of your own; you hand over the cash while your eager partner goes off to change the bills into larger digits and you're left holding the wallet—until you discover that the original bills have been replaced with strips of paper. We've read about the pleasant young red-haired black man who says you knew his father/uncle/older brother and asks for some $30 for a bus ticket because his car has conked out. And there's an expert schemer who phones families to tell them that their son or grandson has just been arrested on unnamed charges; he'll be released from jail when money is wired to a "bail bond agent," who picks it up from Western Union—before the relatives (who fear drunk driving or drug possession) learn that the young man is unblemished and at large.

So in a town awash with inventions, we can be quite sure that natives who weren't conned yesterday probably will be tomorrow. At least thirty of us (chosen at random from the phone book) were fooled by Joseph Calli. All of us live near New York Hospital. Some were told about the injured girlfriend; others heard that his car had been towed after the accident and he needed cash to retrieve it. The detective thinks there are many more unreported cases. Some of Calli's marks—including a blustering auxiliary policewoman—even went to the bank for him; sometimes he accompanied them, waiting patiently by the cash machines. He averaged $350 a hit.

Calli's enterprise succeeded until he roused suspicions in a posh building where his gaunt profile was preserved on the lobby's videotape machine. Hence the police knew what he looked like, though not where to find him. The last person he gulled was a former employee of the phone company who has a caller ID box—which yielded Calli's home number. The detective who elicited Calli's confession observed that most scams play on greed; the marks expect to make some fast money, and grifters expect a willing dupe to be somewhat crooked. But he had not seen people who got taken "out of kindness"—when no dazzling loot was in sight—and this con game was utterly new to him.

In the meantime I enjoyed stalking Calli: checking out the attractive small apartment building in my neighborhood where he lives with a girlfriend and giving him the evil eye in court, hoping he would feel cursed for life. I decided that he would be smitten with rotting toenails and Irritable Bowel Syndrome. Stalking does give you a delightful sense of power: you know the hows and whens of a person's life, his habits and yearnings (he plays the lottery), his favorite coffee shop, his drugstore—but he doesn't know yours.

Calli was convicted of "a scheme to defraud in the first degree" and sentenced to a five-year term of probation; he had to complete an out-patient drug treatment program and pay a $155 fine. He could have gotten four years. Although his pitted face looked seedier each time I saw him in the courtroom, I was surprised by the references to drugs, since his strategies relied on a dexterity that seems scarce among users. (I suspected that the issue of "recreational" drugs and treatment was a lawyer's device for keeping him out of jail, but there was no way to prove that.) Like most defendants, he stood before the judge with his hands clasped behind him, as though wearing invisible cuffs, squaring his shoulders as the sentence was pronounced. Meanwhile my ears buzzed with the words of campaigning politicians who vowed to "take crime out of the streets"—perhaps forgetting that the phone can be a criminal's weapon, that you may be swindled at home just as easily as you can be murdered there by those you know best in the world.

—NORA SAYRE
WINTER 2001

~

In 1968, in a windowless cinderblock dressing room of a small college theater on Philadelphia's Main Line, I saw Sid Caesar in his skivvies and full-calf black socks, listing on one leg while he tried to smooth his hose. Two handlers stood by. The occasion was the opening of a new theater at St. Joseph's College, where I went to school and sometimes earned money crewing for events.

It was no small thing, seeing in the flesh the man I'd known from 1950s television. I loved *Your Show of Shows* and, later, *Caesar's Hour*. One of his best routines was playing the dizzy, disheveled Professor Von Houdinoff, expert on magicians, who always wore a mashed top hat and held a chewed up cigar butt. The skits with his partner, the great horsey-faced comedienne Imogene Coca, were so funny and inventive that I fed off them for days. The shows were live, so you never knew what might happen. The scripts were worked out enough to seem stable, but the medium itself made them combustible. As a comic presence, he was my long-suffering Dauphin of Heebie-Jeebies, his body a wincing, slightly aggrieved shape of energy. Then there was his laugh. No great comic has a straightforward laugh. (Think of Art Carney, Milton Berle, Richard Pryor, Bill Murray.) Sid Caesar's was squirmy, fragile, and hilariously pitiable. Television had made him one of the richest men in show business; by the age of thirty he was earning a million a year.

So why was this brilliant entertainer performing in such a punk venue? At first I hardly recognized him. His skin sagged and was so thinned out that the face looked inadequately glued to the bones. In 1982, when he published his autobiography, *Where Have I Been*, I learned that the Philadelphia gig happened during his lost years. He was by then so far gone on Equanil and Seconal (in the AM) and booze (from noon on) that he was drunk or stoned practically all day every day. The serious drinking started when *Caesar's Hour* was canceled in 1958. He hit bottom in 1978 and decided to dry out. So he went to Canada. Finally clean and sober, he couldn't remember much of what had happened. Big chunks of time, years on end, were erased. Once in a while a fact would float by. About going to Australia in 1975 to do a movie called *Barnaby and Me*, he said: "I don't remember anything about the trip or picture. I lost a whole continent."

Memory is so opportunistic. Sid Caesar was just a hoot and a dream image when I was a kid, but over the years he somehow became in my imagination an all-purpose image of comedic play, *homo ludens* American-style, pinched by self-consciousness. Balancing on one leg in that dressing room, he was someone else. Seeing him in the flesh, I lost him, lost at least my mental image. Irrational and self-serving as it was, I felt a vague betrayal, not just of my own good faith but of all that is comic. I didn't know that while I was watching him he was unconscious, which may have been a cockeyed blessing, since he wouldn't remember the humiliation or the pain of falling out of time. In his sense of things, he wasn't even there.

—W. S. Di Piero

WINTER 2001

~

St. Petersburg is Pushkin's town. There are signs of him everywhere. You can visit the parks, lakes, and villas he praised in his poems and walk the embankments he strode. You can visit the site of his fatal duel. The last of his six residences here is now a museum. The table was just set for dinner when his coach pulled up and delivered the mortally wounded poet to the wife he adored and whose honor he had felt bound to defend. As a guard will tell you, he died exactly forty-six hours later, his head resting on the bolster you can see on the leather divan in his study. His face was turned away from the light. The clock is set at a quarter to three, the hands resting just where his friend Turgenev stopped them. The guard points to a spot to the right of her groin, the location of the wound—until her supervisor, a legatee of the old regime, comes to berate her. Offering information is not allowed, even when it is solicited by visitors from abroad.

I cross Pushkin's shadow everywhere in Petersburg. But what I can't seem to find is a reasonable Russian-language edition of his works, either at the Pushkin museum shop or at Dom Knigi, the city's largest bookstore. There are a couple of period histories, an unserious biography, and a dull monograph or two at the shop. Dom Knigi (the name means "House of Books") has one paperback edition of some of the poetry whose text has no bona fides, along with a three-volume, leather-bound, slipcased edition priced at $200, looking flimsy for all that and affordable these days only by one of the Mercedes-driving "New Russian" elite. It might be the last thing they'd want.

I strike up a conversation with the young man next to me at Dom Knigi, who's examining books with noticeable intensity. "Where can I find an edition of Pushkin's work with a quality text?" In the most casual manner, as though we've known each other for years, we start down the stairs. He guides me towards an antiquarian bookstore further along Nevsky. At the moment it carries several old editions, attractively bound, some incomplete, nothing "truly extraordinary." For that you must know someone—and it might cost $300. He is a book dealer, he says. A book dealer with another job. My impression is that he owns books and knows books and knows people who own books, but has only become a dealer recently—perhaps five minutes ago.

"This is Russia, anything is possible." His gaze is pregnant with meaning. And $100 goes a very long way.

We find a bar and do business the Russian way, discussing literature and life (primarily in English, which he speaks beautifully) over drinks, and ignoring the topic at hand until the bridges go up and the subways are about to stop. In the fresh evening rain he asks what I'm willing to pay. "As much as I must for a good edition, and little enough that I won't cry if it's taken by customs." Anything old of apparent value, including books, requires special authorization to leave the country.

Two days later I'm packing when the phone rings. Can he meet me across from the hotel to exchange gifts? We hurry along Nevsky. In a park several blocks away, in front of the Pushkin Theater, presided over by a famously glorious statue of Catherine the Great, we find a bench and open our plastic bags. He produces a fine three-volume scholarly edition of Pushkin's poetical works, solidly bound in blue cloth over boards, with useful textual annotations. It's from the 1960s. For this he asks a laughably small sum equivalent to eight dollars. When I stare in disbelief he immediately lowers it to four dollars. I hand him forty dollars, much less than what a comparable set would cost at home. I brought to Russia three copies of my firm's newly released *Collected Poems in English* by Joseph Brodsky. I had given one to the Russian National Library and another to the Resource Center at the American Consulate. I offer him the third. "It is magnificent," he slowly intones, like a celebrant at mass. He is transfixed.

Such is the stature of books and writers and writing, still, in this culture. And such is the holdover of habits from Soviet days that this transaction, innocent and entirely legal, is quite naturally conducted as though it were an illicit charade.

—JEFF SEROY
SPRING 2001

Robert Pinsky's technical resources are among the marvels of contemporary literature. In his taste for the high wire, the test, the dare, he seems a cross between his Renaissance precursors (the improvisers, the mercurial performers, the bravura solvers of impossible problems) and the junior high school shortstop, crouched, ready for anything. So dazzling, in fact, is his mastery of diverse forms as to obscure his preference for one shape: the paradigmatic Pinsky poem makes a circle. The reader ends where he began, a place made different, changed by the poem. In Pinsky's hands, the form itself becomes a figure for both stability and flux; it is shaped by recurrence but (characteristically) by inexact recurrence.

"Shirt" is, in two ways, a poem about an article. It is, on the level of subject, a poem about a material object, a thing in the world. If another poet would seize on the artisanal shirt, Pinsky's taste, as maker, runs to the mass-produced, the object that exists in multiple to which access is not privileged. In the second sense, "Shirt" is about the process by which the elemental, monolithic shirt of the title, the ur-noun, immobile, comprehensive, the preemptor of the verb, becomes *the* shirt, the shirt resonant enough to stand as archetype.

It is a peculiar question, recurring in Pinsky's work: how does the mass-produced object acquire character (and the process by which *shirt* becomes *the shirt* is the process by which it becomes as well *my shirt*).

In this magnificent poem, at once rich and compressed, it does so through the opulence (and variety) of association. It stands to reason that Pinsky's interest is in the mass-produced: he is interested, almost invariably, in multiplicity. "Shirt," for Pinsky, is a sum: the sum, more properly, of its individual pieces ("The back, the yoke," the "lapped seams"), the mesh of individual fibers. Each of these elements is in a certain way whole, intact in itself. And each intact thread or shape generates a world, the litany of naming echoing the labor of "[t]he planter, the picker, the sorter." Echoing and memorializing or praising. Pinsky's taste for the unsung is unsentimental; it is his taste for the new ground, the unexploited.

What makes this poem, for me, is the interruption of incantation with specific historical memory, a memory not of making at all but of

> . . . The infamous blaze
>
> At the Triangle Factory in nineteen-eleven.
> One hundred and forty-six died in the flames
> On the ninth floor, no hydrants, no fire escapes—
>
> The witness in a building across the street
> Who watched how a young man helped a girl to step
> up to the windowsill, then held her out

Away from the masonry wall and let her drop.
And then another. As if he were helping them up
To enter a streetcar and not eternity.

A third before he dropped her put her arms
Around his neck and kissed him . . .

Against the worldly, the material, the alternative of conflagration, of non-being. I say "memory" but it is not, of course, Pinsky's memory, drawn hopefully from his private arsenal. It is the testimony of "the witness," the one who saw, the material of legend given, via that authority, the force and immediacy of the real.

It is critical to the poem that the world of making be set in a context of unmaking; the image of the fire dominates the poem, in duration and specificity; it is essential, lest the poem be misread as a sort of hymn to labor, that the most vivid of its figures no longer exist: whereas almost nothing is known of "Irma," and only generic images suggested (if any at all) for "the picker" and "laborer" (Pinsky's point is exactly *not* to imagine them), the figures who perish in that fire have, in their singleness, indelible presence. They seem to me the poignant analogue to the shirt, whose triumphant (if often repeated) wholeness coexists with its fragility.

An object, in this poem, takes form. But the figures in the Triangle fire insure that we read the second poem that informs the first, the poem of chaos, of unraveling, of dissolution. The poem of eternity.

—Louise Glück
summer 2001

The best part of being a writer is, I think, not having to go to work in the morning. There are other pleasures, to be sure, like the act of writing itself when it's all going your way, when you're pulling rabbit after rabbit out of the hat—or they're simply jumping out by themselves wearing bowlers and trilbys. But that sort of thing, for a poet, at least, happens only a handful of times a year, if that. Like infatuations. I can't really see the glamour of it: a bit of desultory typing and a lot of staring out the window. It's surely not the social life; a roomful of writers is like the last fifteen minutes of a birthday party for five-year-olds, with the mothers all looking feverishly for the mittens and hats.

No, as far as I'm concerned, the best part is not having to go to work in the morning. I thought about this, Friday last, sitting in the bathtub with the rain pouring down outside and the fat old mourning dove with greasy iridescent neck feathers cooing on a ledge in the airshaft. If I had a B.B. gun I'd probably have killed that bird long ago, but I don't have a B.B. gun and I've grown to feel almost comradely towards him.

I could hear the cars and trucks and SUVs sloshing down the hill outside en route to their appointments and daily rounds. Inside of those SUVs were frantic twenty-eight-year-old website designers and Internet consultants screaming into their cell phones. Things have gone terribly wrong for them of late, terribly wrong, and it occurred to me that if they weren't careful they might well miss the stop sign at the foot of the hill.

But they were not my concern. I was sitting in the tub in the dark listening to the late Neapolitan pianist Aldo Ciccolini work his way through a program of Chabrier, Grieg, Rossini, Satie, Schubert, and Debussy. It turns out I used to listen to a fair bit of *il signor* twenty-five years ago in my bathtub on rue Aylmer in Montreal. The fellow on CBC radio in those days who presided over the music hour was mad for Aldo. For Neville Marriner, too, and the Academy of St.-Martin-in-the-Field. Vivaldi's *Four Seasons* got a pretty heavy workout on that show, as I recall. With Satie it was almost always the *Gymnopédies* and *Gnossiennes*. There are no good winters in Montreal but that one was less good, given the weather and other circumstances. I spent a lot of time in the tub that particular winter listening to Aldo Ciccolini and M. Satie.

Apparently, young Aldo, something of a prodigy at the local conservatoire, became gloomy in his mid-twenties. His momma told him: "Aldo, maybe you should go to Paris *pour se changer les idées*." What an inspired suggestion. This is not something that would have even occurred to my own mother to suggest to me in my gloomy mid-twenties. In any event, Aldo loved Paris and was a big success. Who doesn't love Paris? Even Hitler loved Paris. Among Aldo's achievements in Paris (he became a musical francophile straightaway) was his popularizing the piano music of Erik Satie.

Satie began composing the three *Gymnopédies* in his twenty-first year while convalescing at his parents' home from a bout of bronchitis, which he had deliberately contracted in order to secure a discharge from the military. Shortly thereafter, his parents threw young Satie out of the house after an amorous incident with the maid. One doesn't ordinarily think of Satie as a *chaud lapin*, but there you have it. The youth moved to Montmartre, got a job at the Chat Noir, and commenced wearing a velvet coat, soft felt hat, and flowing cravat. It was during this time that Satie made friends with Alphonse Allais, who had a plan to cover all the lakes and seas of the world with cork in order to expedite travel. Around the time Satie was completing his six *Gnossiennes* in 1890, he became involved with the Rosicrucians. It was also around this time that he lost his piano job at the Chat Noir for drunkenness.

Epater le bourgeois, that was Erik Satie:

> . . . I go to bed regularly at 10:47. Once a week I wake up with a start at 3:14 AM. (Tuesdays.)
>
> I eat only white foods: eggs, sugar, shredded bones, the fat of dead animals, rice, turnips, sausages in camphor, pastry, cheese (the white varieties), cotton salad, and certain kinds of fish (skinned).
>
> I boil my wine and drink it cold mixed with fuchsia juice. I have a good appetite but never talk while eating for fear of strangling.
>
> I breathe carefully (a little at a time) and dance very rarely. When walking I hold my sides and look steadily behind me . . .

Satie's music is something like that, too, with its exotic modes and unresolved melodies. There are at least two recordings of Ciccolini playing the *Gymnopédies* and *Gnossiennes*, one in mono from 1966 and a stereo performance from 1983, the latter with a brighter, more forward sound and a good deal more fortissimo in its dynamics. The older performance, much favored by aficionados, is gauzier, more recessed, lending further mystery to the atmosphere of the pieces, which are made almost entirely of atmosphere.

And that was to be my day's work, to compare those two performances and to write about them, which would involve my having to get up, at some point, and change discs. By the side of the tub I had the liner notes to the respective performances, each with a picture of Ciccolini, one taken at about the time he would first have arrived in Paris, and the other from his late middle-age, when he recorded Satie in stereo. A nice-looking man: something like Marcello Mastroianni, with those luxurious eyelids, but with too much nose to be a movie idol. The younger musician, in profile, looks fragile, perhaps neurasthenic. The more recent portrait shows a solidly built man in a Lacoste polo shirt looking quite pleased at the prospect of being photographed.

But I was determined not to allow those photos, nor the opinion of any expert, to color my judgment. I was resolved to simply sit there in the bath, in the dark, with the rain pouring down outside, and listen. At least until the hot water ran out.

—AUGUST KLEINZAHLER
FALL 2001

~

Icarus falls unseen. At least that's how Bruegel saw it, in the painting now in Brussels: a ploughman with his cart and horse, a shepherd with his staff and flock, a tall ship with billowing sails, a fisherman with bowed head—and there in the corner, sinking beneath the waves, a pair of pale legs. Auden famously used Bruegel's painting to illustrate how, preoccupied by the personal, we overlook the epochal. For the painter himself, though, the subject matter may have evoked a more parochial question of perspective. There is so much in the world to see. What do you highlight in the foreground, what do you obscure, what do you omit entirely?

I thought of the painting and the poem when I saw the Ballett Frankfurt dance in December at the Brooklyn Academy of Music. It was as if we were all in obstructed-view seats. In the first piece, a duet called *Woolf Phrase*, the performers were speaking as well as dancing. They also moved two full-length microphones around the stage. As they came closer to the mikes, the words—a fragmented passage from *Mrs. Dalloway*—grew louder. More strikingly, the duo moved in and out of pools of light, so that at times they were dancing in the dark.

I remember what a kick I got, some thirty years ago, when I realized that Robert Altman had deliberately muddied parts of the dialogue of *McCabe and Mrs. Miller* into incomprehensibility. Brian Eno was onto much the same idea in his creation of "ambient music," which drifts in and out of audibility. The human race divides between those who strain to hear every word, every note, and those who relax in the belief that they will hear what they are meant to hear.

The Ballett Frankfurt dancers were very good, shifting without warning from the classical positions of Balanchine to a Paul Taylor stride, and I would like to have seen all their moves. Yet there was something powerful in the notion that they would extend themselves with no one able to see them. In the second piece, *Enemy in the Figure*, a line of dancers disappeared behind a sinuous wooden screen; the last one was only half-visible, and my fancy was that the line might continue indefinitely beyond my view. Other dancers were on the sidelines, as if warming up. The dance ends with a duet proceeding in a tenebrous corner of the stage. Might it continue after the curtain drops, even though we are no longer watching?

Medieval masons, when they constructed cathedrals, included details that no human eye could ever observe—all for the greater glory of God. But that wasn't quite what was happening here. Although the work was invisible, this was ongoing, tiring work. It resembled the unstopping toil of the unconscious mind, forever spinning outside our ken, mysterious and yet essential to our conscious life. Put another way, it was like stage machinery that was exposed to sight. That comparison seemed particularly apt, because the light source for *Enemy* was saliently on stage; rolled from place to place, it scattered illumination here and there.

The key component of the stage set in the third piece, *Quintett*, was a trapdoor through which members of the five-person ensemble would vanish and reappear. Since the recurring movement of the dance was a fall or collapse, a contagious swoon, these resurrections were subtly moving. It was as if Hermione's transformation from stone to life in *The Winter's Tale* had been choreographed into a repetitive loop. (The music, Gavin Bryars' "Jesus' Blood Never Failed Me Yet," is built around such a loop.) Swooning, rising, disappearing: you might say those three movements are the vocabulary out of which life is constructed. From wherever we are seated, much of the dance remains out of view.

—Arthur Lubow
SPRING 2002

The National Museum of Health and Medicine occupies a corner of the vast Walter Reed Army Hospital Complex at 6900 Georgia Avenue in northwest Washington, some five miles north of the White House. When I first visited, it was still located in an old red brick building behind the Smithsonian Museum and in sight of the National Gallery on the monumental Mall that is at the heart of our capital city; I liked that all its diseased organs and deformed bones were so near the temples of our civic culture. In fact, the museum I visited as a boy no longer exists as the uncompromising repository of morbidity that was then called, less benignly, "The Medical Museum of the Armed Forces Institute of Pathology." The Surgeon General during the American Civil War had called on army doctors to send him "specimens of morbid anatomy—together with projectiles and foreign bodies," and his successors had asked for much the same. Only in 1988 did the museum drop "pathology" from its name and replace it with "health and medicine."

I must make a confession: I have not actually been to the new venue nor have I seen the collections for more than forty years. I did go often in the 1950s and early 1960s, and perhaps the long interval between my last visit and this report is not so shameful, for if museums are the sieves of history—keeping and arranging artifacts from the past to make them culturally exigent in the present—then memories of museums are but a further refinement. In any case, this is my excuse.

A second confession: my father was a pathologist. He fulfilled all the requirements for his M.D. at the University of Hamburg in 1934 except, as one of his certificates says with what I interpret as an ironic dig at the Nazis, "being of Aryan descent." He ended up training for his specialty in Istanbul, teaching there, and, after 1950, practicing in a series of small towns in the remote West Virginia coalfields. Pathology was the great German medical discipline of the nineteenth century, the most scientific branch of the profession, the hard, ineradicable bottom of disease, poverty, war, and work as they made themselves felt on cells, tissues, and fluids. He loved it. It was his lifeline in a new land he never quite understood. His best friends were other German pathologists in the Diaspora; morbid changes in long-dead patients were what they talked about.

The Armed Forces Institute of Pathology was the mother church of these hardened specialties. I think that one of the few intellectual pleasures of his professional life was studying the slide sets that the Institute sent out and that he returned with what were, every so often, acknowledged to be astute diagnoses. The AFIP was a distant but palpable substitute for a world he had lost. I went with him when he attended courses and it is in this context that I visited the museum of bones and organs on the Washington, D.C. Mall. Although its artifacts are all of indubitable American provenance its organizing principles were those of enlightenment rationality as my father imagined them in a Germany he had lost. His father's microscope was one of the few possessions he had taken with him in his flight, not as a tool of his trade—he had modern instruments—but as an icon to this ideal.

The museum as I remember it was a reliquary in the worship of secular reason. It had few beautiful artifacts and no beautiful displays. There was nothing comparable to the exquisite dissections of the fetal eye sitting in a crystalline little bottle that one finds in Leiden. There were, and are still, fetuses in jars, some still in the disembodied uterus from which they had not emerged. But these are working specimens, not examples of divine contrivance or fleshly flowers to delight the eye. Displays today (or so I gather from the museum's website) are workmanlike and attractive; in the 1950s they were comfortably old-fashioned, rows of bottles and mounted bones on dark wood shelves, like the porcelain or pottery shard collections in unrenovated museums. There was nothing then to detract from the reality of the artifacts, at least half of which came from the century before last. Today a story of medical triumph organizes many exhibits: we no longer suffer from what people in the past suffered from, and we have medicine to thank. Specimens illustrate systems with didactic clarity. There was really no theme in the 1950s, as I remember, and that was all to the good as far as I was concerned.

Fundamentally, the museum was, and at its core still is, a shrine to facticity. Each of the million or so items—whether organs or instruments—bears testimony to a single, almost atomistic reality and to its connections. This bowel rotted from gangrene; that scrotum grown to grotesque size from elephantiasis; that skull eaten away by syphilis. Instruments may broaden the picture a bit, but most of these are for seeing or affecting something very particular. The museum doctors invented photomicroscopy in the late nineteenth century and their work is on display. But the point of all the effort was to document specific diseased tissue.

It is a shrine also to empiricism, to how facts connect with one another from inductive inference. In one exhibit that is something of a real icon—the bullet, specks of blood, and pieces of bone from President Abraham Lincoln (an early director of the museum was there at the autopsy)—what interested me was how compacted the .44 caliber bullet from John Wilkes Booth's derringer pistol had become when it hit Lincoln's spine. (Booth's own third, fourth, and fifth cervical vertebrae are here as well, with a glass probe showing how the bullet passed through.) Also on show are the particulars of mass death: this soldier died from a bullet through his head at the Battle of the Wilderness.

The museum has continued to gather facts and small narratives; it received, for example, the collections of the New York City Medical Examiner, which include such curiosities as the esophagus of a man who died from swallowing his dentures—still in place. Mostly, however, the stories are more edifying. The Medical Examiner's collection offers us the lungs of a man who died of cancer; elsewhere, visitors can compare the lungs of smokers and non-smokers, miners and those who do not work underground. The inferences are obvious. Artifacts have also been re-arranged to create new stories: the collected broken bones from individually identified black Civil War soldiers speak to new interests in racial justice. A great collection of more than two thousand human brains came to the museum in the 1970s and specimens of over two hundred different mammalian brains are about to join them. AIDs and women in medicine and the story of identifying the last of a line of unknown soldiers—from the Vietnam War—were or are being told in temporary exhibits.

Museums teach lessons and this one's is simple: *memento mori*. Yes, modern medicine makes death call on another day for some among us. But it *will* call, and a million examples of the body's fragility remind us that the visit may not be a pleasant one. We warm ourselves at the deathbeds of others, said the literary critic Walter Benjamin about scenes in nineteenth-century novels; we might also warm ourselves among the mortal remains of real people at 6900 Georgia Avenue.

—THOMAS LAQUEUR
SPRING 2002

~

Taipei is possibly one of the ugliest cities in the world. It is all function and neon lights, no noticeable form, and the dominant design element is tile—not the hand-painted glazed kind you're thinking of but bathroom tile in colors so drab that they have no name. The city lacks murals and greenery of any kind; even the graffiti, though often done in nice shades of colored chalk, is strictly practical: advertisements, threats, and one long crazed complaint written in tiny characters on the side of a burnt-out shed. Whether the architecture has cast its pall on the inhabitants or vice versa, there is no denying that Taipei feels temporary and liquid, and in some ways it really is; the city is full of expats who have gotten stuck here, some by choice but most of them by pure happenstance, having simply run out of money while on their way to somewhere else. Now they teach English, draw unreasonably high salaries, smoke joints, and amuse themselves with drugs and experimental cookery on the weekends, saving money for travel and biding their time until something better turns up. There is no marked ghetto for foreigners, but despite this, a whole invisible network of English speakers exists here that has nothing to do with the surrounding culture.

Occasionally, however, one does comes across a real exchange between East and West based on neither business nor fate. I am thinking specifically here of the Cloud Gate Dance Theater, which has been my antidote to the unremitting lack of beautiful things in Taipei. Cloud Gate is a Taiwanese dance theater, the first modern dance group in the country. Although trained in Europe over twenty years ago, their dancers have since developed a separate kind of dance language that incorporates Martha Graham along with movements adapted from Peking opera and *taiqi* and other Eastern art forms. The last performance I saw featured a work called *Cursive*, in which the dancers' bodies bent to describe the brushstrokes of brush calligraphy. Each movement of the work was titled with a separate character projected onto shifting curtains and screens, and the beauty of these backdrops, some spare and others completely baroque, enhanced the tone of the dance far more than the minimal music. One particularly gorgeous segment of *Cursive* was called "yong," a character which consists of a straight line with a hook at the bottom and a dot at the top, with four flowing strokes coming off the center. This piece had only one dancer, a woman in a black dress with gauzy sleeves trailing down past her fingertips, and with these she managed to describe not only the contours of *yong* but also, through the flowing, figure-eight motion of her arms, its meaning: perpetual, forever, everlasting. Most of the audience was Taiwanese, so they would have understood the definition of the character in any case, but this was perhaps the first time in my months here that the written word, the spoken word felt completely unnecessary; movement was all, and quite enough to convey meaning in itself.

—FRANCIE LIN
SUMMER 2002

~

It was curious the other evening how I started to look at the women around me. But only those talking on cell phones. It was rush hour and I was on my way home on the Fifth Avenue bus. (The magic of imagining what people might be thinking has been destroyed by cell phones. But that is another story.) To distract myself from listening I started looking at two talkers with mobiles traveling south on the bus with me.

One woman, middle-aged, thin in a little floating skirt, was still yakking as she got off. The other, finishing her conversation, flipped her mobile shut and held onto it like a Fabergé egg as she tripped down the street. Both had eyes tipped back in a pre-orgasmic look of self-absorption. Mobiles have replaced handbags and cigarettes as comfort fashion. It is also a way of saying, *I am not a face in a crowd. I have a private life.*

It was my stop too so I got off, still watching and more closely now. What struck me then was how the women with the mobiles were walking. Theirs was a strange half-walk, more like a slither or a slide. I looked down and what I saw intrigued me. For both were wearing backless shoes, the kind that used to be called mules and were worn indoors or poolside. In the 1950s mules had wedge heels and came in pastel colors with a pompom at the toe box. My mother never wore them. Now Prada and rip-off companies market them. They come backless with mean toes, like the nose of a Concorde. Sneakers now come backless too, which means they are no longer sneakers. Maybe hiking boots are next.

I was excited, for I knew I was on to something. And yes, every woman I saw talking on a cell phone between Fifth Avenue and the West Village, where I live—ten in all—was sliding down the street in open-heeled shoes as if in her boudoir. I could imagine each and every one of them lying in bed, talking and twirling a backless sneaker or hiking boot with her big toe. In the week since I made this capital discovery, I have seen literally hundreds of women in New York City talking on cell phones, all of them in mules. They may think they're up and vertical but they're really horizontal.

—HARRIET SHAPIRO
SUMMER 2002

~

Last year, in the course of four months of travel in southeast Asia, my wife and I regularly found ourselves in places where there was, as they say, nothing to do of an evening. We'd have dinner, read, read some more, then sleep. Turning this entertainment-less situation to advantage, we decided to read Shakespeare aloud, perform it for ourselves. We swapped a copy of *Mr.*

Nice for one of the plays we didn't know so well: *Antony and Cleopatra*. I was Antony, obviously, and my wife was Cleopatra. The rest of the parts we divided up arbitrarily, taking turns to speak whichever lines came our way.

We hadn't read any Shakespeare for years but were both entirely unsympathetic to the philistine argument that he—let alone Spenser or Chaucer—no longer has anything to say to kids from the inner city, that an appropriate education demands something more relevant to their own situation and experience than *Coriolanus* or *As You Like It*. It came as a shock, then, to discover that he no longer had anything to say to *us*. It was unbelievably boring, for starters, and we had trouble making sense of a lot of what was being said. The play seemed to consist entirely of messengers coming and going, delivering reports on what was going to happen later. Off traipsed one messenger, in trudged another. It was like a cross between a cable news channel ("Coming up on CNN . . . ") and a toga party. Then there were the passages where the characters competed with each other to dress some commonplace observations in all the rhetorical finery they could muster. The famous bits ("The barge she sat in, like a burnished throne . . . ") seemed to come shrink-wrapped in quotation marks and sounded like they had been lifted from *The Waste Land*. We made only halting progress. Weakened by the end of the first act, our resolve collapsed entirely midway through the third. We started skipping and then we ground to a halt. Even with nothing else to do, reading *Antony and Cleopatra* seemed a pretty poor option compared with sleep.

Three months later, we were in Nevada for the Burning Man Festival. We arrived at the gates of the temporary city of Black Rock and were greeted with the words "Welcome home." That's what Burning Man is to me and the thousands of others who each year make this trek to the desert. Burning Man is the defining center of my life. Asked recently by an Italian literary magazine if I considered myself a Londoner, English, British, or European, I responded that I am, first and foremost, a citizen of Black Rock City. When I die I want my ashes to be scattered on one of the communal fires there. On several occasions I've written little things about Burning Man, but what happens there exceeds all imagining. If you boiled down everything that was best about a year in London, you could trade it for about an hour here. An ideal city—as fantastic as one of Calvino's *Invisible Cities*—comes into existence and then, at the end of the week, disappears, leaving no trace in the white emptiness of the desert.

The Man burned on Saturday; other structures and artworks were due to be burned on Sunday evening, but we had to be back in San Francisco and left at midday. The temperature was close to a hundred degrees. However slowly the traffic moved, the dust was thick, choking. To organize the exodus, volunteers stood in the middle of the scorching desert, swathed in dust, directing traffic with endless patience and humor. I was exhausted from lack of sleep, feeling, as D. H. Lawrence put it when he was near this part of the world, that "I might drop dead if any more stupendousness assailed me." A few days earlier my wife had become so dehydrated she had to spend hours on an IV drip. It felt as if we had lived several lifetimes in the course of six days. We had seen and participated in something miraculous, but the most intense experience of the week still awaited us—and it was a literary one.

As you head towards Black Rock City, little messages of about five to ten words are written on signs. These signs are spaced at ten-yard intervals so that sentences emerge as you drive by. On the way out there are usually none of these signs, but this year there was one small sequence, barely legible through the swirling dust. On the first sign I read: "Our revels now are ended . . . " It was the beginning of Prospero's famous speech from *The Tempest*. How many times have I read this speech? I've lost count—enough, certainly, to mean that I don't read it so much as recognize it. I know it so well I'm almost oblivious to it. Except now, as we drove slowly by, the lines unfolded in a new way. Each measured phrase was framed and isolated by a single sign. Cadence followed majestic cadence, exactly describing the indescribable wonders of which we had been a part:

> Our revels now are ended. These our actors,
> As I foretold you, were all spirits, and
> Are melted into air, into thin air;
> And, like the baseless fabric of this vision,
> The cloud-capped towers, the gorgeous palaces,
> The solemn temples, the great globe itself,
> Yea, all which it inherit, shall dissolve,
> And, like this insubstantial pageant faded,
> Leave not a rack behind.
> We are such stuff
> As dreams are made on, and our little life
> Is rounded with a sleep.

I was in floods of tears—of awe, gratitude, love. Now, I am not one of nature's huggers, but as I got out of the car to hand a sixpack of Calistoga to one of the guys—pierced, tattooed, as wild-looking as Caliban—directing traffic, I found myself embracing him as though he were a brother from whom I'd been separated at birth. Totally unfazed, looking at my tear- and dust-smeared face, still managing to direct traffic, he said, "You should stick around longer, man. We're gonna burn the rest of this shit tonight."

Shakespeare himself could not have come up with a better response.

—GEOFF DYER
SUMMER 2002

~

The other day I passed a shop where they sold "Natural Toys for Children," which are, naturally, made of wood. Unnatural toys—you guessed it—are naturally made of plastic. This species of talk about nature can also be heard at the bedside of dying patients. People in that situation often come up, in all seriousness, with the suggestion "to let nature take its course." Well, if that is really what you think we should do, we'll have to leave the patient somewhere in nature (plenty of woodland around here) and ourselves dash back to town. Then nature can, and will, take its course. That's not what they mean, though. They mean: please stop intervening, avoid the intensive care, don't make her suffer, and do your best to alleviate any pain or discomfort.

People think of it as quite a statement when they say that something is unnatural. It sounds much more impressive than: I don't like that. And things or matters which are said to be natural, or even "completely natural," are thought to be more than just a little okay; no, such matters are thought of as good in an interesting way.

Blushing is natural, and so is growing a beard. Shaving and eye shadow are of course highly unnatural. There are degrees here. The Pill is exceedingly unnatural, the Pope thinks. But to withdraw your member just before discharging is, well, not wholly, but certainly a lot more natural. What is "really natural" under those circumstances is something we should maybe discuss some other time.

There are also degrees of unnaturalness.

Consider the business of writing, in the sense of "making marks on a surface." You can classify ways of writing, starting at the height of unnaturalness—on a computer screen—and then proceeding downward to less unnatural—using a pencil and paper, a slate with chalk, goose quill and parchment; scratching into wax on a piece of wood—and then gradually sliding back into the almost natural: writing with your toe in the sand. Going one step further in this direction lands us safely back in nature: just leave a footprint in the sand (of an unshod foot, naturally). This last step frees us also from the whole contrived business of writing, to which something unnatural still clings. I would say that the guaranteed maximum of naturalness in this direction will be found in the footprint of an animal. No mark was ever made more naturally.

There are instances in which this Deeply Dotty Classification System breaks down in a most enlightening manner. For instance, when we try to find a place for human insulin. Until about fifteen years ago, diabetics injected themselves with insulin derived from pigs. Nowadays there is only human insulin on the market. This is not manufactured by humans, but by bacteria into whose genome a bit of human DNA, coding for insulin, has been inserted. The microbe thus modified cannot help producing an insulin which is, down to the last atom, identical to the "real" thing.

You cannot get it more natural, or unnatural, than that.

There are varying degrees of nature thought to be present in shampoos, cereals, and shoes, in gasoline, holidays, and medical regimes, in shirts, shorts, and some sports, in bikes, yogurts, and hikes. And around death, too, nature naturally has its role to play, though this is sometimes thwarted when death is ushered in by "unnatural causes."

Recently I was involved in a tussle about the amount of nature present in the vitamin C pills my daughter takes. She reckons it works against a cold.

A friend explained to us that those pills contain chemical vitamin C, which is an unnatural substance. She wondered why the poor girl had to swallow this artificial stuff when you can get the real vitamin C at any health-food store.

I explained to her that stones and plants and dogs and hairs and hands and heads are all of them chemical substances, made of molecules—made of the same stuff, in a sense. She found that an eerie notion.

But a couple of days later she phoned me, greatly relieved, because she doesn't want me to think of her as slightly gaga: "I had the wrong word earlier this week. I didn't mean *chemical*, I meant *synthetic*."

"Marvelous," I said, "now we're out of the woods!" But still in the dark, I did not add. I think there are, among others, two meanings of the term "natural" in this context. First: not manufactured or in any sense meddled with by man; untainted, you might say. And the second: made by man, but in an era, or by a method from an era, "when things were still all right." Thus we can hang on to wooden toys, the stage coach, wool, candlelight, muesli, leather boots, bow and arrow, wine, etc. The thought, if you'll pardon the expression, behind all this is that somewhere in the eighteenth century, say around 1770, events took a wrong turn and the unnatural started on its relentless march. One of the first disasters following in its wake being the steam engine. From there on, things only got worse.

The word "natural" harbors a sigh of nostalgia; it reminds us of an imaginary world we think we have been thrown out of.

That we have been thrown out of some place is, after all, the basic feeling pervading our tattered sense of identity as humans, ever since Genesis. There remains the vexing question of how something as unnatural as a health-food store ever arose out of nature.

—BERT KEIZER
FALL 2002

~

Last night I watched two films. (Or, rather, re-watched; I had seen each in a theater, and was now viewing them on cassette.) One was 89 minutes long, the other 99 minutes and 20 seconds. When I was done, I had "used up" 188 minutes of my life; I was 188 minutes (and 20 seconds) closer to my death.

When we read a book we have no idea how many hours it will take us to do so; when we view a painting or a photograph, we decide, though almost never in advance, when to stop looking. Few of us know exactly how long a play is, and in any case this can vary from performance to performance. But film trumps—or, one might say, cheats—the uncertainty of time. In fact, a film's finite duration may be one of its chief comforts, for uncertainty about time—which is to say about what we do with time, which is to say about death, which is to say about loss—is a specter that haunts us. What else prompts that anxious, ludicrous question about romantic relationships that has spawned a hundred women's magazine articles, quite a few books, and untold thousands of conversations: "Will it last?"

Yet who among us would want to know? What if "it" is unimaginably wonderful, but *won't* last? Or will last three weeks but not four, or two decades but not three? What if something less wonderful would last longer? Which would you choose? These are stupid questions. You do not get to choose. Or, rather, you do not get to know before you choose; you must act (often again and again) in the absence of such knowledge. (Knowledge follows action, rarely vice versa.) No article, no book, no conversation can change this—though many promise that they will.

With a film, it's different. We do not know what the experience will hold, but we know *exactly* how long it will last. We know how much older—if not how much wiser—we'll be when the last frame flickers. There is something reassuring in this, but something sad and defeated, too. For embedded in the anxiety of not-knowing is also an excitement, indeed an eroticism, of not-knowing.

John Berger has written that every photograph records not an event, but a decision: that of the photographer to shoot a particular image at a particular moment. (A good photograph, he suggests, is one that can explain its decision: "Photography is the process of rendering observation self-conscious.") Similarly, a film, especially a documentary film, is not so much the telling of a story as a meditation on time. It is the complex interplay between what we, the viewers, "know"—which is always essentially a function of time—and what the people on the screen don't that accelerates the film's tension as it unfolds. (Such knowledge can sometimes function equally well in fictional films, when what we know is that the wife is cheating on her husband or that the murderer is lurking in the cellar.) This knowledge is the connective membrane between the viewers, who are in some sense always old, and the film's characters, who are in some sense always young. But it is, oddly and simultaneously, also a distancing device—which is why we so often view older films, whether trashy romances or classic documentaries, with a condescension that borders on smugness and turns the human drama into quaintness.

We shouldn't. Far better to guard against such arrogance—against the specious assumption that we are better than, say, Spanish Loyalists, Chinese peasants, or Russian revolutionaries because we know some things they didn't. For the truth is that they knew some things, too, that we have yet to learn—or perhaps forgot. One could ask of any revolution: Will it last? Or, better: Will it turn out "right"? These are stupid questions. You do not get to know before you choose; you must act (often again and again) in the absence of such knowledge.

And one of the things that Spanish Loyalists, Chinese peasants, and Russian revolutionaries may have known, and that we don't, is the ways in which we belong to time and human history (though never they to us). Every life ends with death, yet no life ends with death. Despite the jumpy, dissociated, increasingly hysterical texture of modern life—in which continuities between the living and the dead are so ably disguised—we can never sever the thick, knotty cords that coil us to the past and the future, to lives and generations other than our own.

—Susie Linfield
SPRING 2003

~

I get my hair cut at a Dominican barbershop on the Upper West Side. You have to go down some metal stairs to get there. It's kind of like a cave. There are crucifixes and postcards and a three-foot plaster statue of a naked goddess. On the mirrors they've Scotch-taped photos of guys with hairdos, and the chairs must be at least fifty years old.

It's usually chaotic. People come to hang out and the TV is always on too loud, blasting in Spanish. Depending on when you show up, there are anywhere from one to four barbers, two young and two old. None of them speak English. I'm always the only non-Latino there. I like the place because you don't have to make an appointment and it's cheap, just twelve bucks for a decent haircut.

You never know which barber you're going to get, but the other day I got one of the old guys, the one they call El Maestro. El Maestro is short and stocky with sloping shoulders. He has a bullfrog face and wears huge glasses and a gold necklace. There's a big ring on each hand. I've never seen his hair because he's always got a cap on, the kind newsboys wear in old movies. His hands are stubby but he's so gentle I usually nod off a couple of times during the cut.

He went at my hair with his electric razor first, changing the head several times, then got out the comb and scissors. It took about thirty minutes. Along the way, he used a variety of strong-smelling gels and lotions that he brushed and rubbed into my head hard, stimulating the scalp, I guess. He trimmed my ears, my nose, and my eyebrows. The guy's a total perfectionist.

It's always the same routine, so I knew El Maestro was almost done when he unwrapped a fresh straight-edge razor and meticulously cut the hairline around my ears and neck, making it sharp and clean. Then he toweled the goo from my head, turned on the blow dryer and, after a last go-round with the scissors and a quick fluffling with talcum powder, I was done. He'd never said a word.

When he picked up the mirror to show me how it looked in back, I nodded approval, then gave him a five-dollar tip and left. Normally, I would have headed straight home to shower the stink from my hair, but it was getting late and I had to stop by Bergdorf Goodman before catching a train to visit a friend who'd asked me to bring her something called Perfect Air. "It's a spray that makes your hair amazingly silky," she'd told me. "It's only sold at Bergdorf's. You'll find it on the Beauty Level."

The Beauty Level?

Like Dante's Inferno, Bergdorf Goodman has nine floors, but the Beauty Level is in the basement. It's a sleek and sterile place, lots of glass and nothing on the walls, the eyeliner containers and lipstick tubes lined up perfectly, a museum for makeup. There weren't many customers, everything was hushed, and the bored eyes of the sales force sized me up. "We're out of Perfect Air," one told me. "Take the elevator to nine."

I traveled to the ninth floor, where the elevator doors opened onto the John Barrett Hair Salon. The reception area was spacious, with high ceilings, lots of polished wood, and a view of Central Park. You'd never know hair was cut there; that's done somewhere out of sight, behind closed doors.

A friendly young woman asked if she could help me. When I told her I was looking for some Perfect Air, she fetched a tiny dark blue bottle from a shelf. At first I thought it was glass, very classy, but it turned out to be plastic. (What could I expect, though, since the price was only nineteen dollars and therefore something of a bargain, considering the surroundings.) As the clerk slipped my Perfect Air into a Bergdorf shopping bag the size of a purse, I asked what haircuts cost at the John Barrett Salon. "It depends on the stylist," she explained. "A Level One stylist costs $100, but if John Barrett himself does your hair, it's $350. Would you like to make an appointment?"

"Not today," I said. "But thanks."

"Come again," she told me.

I got on the elevator with a woman with an impressive mane. I'd noticed her as she paid her bill. Her cut was elaborate and sculptural, with a spiky thing on top, then some layered business, and the ends were intentionally ragged. The word postmodern came to mind, like those 1980s skyscrapers that mixed together several styles. The elevator doors closed and we headed down. I felt her scrutinizing me. When we passed floor five, she said, "Excuse me, but I have to ask: Which stylist did your hair? It's fabulous!"

"El Maestro," I told her, and she nodded in a way that said ah, yes, of course, she knew just who I meant.

—SAM SWOPE
SUMMER 2003

About a thousand years ago, English began to lose most of its inflections—suffixes that indicated the gender, number, and case of nouns, the tense of verbs, and the person and number of the verbs' subjects. Without the system of inflections for its grammar, English gradually evolved to a fixed word-order to distinguish subjects from objects and the relationships among phrases: S-V-O. Subject-verb-object. Its influence on English speakers can hardly be overstated. S-V-O is our expectation for a sentence every time we hear one or read one, and channels our thinking every time we speak one or write one. Every English sentence occurs against the S-V-O grid: fulfilling it, frustrating it, playing with it or against it. Every English sentence is a mystery novel whose plot we already know. The suspense usually comes not from who did it but from what they did to whom, although we certainly want to know who did it right away. If the subject is suspended by introductory clauses, we wait for it, sometimes impatiently, and we want the subject to be the main character, unless we understand from the context why it isn't. We then want the verb to follow quickly after the subject. We want to know what the who did. And we like those actions to be specific, even if they're conceptual or metaphorical actions. If the verb is transitive, we'd like to have the object follow the verb quickly, too. We are eager to understand, to learn, to know (spend ten minutes with my three-year-old daughter and you'll see how eager). We want our S-V-O fix. That we want it so much allows for all sorts of suspensions and elaborations and fine-tunings of opposite kinds: from James and Faulkner at the one end to Hemingway and Carver at the other.

One could also graph the sentences in poems across the same stylistic range, according to how they fulfill-frustrate-play-with-or-against our S-V-O expectation. Poems no less than prose are made of sentences, and expectation of sentences (by the reader), and avoidances of sentences (by the writer). But they are also made of lines that alter our experiences of sentences, by foregrounding the sounds of the words, phrases, and pauses which make up sentences but which we don't attend to until these sounds are highly organized and orchestrated. The primary instrument of this orchestration is the lines, and lines can also be arranged in stanzas, which may further foreground the lines by signifying their own organization independent of the sentences. The difference between metered and un-metered lines, from strict stanza forms to free verse, is no more than the difference between the degree of foregrounding of the lines against the sentences, and therefore the degree to which our attention to those sentences is complicated.

The sentences are nonetheless always primary. As every reader of this magazine knows, the way to read a poem is to read the sentences (not the lines)—and you parse each sentence as you read it, from phrase to phrase, gambling on the relationships of the phrases, constructing a multidimensional Lego, making larger pieces of the smaller pieces as they click into place. We perform this in nanoseconds. We not only understand grammar automatically, we do so at the speed of light, integrating semantics, grammar, and lexicon simultaneously and interactively. When we enter Grammar World we enter inner space at warp speed, brain speed, firing synapses and lighting up neurons still well beyond the understanding of linguistics or neurobiology. We translate soundbits and nanopauses into words, and group words into phrases. We gamble on the meaning of the phrases, according to not only their grammatical relationships but also the context they create among themselves, and the context of our own individual experience (variable and idiosyncratic as it may be), experience that's being changed even as we read. We interpret, and reinterpret if we have to, and wait to understand. And we provide connections when we have to—among the multiple and variable conceptual, connotative, and metaphorical meanings that words have individually and in conjunction with one another. We provide the mind for the protean organism of language, with its indistinct categories, fuzzy boundaries, inconsistent rules, and bizarre idioms.

Most people learn how to do this before they're two years old. This is why the sentences rather than the lines of poems are the primary focus of our attention: the function of language is the transmission of meaning, and we've attended to sentences as the life-giving instrument of meaning since infancy, long before we ever started reading poems. But language is also a system in which everything is connected to everything else—*tout se tient*, in de Saussure's words—which is why the orchestration of sentences through the agency of lines may produce a unique kind of musical meaning that expands the meaning of sentences as they unfold.

—Michael Ryan
winter 2004

~

This account (begun in the third person to protect the middle-aged) finds an American student abroad: a young Wagnerite seated in a Viennese coffeehouse named, singularly inappropriately, the Café Aida. Two college friends sit beside him. It is late July, 1976. They peruse an issue of the *International Herald Tribune*. The centennial season of the Bayreuth Festival has just opened with the long-awaited new production of Wagner's *Ring of the Nibelung*, now in the hands of Patrice Chéreau (director), Richard Peduzzi (designer), and Pierre Boulez (conductor). The paper carries a review of the performance—no, the event. It records the general shock of the audience. It displays a photograph from the opening performance of *Götterdämmerung*, Act Two. The Hall of the Gibichungs is now a tenement on the waterfront; the Nibelung villain Hagen resembles Lee J. Cobb. He wears a rumpled grey suit but carries a spear. The banks of the river Rhine, the review recounts, have been transformed into an industrial landscape, replete with a hydraulic dam. The Rhinemaidens are factory prostitutes. The gods are scions of a decadent industrial elite. Siegfried wears denim.

Cut to the following Monday morning at five AM: dawn on the day of the conclusion of the second *Ring* cycle, the second performance of *Götterdämmerung*. Indignant but exhilarated, two of the Wagnerites have decided that Wagner needs them, or rather, us. We have spent a long night on the train. From the early-morning scene at the Bayreuth train station (where everyone else is drinking beer), we make our way up the green hill to the festival hall. This is the correct route of the Bayreuth pilgrimage, but the climb is supposed to be taken slowly, in the pious company of other devotees, circa three PM, following the ritually prescribed visit to the Master's home and grave in the town below. Now the hill and its festival theater are empty. The box office will open at ten. The performance has been sold out for years. Years: this is the centennial production. A few other scavengers are about, mostly students. At ten sharp, the box office behind me appears to remain closed.

But now an apparition seems to form on the empty roadway in front of me, leading up to the theater. It is a procession of four or five silver-blue Mercedes sedans—indistinguishable one from the next, at least in my memory. As they approach the curb, it becomes clear that they are all driven by solitary women—stately, elderly women. Not, clearly, the normally designated drivers of these vehicles, we surmise. No, these are Valkyries—or rather Valkyries *emeritae*: they have been sent forth from Valhalla on their high-tech noble steeds by the guardian gods of Old Germany; they are on a mission. From the window of the car nearest me, two tickets are hurled to the ground. I pick them up. They are very expensive orchestra seats.

This is indeed a report from Valhalla, I tell myself. This particular Mr. and Mrs. Wotan will likely have some difficulty with any rendition of the twilight of the gods. Certainly they will not tolerate the debacle imagined in a decayed industrial landscape by a young, French, gay director—one, moreover, who had told the press that until he received the current assignment, he had never heard a note of Wagner.

So that evening, between four PM and eleven, I saw the second performance of the Chéreau/Peduzzi/Boulez *Götterdämmerung*, from a center seat in the fourth row. I was convinced—transformed, educated—within minutes. Wagner himself was held up as both poet and criminal, and we, the audience, became bystanders—perhaps not guilty but implicated nonetheless in the story we were watching and hearing. It was too much for many. The Fricka and Wotan seated to my left burst into tears during the third act, as Hagen's hunting party appeared in the forest in dinner jackets and were offered ivory washbowls by their attendants—a nightmare perhaps first visualized by Thomas Mann and after him by Luchino Visconti. When Gunter wiped his hands with a linen towel, several people screamed out from around me that the performance should be halted. To which a Frenchman behind me murmured, "*C'est indigne, ces gens*"—terrible, these people who don't behave at the opera. The final cataclysm showed us not the empty stage Wagner had ordered, but a crowd of proletarians who slowly turned and faced the audience in an accusatory glare. Pandemonium swept through the curtain calls that followed, calling to mind the standard accounts of the 1913 premiere of Stravinsky's *Rite of Spring*. I promise you that I saw several drops of blood on the floor, near an exit.

The Chéreau *Ring* stays in my mind as the foundation and greatest example of the practice—or rather the argument—of *Regieoper*, or director's opera, wherein the revival of a great work must come from having something to say to and about that work, something new, something transhistorical, connecting a moment of the past to a concern of the present. When *Regieoper* fails, as it so often does, it is because its concepts stumble into cheap shots and clichés, of which the anecdotes are legion and usually told competitively. Devotees of the Chéreau *Ring* can also cite a notorious space-age *Ring* staged in Kassel, in which the earth goddess Erda appeared in the form of a singing computer. Or a Covent Garden *Ring* set, apparently, among American Indians. *Was hat das mit der Musik zu tun* ("What's that got to do with the music?"), to cite the legendary repartee of the aging conductor, on being informed by his concertmaster that his fly was open. "What's it got to do with the world?" is the analogous question asked by the serious opera-goer. At Bayreuth in 1976, I first heard it answered.

—MICHAEL P. STEINBERG
SPRING 2004

It must have rolled over on its back the moment it succumbed to the great reaper. How else could it have landed on the woodpile in the cellar with its paws in the air? Or did it try a position it had never tried before in the hope of alleviating the pain? It lay on the wood surrounded by shredded newspaper and other signs of nest-building, so that one wondered what extravagant ideas had filled its restless brain at the instant disaster struck.

Was it an instant, or was it a case of long-drawn-out death throes?

A Rat surrendered here
A brief career of Cheer
And Fraud and Fear.

Of Ignominy's due
Let all addicted to
Beware.

The most obliging Trap
Its tendency to snap
Cannot resist—

Temptation is the Friend
Repugnantly resigned
At last.

Is Emily Dickinson's poem as good as I once thought? Or is it a bit over the top? It is not often that Dickinson goes in for so much sound; what got into her? She doesn't see a rat at all, neither dead nor living. She has let an idea fall into her trap, a cliché notion. In the last stanza the evilness of the rat is equated with that of the person who exterminated it. The poet who could write so movingly about pain, "After great pain, a formal feeling comes—," does not mention the death pangs that led to the dried-out remains I held in my hand, eighteen centimeters long measured from the tip of its nose to the root of its curled back tail. We both yielded to temptation—I to my desire to be rid of the creature. Reassuring words had been printed on the box: in contrast with other pellets, these pellets would ensure the rat's natural death. The rat was nervous and quick in the cellar full of food where I once stood eye to eye with it, I near the door, the rat stock still on a rickety table in the far corner, its eye glistening feverishly in the weak light: an unparalleled face-off from which I withdrew leaving it to do as it pleased with its Cheer and its Fraud and its Fear, which rapidly declined so that it sometimes leapt straight over my foot when I disturbed its gnawing—straight over my foot into the woodpile, where it was always safe.

I look at it the same way up as I found it on the wood; I place it on a newspaper. I had read on the box that the rat would not die a natural death instantly but some four days after eating this last supper. Four long days after its "brief career"—had I read the conscience-assuaging text properly? In those four days its intestines would cease to function naturally, painless internal hemorrhages would occur, etc. Had this cold-blooded prose really penetrated to me?

The ethology course I took for a while was so scientific that we were forbidden to explain an action observed in an animal in terms of human reactions. For example: if a dog runs away from you howling because you kicked it or hit it with a stick, you shouldn't simply assume that it is howling with pain. This has not yet been proven. How do I now prove posthumously that my rat died a natural death? How can the pellet manufacturer prove it to me?

It lies on the newspaper, its skin hard, dried-out leather, as if baked dry from within. Its head is hollow, eaten away or pulverized. On either side of a nose with one blocked nostril are withered straggly whiskers. No trace of an eye. A big black hole is half bridged by worn-down upper incisors and two slightly bent lower teeth three times as long, sharp and shiny, discolored and stained as after a lifetime of heavy smoking. They have remained in place like the warning in Dante's *Inferno*: "Abandon all hope ye who enter here." The mouth cavity has something of a bomb crater in which an indescribable black growth has developed, nature off the rails, a proliferation of leaf fibers. Are they the skeleton of the painless, internal hemorrhages? Below the head, the two forepaws are raised half-spread, as if praying for forgiveness, a gesture of ultimate despair, paws raised against blinding light or a sea of fire, the claws almost as long as half the limb. Regarded from a distance, the impression of a scream of agony is toned down to a perfect dance of death.

And then the newspaper snippets: what do these shreds tell us? That the rat started to work like crazy the moment it started to feel off-color, driven by a sense of duty, the need for a home, a family, before it was too late? Was it male or female—who could tell?

The natural death leaves nothing to chance; it is a thorough job. Five black bomb craters have been blasted into the body, all grown together again in the same way. A dead animal is an indictment and a treasure. You can make of it what you will. On the hard skin between the holes, there is still some hair that looks like miniature blades of flattened beach grass. As soon as I touch it, it falls out in tufts, like hair after radiation therapy. The bone of one of the back paws sticks through the skin: that must have happened before it dried out and went stiff. Was the rat still conscious then? Did it think: what is happening to me, I must run for it. Or did the skin suddenly become too taut for the skeleton so that the bones burst through it as the natural death was taking place? (The tuft of hair that I touch moves and starts to scurry off: vermin, I can't leave my find on my table any longer.)

It has huge paws on highly developed back legs, and long, strong toes, as if, like a bat, it used them as hooks to hang on.

Emily Dickinson's rat lacks paws, teeth, and body weight. Although there is no mention of it in her biography, there is little doubt that she set the trap herself, just as I, after lengthy hesitation, placed the pellets in a strategic spot. I'm convinced that she set the trap herself, and then atoned for her bloodthirstiness with an easygoing Puritan moral.

—Henk Romijn Meijer
SUMMER 2004

"So have you met any famous people in your life?" he asked. He was Eli, a Berkeley freshman who had just dyed his hair yellow. I was a token faculty guest at the annual dinner hosted by a group of freshman dorms. At my table were Eli, four Chinese-American girls, and me.

I was momentarily flummoxed by the question. I have met many famous people in my life. The most famous ones were in my dreams. Over the past several decades, I have had serious, substantive conversations with world leaders like Charles de Gaulle, Richard Nixon, Jimmy Carter and every president until George W, and Walter Cronkite. In each of the dreams the leader asks for my advice on some important issue and listens attentively as I explain what he should do. Each leader seems to be impressed with what I have to say. When I asked de Gaulle, once we had established a relationship, how I should address him, he said: "Call me *mon General.*" (The conversation was in French.)

In the Cronkite dream, I was guiding the anchor and Most Trusted Man across a perilously slippery field of ice and crusty snow in the dark, holding him by the arm. He seemed frail and much older than he was at the time. He volunteered that he was seventy-six years old. (In real life he was much younger.) He, like the other famous people in my dreams, seemed to think I was someone worth listening to.

When I recounted the Cronkite dream and its predecessors to a friend who knew something about psychoanalysis, she immediately asked: "How old is your father?" Oh. So all these conversations were really with my father . . .

I didn't tell Eli about my dreams. I don't think that's what he was looking for. Instead, I inventoried my memory for someone I had met that he might agree was famous. I started with Warren Beatty, who was a college fraternity brother. Eli had never heard of him. Struggling for a more current celeb, I said that I had just met General Wesley Clark at a political event. Eli didn't know who Clark was either. Neither did any of our other dinner partners. Well, then, who would this generation of college freshmen know that I might have met over the years? I've never met a rap artist, Britney Spears, or Kobe Bryant. Also, not to be too Clintonian about it, but it may depend on what you mean by "famous."

I turned the conversation to the Diego Rivera mural in the adjoining room, expressing my surprise at its presence in a postwar building. Eli and his classmates had not noticed it, and wanted to know why I was surprised.

I didn't find any of these disconnects discouraging. In fact these kids were uniformly bright, interesting people, who came from varied places. (One of the Asian girls had been born in China but had spent several years in Skokie, Illinois; she knew nothing of the Skokie Jewish demographics or the famous Nazi march there.) They were genuinely curious about what I'd done and where I'd been. I was flattered that they thought I had something to tell them about the world, my world, the one inhabited by old white men. Maybe I'll show up in their dreams.

—William Bennett Turner
SUMMER 2004

~

The stagy moment of fear in *Robinson Crusoe* is the single footprint in the sand. How there can be just one, how it got there, what it signifies are all questions that get endless discussion among readers. It is a brilliant stroke on Defoe's part, a human trace as lonely as the man who finds it after all those years on the island. Not the tracks of many human visitors, just one footprint.

But it is not the most frightening moment in the novel, or at least not to the reader who is also a writer. That comes much earlier in the novel when Crusoe says:

> . . . I began to keep my Journal, of which I shall here give you the Copy (tho' in it will be told all these Particulars over again) as long as it lasted, for having no more Ink I was forc'd to leave it off.

No liquid compounded from oak galls or berries or soot or clay or anything else that fell to hand could serve his purpose. Crusoe tells us of the ink he salvaged from the shipwreck, that he "eek'd [it] out with Water a little and a little, till it was so pale it scarce left any Appearance of black upon the Paper." The ink grows pale, the traces on the page become no more than the indentation of the nib, the journal is abandoned. Perhaps for his novelistic reasons, Defoe did not want Crusoe to keep a journal. But think for a moment of what Crusoe says: his ink gave out, his journal ceased, and the only record of his life, apart from his own memory, was in the world he made for himself on the island.

Crusoe is in the event rescued and returns to Europe, where there is no lack of paper, pens, or ink. There he writes his account. But imagine that no such rescue happened. His only audience being the animals and birds of the island, he tells stories of his life that disappear into the air. Perhaps he arranges his settlement in such a way that the scraps of his life—the partial journal among them—would speak of his time on the island to anyone who found them. But he leaves no written trace of his later years. His lack of ink comes to seem like the drying up of a necessary bodily fluid.

It's the Crusoe without ink and rescue that is so haunting. Some vague memory of this scene may explain why many writers hoard pens on their desks, from the cheapies given away by motels to elegant fountain pens. That way there will always be something to write with. The appearance of computers and printers hasn't changed this habit of hoarding. If anything, it's cursed us with a high-tech version of Crusoe's predicament: one crash of a hard drive, one tonerless printer, and you are back on the island without ink. To think about Crusoe in this way is to recover the novel from its reputation as a boy's book, because for boys it's that stagy moment that gives them the creeps and makes it all a true adventure, not simply a do-it-yourself course on domesticating the wilderness. This fear of being without the means to write comes only with rereading, with recognizing the sheer contingency of Crusoe's account. The knowledge that one's stay against being forgotten is the available supply of ink seems far more sobering than that footprint.

The mystery, though, is why Crusoe can't make ink. He makes virtually everything else he needs to survive and indeed to live comfortably. He learns to breed goats so he won't be dependent on his dwindling supply of gunpowder; he divides his herds so that no disaster will leave him without a supply of meat. He makes pottery vessels to hold his grain and rice, as well as tiles on which to bake his little cakes. He learns to weave baskets so he can have a variety of containers to organize his life. Perhaps it's that he doesn't *want* to make ink and keep his journal any longer. He is an active figure who reenacts, in his own time on the island, the history of human beings from hunter-gatherers to settled agriculturalists. He is not given to brooding on the meaning of life as he lives it. Perhaps, finally, he knows that writing to one's self on an otherwise uninhabited island is too dangerous a form of introspection. Put another way: to write an account while still on the island is to renounce any hope of being rescued. Better to keep the stories unwritten so they can be told fresh to rescuers. Then, once Crusoe gets back to England, he can write his island story at length and add his later adventures in parts elsewhere.

It must have been a great relief to Defoe, who wrote prolifically and under all sorts of guises, to get his hero home to where running out of ink meant no more than an errand to the local stationer's. But I keep thinking of him on the island, without ink, as he lives his life so that he can remember it in the hope of writing it all down in his precise, account-book style.

—NICHOLAS HOWE
WINTER 2005

The top-down convertible slows, or seems to, as it passes. The woman inside, as I remember this, moves in slow motion, too. In her late twenties, early thirties maybe, though it's hard to tell, was hard to tell even then in the blurred action of car and face as they creamed into the night air, summertime, our car windows open, my father at the wheel, as background the dark green of a city park, a storybook forest children vanish into. She was shouting "Help. Help me." A Shakespeare character would shout back: "What kind of help?" That's what I wanted to know, what kind. Though the man driving wasn't holding her, the terror and desperation sounded real, though she was also smiling, as if it were all a joke or ruse. They were pulling past and away from us, while I asked my father what was happening to her. "Nothing probably," he said. "How would I know?" I felt confused and sinful in my ignorance. Not taking action to save her was an act. But we invent or contrive possible actions in the wake of bad events. What could I have done? Or my father? I must have been ten or eleven years old. Those questions even then were tuning conscience to nerves. Some of memory's picture-strips stay more immediately available all one's life than others that may be even more momentous in consequence. This had to do vaguely—its vagueness is essential to its tenacity in memory—with panicked recognition of horror and danger attached to love, and love (or passion, anyway) attached to speed, hilarity, and ignorance.

For my family, New Year's Eve was always an event of strained celebration. People lived such aggrieved lives all year long that year's end was an occasion to let grievances go, for a while, and pretend noisily that promise and hope awaited. Our entire large family gathered at someone's house. Women got tipsy, which was unusual. Men had license to drink harder than usual. Husbands smoked Camels, their wives Pall Malls or Chesterfields. Everybody craved reassurance—who does not?—that they had reasons to be happy in their lives. I was young, and it's normal for children to feel excluded from adult rituals, so the celebratory mood, forced as it may have been, was like a party in a house across the way to which I hadn't been invited, and even if I were I wouldn't know how to behave. I wanted the New Year already to be over with. The ball over Times Square glittered on TV, and the adults watched in wonderment and anticipation as if watching not from Philadelphia but from India or Egypt. I could never be sure if they were celebrating the end of an old year or the beginning of a new one, if the dominant tone was relief or foreboding. Nobody died this year, thank God. God is good even if he treats us bad, that God who, in Sinatra theology, was The Man Upstairs. Champagne, of course, the only time of year a beer-and-shot culture so indulged.

Once, while people up and down the street stumbled outdoors, banging pots and pans, kissing neighbors, throwing fireworks (or not—my father nearly blew off his thumb lighting a firecracker in his hand), I tracked a scene: Bridget, a black-haired beauty who lived down the street, was running from her boyfriend (a tough, hard-muscled Irishman), fear and rage in her face, while the boyfriend chased after, caught up, and grabbed her by the arm so hard she winced and started to cry. They struggled and were in each other's face so fiercely it looked as if all the celebratory energy of the night was suddenly channeled darkly between them. Everybody else is filled with the enthusiasm of the moment and doesn't see what's happening. The memory-strip runs out there, dissolves into whistles, smoke, hooting and horn-blowing.

Jump forward twenty years. I'm coming home after midnight, struggling to walk with canes because of a crippling ailment. Again, a woman goes past me, shouting, running, behind her a young guy who, like Bridget's boyfriend, finally grabs her. Then he slaps her. She groans and starts to run again. I give chase. That is, I mince pathetically behind, shouting at the guy to leave her alone, shouting so loudly that neighbors poke their heads from doors. This was an old-style working-class self-policing sort of neighborhood. Within seconds, it seemed, a half dozen men, some in pajamas, a few carrying baseball bats, are running down the guy to step between him and the girl, though the guy, temper aflame from the booze we all smell, is prepared to take it to the baseball bats, by which time a couple of squad cars pull up to settle the trouble. The pain that prevented me from moving and the immobility itself—like the sustained pause between times that is New Year's Eve—fuses to the running men, the girl, and her wolverine boyfriend.

Some years later the convertible girl in distress revisited me. This time I was on foot, walking by a city park; a sedan rolled past, windows open. A shrill cry, like wind gashing the air, warped through space and for that instant filled it. I couldn't tell if it was another call for help or a shout of gaiety. Just like the convertible girl. I wasn't alone. I was walking with a woman. We were in love and breaking up, croaking stupid words we hoped would never become too consequential, to fill time until we got to the train she would board that would take her far away. Emotional trauma so fills consciousness that the smallest details—leaf, gravel, dust—seem fraught, and we feel that the slightest twitch in the order of things will have awful consequences. When I asked what to do about the wailing woman, she didn't understand. She didn't hear it, she said, she thought it was the wind. I was in so much chaos, had so much noise in my consciousness, that just then I began to doubt I'd even heard the voice at all.

—W. S. Di Piero
WINTER 2005

Like many older people, I read slowly. This is not, however, because of aging. For me it has always been so. Slow reading was a youthful and intellectual necessity that became an art; for many in my generation, likewise. We did not read to get at an idea, to extract a dominant thought or even an ideal, such as social justice. What did we read for, then? Why did we read? This, even in retrospect, is a difficult question to answer.

Every youngster is in a hurry, but we knew we had a ways to go. When it came to detective novels and highly plotted suspenseful fiction, I am sure we read as excitedly as anyone else.

But for those of us maturing in the years immediately after a World War and the Holocaust, what was foremost was a vision of peace, a definitive elimination of the disasters just possibly ended, and a restoration of the culture that had failed, or been kidnapped, rather, for evil purposes.

Reading was, first of all, a mode of acculturation—all the more so for an immigrant like myself. It promised a way of learning whatever had to be learned, of absorbing its strangeness, of hoarding new expressions and puzzling out the direction from which they hit or the source of their appeal. The plot was words themselves, as changeable in context as the look of seductive models, those film stars or singers who surprise us each year with a new face, coiffure, dress, character—even, it almost seems, body.

At some point, my academic "cohort," as sociologists say (though we lacked, I think, until well into the Sixties, the wish to be defined as a generation, whether yuppie or popping or rocking or X-rated: we lacked even the consciousness that we were anything special)—my cohort, then, fortified by modernist literature and by the New Criticism too, with its clean enthusiasm for literary technique as a mode of discovery, began to read for the plot in a peculiar way. It wasn't the story-plot, but the writer's own devices and manipulations. Technique and strategy became hot-button terms. We indulged in the literary equivalent of war games. Eventually we came to resent such designs, and turned into pre-deconstructionists who wished to demystify every text, motivated by regret for our own (lost) spontaneity and sometimes by a self-righteous ideology borrowed from reigning literary pundits.

In my case, that stage was skipped. I had come under the sway of European stylistics, with its immense respect for the evolution of the literary vernaculars and the struggle between (or, at best, symbiosis of) the writer and the ever-evolving language—as well as its instinctive Freudian feel for overdetermined meanings, all of which had to be given mental space, so that interpretation became a feast rather than a fast. When practiced by such masters as Auerbach and Spitzer, this approach made such rhetorical counters as "irony," "paradox," even "ambiguity" (except in Empson's famous book) seem pale reflections of a boundless and bountiful play of language. Nor did I fret much about issues of unity, coherence, and a so-called "tough lyric grace."

Yet I did begin to read for the wound—that is, for some defining, even too definitive, dubiously unifying imprint, incurred early and returning sporadically to inflame and inspire, like a forgotten injury. Might a psychic mark of that kind have mysteriously strengthened the artist, as Edmund Wilson argued in *The Wound and the Bow*? Did such a mark become the artist's signature, and was it a peculiarly post-romantic idea that this torment may have been self-inflicted—a necessary, emancipatory act of individuation?

So in Coleridge's famous poem, the Ancient Mariner's apparently gratuitous killing of the albatross brings on "all that consequence," including (today) the theoretical issue of how to understand the relation of unconscious motivation to the highly organized qualities of the work of art. In Wordsworth's development, too, individuation was not only the place of injury but virtually that of healing. Whatever trauma, in childhood or adulthood, raised Wordsworth's self-consciousness to apocalyptic pitch, to his being haunted by spots in the rural world that addressed him mutely, like navel-points of the earth on which ancient shrines were built, he credited the fearful as well as beautiful impact of England's rural scenery with a "renovating virtue." What he came to call Nature (which, as a youngster, he had treated thoughtlessly or even with destructive abandon) was depicted in the autobiographical *Prelude* as a conscious, guiding, suffering presence. He insisted that it had saved him from psychic and sensory fixations.

In my own critical writing, I speculated that some anguish of socialization must have entered the process. Even if elided, deeply shaming or embarrassing moments, accompanied by words actually uttered, surely played a part, so that only further words (poetry itself) could help to heal the wounds words had made. My psycho-aesthetics tried to show how integral poetry and artistic creation were to sanity, to negotiating the precarious, bewildering passage leading through childhood and youth. I wanted, like Paul Ricoeur, to reconcile a hermeneutics of suspicion that enveloped every grand narrative with an affirmative outcome that left the motivation to narrate intact.

That phase soon became more complex. Was there any commonality between this focus on ordinary if troubling issues of socialization, and my desire to concentrate, as I did more and more, on the traumatic experience of the survivors of the camps and related mass murders? How could these experiences, which now came home to my consciousness, be honestly listened to? What kind of intellectual witnessing was called for, and might these testimonial narratives play a significant role in the life of the survivors as well as in the public pursuit of human rights?

Perhaps, though, I was more of a loner than this account implies. My turning to the interpretive daring of psychoanalysis, and later to trauma studies, even if all this was not unusual, suggests a personal need. One pretends, retroactively, to be part of a collective movement, less out of modesty than in order to think of oneself as having been at the crest of a gathering wave. There, as friends and colleagues die, I hover still, disenchanted by the waning force of a once self-defining, now vague generation whose coherence may never have existed except in the very branding it no longer acknowledges.

—Geoffrey Hartman
SPRING 2005

~

The summer before I went to college, the horse trainer for whom I had been working told me, flippantly, that I could take the few months I had before I left to work with a little mare she had, that she didn't have time for. It would be good experience for me, she said, and good for her because I would get the mare into condition to be sold. She put special stress on the word "sold"—she had always been bothered by the attachments I developed to horses, by my tendency to anthropomorphize. I used to feel stung by the digs she would make at me over it, but retrospectively I can see the sense to her view; sentiment can sometimes be unintentionally cruel, or inescapable once invoked.

She had put the mare I would be riding in a pipe corral at a distant end of the stables that was a trek from the main barns and from the cross-ties where we groomed the horses and tacked them up. The mare was four years old, bay with a star, and newly arrived from the racetrack, where she had been a failure. She wasn't fast enough, and she was probably too small to have ever warranted serious attention, in any case. She was only fifteen hands high, and the bones in her legs were as thin and delicate as those found in birds' wings. Her legs were the first thing I noticed about her and the first part of her I touched, because it was obvious that she had been kicking, repeatedly, against the metal bars of her pipe corral. There were scratches and raw, bloody places, and I felt a wincing heat under my hand when I touched her. She lifted her toy-sized hoof, and I realized that I had already made a mistake: there I was, crouching at her feet, an easy target, and I had not even bothered to put on her halter or to tie her against the rail.

That first careless contact, my thoughtless and automatic reach for her leg, seems now to have established me with Eve—that was her name—in some irrevocable way. The other horses with whom I had had a kind of intimacy had learned to nicker for me when they saw me approaching, to be stroked and fondled and baby-talked. The parameters of affection I'd experienced before as a typical girl who loved horses, and whose love for horses had carried over past the age of twelve or so, were torn down in my relationship to Eve. We had a strange and lawless physical intimacy—anonymous and rather fierce. She must have been able to feel my heartbeat through her thin Thoroughbred skin while I had my hand on her swollen leg, curled around her suspensory ligament, her cannon bone, her flexor tendons, and her delicate little sesamoid bones. She looked down at me with wide, dewy brown eyes.

I couldn't ride her at all that first week. I would walk her all the way down to the cross-ties, with her shying, whirling around, and even flinging herself into me and bruising my ribs, and then I would clean and medicate her cuts and bandage her legs. This routine was a welcome break from my state of generalized listlessness. I was living in a kind of anticipatory despair; I would spend hours and hours just driving, peering at the coils of heat that appeared above the asphalt ahead of me. That summer was full of my sense of the impending unknown—of impending adult life, I suppose—but everything lay ahead, invisible, while I had to sit parked for a few months more, full of a destructive nostalgia and desperate for velocity. There were wildfires that summer, and

I breathed their smoke with a vague sense of symbolic fulfillment, just as I took pleasure in the clouds of choking dust at the stables and in the tumbleweeds trapped in the barbed-wire fence along its perimeter. I was simultaneously full of a keening attachment to home and an urge for revolution, and these home-specific emblems of disintegration held a kind of glitter for me. They seemed to fulfill my listless, in-between aesthetic and sneer at it at the same time, and to be expressions of my bitter and unrealized urge for impact—for impact of any kind. I felt like smashing my hands with bricks most of the time, so I was sympathetic to Eve's kicking, and the precision required in bandaging her legs—the pressure just right, the strips smooth and crossing each other just so—was oddly soothing, at once numbing and engaging, a respite from my unrest.

When Eve was sound enough to ride, my trainer told me to be careful—to start out riding her in one of the twenty-meter round pens, and to be very wary of touching her back, especially when getting on. This seemed sensible enough when I was walking her, trying to cope with the way she leapt around, but she would always stand so amenably in the cross-ties that by the time I had finished grooming and bandaging her she would have convinced me that she was, in fact, quiet rather than pistol-hot. It was always a surprise, maybe even an affront, to discover the opposite. She had been well behaved while I curried and brushed her, and hadn't reacted noticeably when I placed the saddle on her back, or tightened the girth around her belly, or slipped the bit into her mouth, and so on that first riding day I entered into one of my states of denial. I climbed up and settled onto her back without thinking too much about it, and she immediately shuddered indignantly and clenched up. She bolted like a shot.

She had nowhere to bolt to. She went barreling around the little round pen, her speed choked by the tightness of the circle.

Clods of dirt flung out from under her scrabbling hooves. She ran without breathing quickly or emoting in any way, but with a feverish intensity. *Eve, ho*, I told her, *Easy*, and even *Good gir-rul*, in a false, wheedling voice, but she did not condescend to listen. She ran right through the bit as well. The speed and the metal of the fence that would sometimes clang against the toe of my boot frightened me, and at first I sobbed and choked a bit and pulled desperately at her mouth, but eventually her movement took on a strange kind of abstraction, and my fear disappeared. We were suspended in this pounding speed, oddly outside time, and each contraction of her muscles felt like a little bit of explosive joy. This was the velocity I had been craving. I touched down lightly onto her back for a stride and then lifted up again, and then touched down again for two strides, and I was even training her—I was teaching her something, making her softer. At last she grew tired, and she fell into a trot and then broke to a walk. She was lathered in sweat, and she staggered a bit as I cooled her out, as if she had gone through a ritual of purification.

My rides on Eve—the galloping and speed of them—were the most vivid things to emerge out of that summer's haze of smoke and tumbleweeds. The feel of Eve's back became something that entered into my dreams, that had singed the nerve endings in my thighs. She felt more like some supple sea creature than she felt like a horse, always dynamic, and I tried to invoke her whenever I felt one of my petulant desolations set in—when I would find myself being cruel to my mother or one of my friends, wanting to scratch and scratch until I got to something raw. The sensation of her was a kind of limber humming in the hips—a feeling my trainer had only been able to try to indicate by chanting, "whup, whup, whup," when my seat would lock and make me lose the elasticity and impulsion of whatever horse I happened to be riding. It was so novel and lovely, I would chant it to myself to make sure that it was real and that I actually had come to own it—"whup, whup, whup."

I was reading *Anna Karenina* that summer, as well. Someone had told me that the book was about inevitability, about convergence, that it began with someone dying, struck by a train, and that it ended the same way: a cycle of suicide. This idea was appealing; it seemed akin to the wildfires, but significant instead of merely random, as they were—it converted what was for me nothing more than remote, observed destruction into intimate, experienced destruction, and therefore it converted half-life into life. The idea of destination, of destiny, of having something grasping onto me and pulling me forward, seemed critical. It was a release from my feeling of entropy, and of being subject to dispersion at any time—of being lighter than air. I realized, though, that Anna's destination was in fact accidental, even circular, and it struck me as being somehow bound up with my endless, exhausting gallops with Eve around the round pen, that wore both of us down to an elemental edge. When I got to the passage about Vronsky's little mare, Frou-Frou—hot, narrow, and dancing, just as Eve was—I imagined her as Eve, and nothing I have read horrified me so much as her sudden death. My identification with Vronsky and Frou-Frou, and with their steeplechase race, made the accident seem completely shocking, like a tear in the essential fabric of things. Frou-Frou's broken back, her helplessness as she lies on the ground, galloping seconds before, and what Tolstoy describes as her "speaking eyes" have, for me, a devastating proximity. The passage suggests that suspension, that the paradoxical feeling of galloping that felt so crucial to me, is fallible and mortal even at its most potent—that it is as ephemeral as breath.

After reading, it was hard to look at Eve's little feet, or the thin blade of her backbone. She was sold the week before I left, and before that every day when I went to get her I would jog anxiously to her corral, afraid that I would find her down and crippled, or with her legs smashed up to bits. In the midst of my embrace of the dissolution and destruction that seemed so appealing during that last summer—in the midst of my drive to cast off everything around me—I pined for a stasis that could make its place within movement. I wanted Eve to have her own sanctity in all her vulnerable, inadequate speed.

I have never asked what became of her. There is no legitimate reason for believing her to be injured or dead; she had settled down a good deal by the end of the summer, and probably wouldn't have done anything to hurt herself. I think what I'm after in avoiding news of her is a puncturing of the screen that separated me from Anna Karenina that summer after high school; I would prefer to be blind, hurling myself toward meaning I cannot see, than to be all-seeing and stationary, sitting in the dust, smirking, and watching the world through a pane of faintly shattered glass. It strikes me as better to be Vronsky, careening unknowingly toward Frou-Frou's dreadful fall, than it was to be my larval self that summer, tongue-tied in a panoramic remoteness that felt like being buried. So when I picture Eve I picture her teetering, hooves pounding, energy nearly spent, and I am able to imagine my own suspension, my dazzling and momentary control, and the life of my body, as things that can still be clutched and exclaimed over, maybe placed between the teeth as one would a pearl, to check its worth.

—MIMI CHUBB
SUMMER 2005

~

A vignette for the fabulous storyteller Lê Thi Diem Thúy:

A Vietnamese woman in her early fifties. She is wearing a floral bathing costume, its pattern a little like English chintz. Her bathing cap is the color of raw ginger when sliced. She walks from the obligatory public showers to the corner of the indoor municipal swimming pool and waits by the short ladder that leads down into the water. The municipality is a Paris suburb.

A Vietnamese man in swimming trunks appears. He is thinner than she and a little shorter. Probably he's her husband. I don't know why I have a slight doubt about this. Is it his deference? He climbs halfway down into the water and she half-sits on his shoulders, facing the side of the pool; then he descends prudently, until the water is over his hips, and she launches herself to swim away. After swimming a couple of lengths himself, the man climbs out and leaves the pool. All this with the greatest discretion and without a word passing between them.

She continues swimming for about an hour. Her legs move as pliantly and strongly as a frog's. When the man returns and gets back into the water, she comes to the corner where the ladder is, and he gently lifts her arse with his hands and the pair of them climb out. His gestures are utterly impersonal, discreet and, at the same time, very precise, as if he were performing a traditional ritual. A ritual perhaps handed down over generations.

The woman walks away from the corner of the pool almost as easily as she swims. Or does she have a slight limp? Vietnam is a country of deltas, rivers, and water, and there may be bathing rituals there which are difficult to imagine on drier land. In the Vietnamese language the word for *water* is the word for *homeland*.

Or is she simply frightened of slipping on the rungs of a ladder? I come each day at the same hour as she does—when everyone else in the suburb is eating their lunch and the pool is relatively empty. As we pass in the water we nod once at one another. It's surely clear that we both enjoy the water. She, however, is more submerged in it than I am, as though for her the water were deeper. The Vietnamese word for water is *nu'ó'c*.

In her wide yet fine face, her narrow eyes are greenish, and I sense that for her the color of the water in the pool is slightly less a cerulean blue than it is for me. For her it has in it a touch more yellow or sunlight, making it a fraction closer to the color of some water beside the faraway, incontrovertible Mekong.

The man's gestures accompanying her immersion and emergence from the pool are unchanging. By now I know them well and could perform the ritual myself. And saying this, I suddenly ask myself whether once I didn't replace him?

—JOHN BERGER
FALL 2005

~

In the mid-1950s, I had a job as a tutor at Sleepy Hollow, an institution in Dobbs Ferry, New York. Sleepy Hollow was partly administered by the Manhattan School Authority and was non-denominational. Most of the children were troubled and lived in cottages with an adult married couple. During the day they saw social workers. Some of them went to the local public schools. Half did not (they were defined as too anti-social by the psychiatrist who visited monthly). They ranged in age from eleven to seventeen.

Frank, who was seventeen, had spent most of his life in foster homes. He had a rootless quality; he always seemed on the point of departure. He perched on the edge of his desk and listened tolerantly while I tried to show him what a complete sentence was, but he was thinking of something else.

If someone had told you Frank was a sociopath, which someone had told me, you might have had difficulty attaching that word to Frank. He loved the talking part of my evenings at Sleepy Hollow, after the work was done in arithmetic or spelling or composition—the stories, the jokes we made, the tides of spoken memories.

I saw him angry only once. That was when the institution children, himself among them, went out to neighborhood schools with special food tickets because, it was said by Sleepy Hollow officials, they frequently spent the money they were allotted for lunch on candy and cigarettes. The local kids did, too. Drugs were rarely available in those days.

Frank and the other children refused to go to their schools until the administration stopped the use of the special food tickets. It was hard enough for them to be known as institution inmates, but to be so dramatically singled out as they were at that moment when they had to hand over their maroon tickets to the cafeteria cashier was intolerable to them. They were often bullied and baited by the local children, who exalted themselves and their own circumstances—whatever those might have really been—at the expense of strangers in their midst, a form of cruelty not restricted to children.

When Frank was seven, he had asked his mother to take him to a movie. She said she couldn't—a friend was driving her to an appointment with a doctor. Frank told her he wished she was dead. She was killed in an automobile accident that afternoon, although the driver, her friend, was not seriously injured. Frank's father had deserted his family several years earlier. There was no one to take care of Frank. He began his institutional life a few weeks after his mother's death.

I don't know how deeply, or in what part of his mind, he felt there was a fatal connection between his fleeting rage, the wish he had expressed, and the death that afternoon. I know he suffered—his very abstractedness was a form of suffering.

One night, Frank lingered at the gatehouse where I held my classes. He asked me if I had ever worked at another place like Sleepy Hollow. I said yes, once. Then for some reason I told him about the concentration camp children I had met ten years earlier in the high Tatra Mountains in Poland. I spoke a little about the Holocaust. We were sitting on a step. It was a clear warm night in spring. The stars were thick.

"I never heard of anything like that," he said. He asked me what had happened to those children in the mountains. I said I didn't know, except what happens to everyone—they would have their lives, they had endured and survived the horror of the camps. Each would make what he or she could of life. He looked up at the sky.

"What's after the stars?" he asked. "What's outside of all we're looking at?"

I named a few constellations I thought I recognized. Although his school grades were low, Frank had read an astronomy textbook on his own. He corrected my star guesses twice. "But what do you think about way past out there?" he urged.

I said there seemed to be a wall in the mind beyond which one couldn't go on imagining infinity—at least, I couldn't. "Me, neither," he said.

We sat for a few more minutes, then said goodnight and walked away from the gatehouse, me to my car, and he to the cottage where he would live a few months longer before he ran away and was not heard from again by anyone at Sleepy Hollow.

The children in that residence accepted a certain amount of discipline—do your homework, eat the carrots before the cupcake—though they complained noisily about it. What they really hated was to be told how and what they were. They had heightened sensitivities to questions that were not questions but sprang from iron-clad assumptions about them and their troubles.

There were many people on the staff who were sure they knew everything. They had forgotten—if they had ever known—that answers were not always synonymous with truth.

—Paula Fox
FALL 2005

~

Lolita isn't about a girl, or about a man with a deviant sexual fixation; it is about the male heart. What do men want? Women. Preferably young women. What do men fear? Other men. Particularly, men more appealing than themselves. Around this triangle, Nabokov constructs his book. Humbert Humbert, our narrator, represents the generic man. Lolita, a sexual vessel fourteen years of age, is his ideal object of desire. Clare Quilty, in the shadowy background for most of the book, is "the other man."

The story begins with the exhilaration and the agony of courtship, followed by the ecstasy of conquest. Humbert gets Lolita. He "has" her many times but, because he cannot possess her completely, his lust for her remains unsatisfied. He suspects that she is unfaithful. Everywhere he turns he perceives the ghostly threat of "the other man." To protect against "the other man" he twice spirits Lolita across America, driving from town to town, living in motels. This is an extreme measure to take but Humbert intuits that a moving target is hardest to hit. And yet, inevitably, he is hit. "The other man" materializes and steals the girl. We, the readers, have felt "the other man's" presence in the book, but we could no more have identified him than could Humbert. This is Nabokov's genius: the genius of implication, tone, and pacing. Who is this "other man"? Not until the very end does Nabokov reveal his face. He is the driver of the mysterious car. He is the stranger at the gas station. He is the voice that emanates from the darkness of a motel porch.

> "Where the devil did you get her?"
>
> "I beg your pardon."
>
> "I said: the weather is getting better."

"The other man" exists, and it is only a matter of time before he prevails.

Then, as in a dream, we meet him. And, as in a dream, our worst fears are realized. "The other man" is superior in every way—smarter, more virile, more charismatic, inspired in his decadence. Because we cannot defeat him or become him, we kill him. Which is cold comfort. He stages an opera of his own death, and the girl remains irretrievable. This is the psychological terrain Nabokov charts. And this—not the prurient accusation of pedophilia—is what continues to make the book provocative. Concealing nothing, Nabokov offers a stark depiction, though not a denunciation, of the male heart—from its illicit desires to its primal fears.

—David Bezmozgis
winter 2006

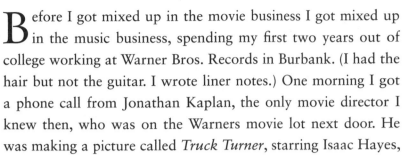

Before I got mixed up in the movie business I got mixed up in the music business, spending my first two years out of college working at Warner Bros. Records in Burbank. (I had the hair but not the guitar. I wrote liner notes.) One morning I got a phone call from Jonathan Kaplan, the only movie director I knew then, who was on the Warners movie lot next door. He was making a picture called *Truck Turner*, starring Isaac Hayes, who'd also composed the score. There was to be a recording session that afternoon, with Mr. Hayes conducting, and did I want to come watch?

It sounded like fun and turned out to be thrilling. An orchestra the size of some Biggest Little City's symphony sat on the scoring stage, surrounding Mr. Hayes, who in recent years had killed the people with the theme from *Shaft* and an emotionally pummeling cover of "Walk On By." The session was like a normal recording date at the record company except for the movie screen on the wall, where clips from the *Truck Turner* work print were shown so that the music could be timed to them. "Bassoons," said the Barry White–trouncing bass voice that had moaned its way through *Hot Buttered Soul*, "you need to be out when the car door closes. Again."

Again, baby! The car door on the screen closed several more times, the bassoons at last caught up with it, Mr. Hayes went on to the next cue, and I was in heaven. The only thing that could have made it better was if, instead of natty casual clothes, he'd been wearing the getup with the chains from the *Black Moses* album cover. This being Hollywood, I soon started remembering it that way. As a bonus, the route to the scoring stage took me down Warners' New York Street, a beautifully detailed block of fake Manhattan, complete with little staircases leading down from the street to basement apartment entrances. As I walked back to work, it occurred to me that some of the inspiration for Disneyland must have come from Walt's seeing the delight of civilians taking their first walk down a back lot's ersatz avenues.

Later, as I say, I got mixed up in the movie business, so mixed up that I sometimes took it seriously. Like the showbiz columnist Army Archerd's fictional studio correspondent Onda Lotalot, I was on the lot a lot. I walked from my car to the office through a dusty village that was Cuzco one week and China the next. I ate at the commissary. I bought discounted Warner-Reprise CDs at the studio store. I wrote monster movies.

I would say that I became intimately familiar with the New York Street during that period, but in fact I was intimately familiar with it before I ever set foot there. Everyone is. It's the setting of a million crime pictures, musicals, TV episodes, and commercials. It's basically 1940s, but with a little signage and some show cars its age can be pushed back or pulled forward by decades. Gangsters tommy-gunned one another from running boards there, and dozens of young strivers burst simultaneously out of their below-grade apartments to do dance numbers about hope up and down the fire escapes. The car chases on New York Street accounted for half the crime in the Valley. It was no place to own a fruit stand.

Years after my first visit, my wife and I went to the Warners lot one night for a screening. "The lots are full," the guard at the gate said. "Park on New York Street." We got the last available space. As we got out of the car my wife said, "We're by a hydrant."

"No, no," I said, "that's not a real hydrant." My wife is brilliant and all, but she's never been in show business. If our marriage had been announced in *Variety*, the item would have listed one or two of my monster movies and, despite all her achievements, added, "Wife is a non-pro." If Curly from the Three Stooges had married Marie Curie, she would have gotten "Wife is a non-pro" too.

Nothing on the New York Street was real, I explained. The apartment house façades looked like gritty real life took place inside, but there was nothing behind them. Gritty real life happened on soundstages, a hundred yards away. I closed the car door, without bassoons, and said, "We'll be late."

When we got back from the screening, there was a ticket on the windshield for parking by the quite real hydrant. I was mortified and didn't know what to do with the ticket, or even who had issued it—studio security? the Burbank police? Karl Malden in *The Wrong Man*?

I showed it to the guard at the gate. "You can't park by a hydrant," he said. "What if there was a fire?" I nodded, cringing at the thought of years of America's memories going up in flames like an over-insured furniture store because some idiot, me, had blocked the fireplug, and with a rented Cavalier at that. "I'm really sorry," I said. "How do I pay it?"

"Pay it?" He took the ticket from me and dropped it in the trash. "No, no. That's not a real ticket."

—Charlie Haas
summer 2006

~

Last week I moved from Massachusetts to my new home here in California. The day after I arrived I did what most people do when they move someplace. I opened a bank account.

You might think this would be easy. I've had an account in Massachusetts for twenty-five years, and there's still money in that one. I would just write a check drawn on my old Massachusetts bank account for deposit in my new California bank account, and the money would be available in no time. Or so I assumed.

The nice young man who was sitting there at a computer in the California bank told me I'd have to wait two weeks for my check to clear.

Two weeks? We're in an electronic age. Money moves from Boston to Bangkok in two seconds. My car and furniture got moved from Massachusetts to California in ten days. Why should it take two weeks for my money to move from Massachusetts to California? The nice young man sitting behind the computer explained that Massachusetts was a different state from California, I was new to California, and, well, various things had to be looked into.

I told him he could look at my Massachusetts bank account right there and then on his computer. If he averted his eyes for a moment I would type in my pass-code on his keyboard and he could see for himself I had more than enough money in my Massachusetts bank account to cover the check I was depositing in his bank. But no, he was sorry. It would take two weeks for my check to clear. So like a chump I said okay, fine. And now I'm well into in my second week waiting for my money.

So where, exactly, is my money? It's no longer in Massachusetts. I looked on the internet. Forty-eight hours after I deposited the check in California the money was already gone from my Massachusetts bank account. So where is it? Hovering aimlessly over Kansas City? Gasping as it crosses the Rockies?

I know where my money is. It's already here in California. The California bank has it. (If truth be told, the California bank isn't really a California bank anymore because it just bought up the major bank in Massachusetts and is now one of America's largest national banks.) This big national bank has been using my money—investing it, getting a nice return on it during these two weeks, while I've been in effect lending it my money at zero-interest. The bank is getting two weeks of "float," as they say in financial circles. It's got my float and presumably the floats of thousands of other new depositors who are moving from one state to another and who also have to wait two weeks to see their money again.

This is exactly why we don't want big bank consolidation of the sort that's going on. It reduces competition, which means this giant bank (okay, I'll name it—the Bank of America) doesn't have to worry I'll walk out and go to another bank that will be more responsive. This bank can pretty much do as it pleases with my money for two weeks and I have no recourse. Except to complain to you.

—Robert Reich
SUMMER 2006

~

I did not go to Marfa, Texas, in search of Donald Judd. I went to putter with poems and essays, and to look at a wide, high sky and desolately outstretching tawny grassland that surround the Lannan Foundation's house for visiting writers. I went to see plants I didn't know: yucca, sotol grass, mesquite, ocotillo. But there was Donald Judd's Chinati Foundation just outside of town, and, obediently, I visited.

My few earlier encounters with Judd's work in New York City galleries had left me cold. So I was taken aback, stopped in my tracks, when I found myself being acted upon by his one hundred aluminum boxes. They are arranged in two long, symmetrical artillery sheds with high ceilings like airplane hangars on the old army base Judd took over in 1979. As in strict metrical form, the effect is one of symmetry and cunning variation. The boxes are all of the same dimension, rectangles about my shoulder height, and they are all made of identical industrial mill aluminum sheets. Each has its own internal order: variously placed vertical or horizontal walls inside each box create subtle shifts in spatial ratios, and the occasional slanting plane increases the range of play. The boxes work inward, toward internal division; they also work outward, from their hallucinatory rows fitting exactly into the concrete slabs on the floor, to the tall rectangular windows that march down both sides of the sheds, to the stretch of almost desert grassland, the spectral mountains, the apparently endless sky.

If the boxes gesture out toward infinity, infinity responds and seems to come visiting in the form of light. The aluminum is grainy enough not to mirror light, but reflective enough to translate sky into a silvery aura inside the sheds. Scale seems reversed, with infinity and the finite changing places. Matter and spirit also flip: metal seems sublimed to air and the boxes hover like Platonic ideas, while the blocks of sunlight framed by the windows look as if each weighed a ton. By his elemental principles rigorously applied—regularity, exclusion, reflection—Judd has organized space and light. Emerging from the visit, I found myself, willy nilly, reorganized as well.

—Rosanna Warren
FALL 2006

TABLE TALK

It was unsettling to encounter a buffalo in the city. If we had been driving across the plains or camped in the foothills of the Rockies I might have been better prepared. But my friend and I were riding bikes through Golden Gate Park, a city park where trees have been carefully planted to naturalize the more anomalous amusements—a Dutch windmill, a Japanese teahouse. I was focused on our destination (the beach) when we came up over the hill in sight of yet another open expanse of grass; this one was comparatively scrubby next to the manicured picnic lawns and terraced greens outside the Conservatory of Flowers. I did not notice at first that this pasture was ringed with chain-link because, in the instant of its unfurling from the crest in the road, I was wobbling over my handlebars, searching for the brakes and instead settling on my shoe, dragging my toe across the asphalt to the gravel to the dirt. There, looking up at me with a mouthful of grass, was a buffalo.

"Bison, actually," my landlady said when I told her of my discovery. But I paid no attention to her correction. Do you know about the buffalo? I kept asking of friends, of strangers. What do you mean? they replied. Of course, everyone knows about the buffalo: we slaughtered forty million of them in one fell destined swoop. Do you know they wallow right in our midst, I repeated, right here in the urban mist? A beast. Fur and horns and hooves.

The natural history I found at the library gave the buffalo's Latin name: *Bison bison*. (The reiterative quality of its scientific classification somehow confirmed my need for hyperbole.) *Bison bison* is the descendant of the *Bison pricus* that crossed into North America from Siberia. Slowly the bison began to colonize the plains, outlasting the mammoth and the mastodon, the saber-toothed cat and the tyrannical "bull-dog bear." In time they evolved into smaller, more efficient animals. Nevertheless, the bison has a formidable stature: from a narrow rear, his back rises to a hump that sits well above his head and gives him a look of impossibly broad shoulders. He wears a regal cloak, brown and woolly. When the Spanish explorers first saw him, they thought he looked like a monstrous composite of lion, sheep, camel, and bull. Once, my library book recounted, a bison swallowed a woman and she was found years later, whole in the belly of the beast. The buffalo from the park began to graze through my dreams. When he turns to me with a dark, intransient glance, I wake up trembling.

Of course, humans proved dominant. The early hunters would dress as wolves and creep up close to the grazing herd. It was an intimate affair. I imagine there were moments before the kill when the buffalo looked up to see a pair of human eyes watching him, like spears, through a furry disguise.

The rest of the story has been well told. The extermination of the buffalo became a means to reduce and contain the indigenous communities while the white population spread westward. Today, the bison have been reappropriated as a symbol of American pride, a representative example of what we can revive and preserve and still manage to consume; bison herds roam free in several of our national parks, while simultaneously bison meat is raised elsewhere as a leaner and hormone-free alternative to beef.

I went back to the paddock several weeks after my initial encounter. This time I dismounted my bike carefully and sat on a park bench. The herd was lounging two hundred yards from the fence; every now and then a bison would get up to drink from a trough set under a little shelter. I watched as a gopher peeked out of a hole to steal some healthy portions of sod and grass—and I was struck by the banality of the scene. A tour bus hissed to a stop behind me. The paddock was an exhibition just like the tulip garden and the windmill. How could I not have understood that the first time?

I struggled for a few moments to remember what it was that had originally been so uncanny. It wasn't simply the titillation of the wild and almost-exotic. Eye to eye with the beast, I had understood creaturely fear. And I could imagine the kind of aggression that might lead to slaughter. The buffalo had appeared in my dreams, after all, and humans have not infrequently committed acts of violence in broad daylight in order to keep a nightmare at bay.

—KATHRYN CRIM
WINTER 2007

~

For many years now, I have been attracting the lost. They approach me in slow-moving cars, they find me in crowds, they question me in subway stations, cafés, museums—all of them, impatiently hopeful, needing directions. It does not seem to matter where I am, or how long I've been there. They've stopped me in San Francisco, Wichita, and Boston, sometimes only hours after I'd seen the city for the first time myself. One summer, vacationing in Paris during a spell of near-tropical heat, I was desperately seeking a cold drink amidst the chic bustle of the Rue de Rivoli—surely looking quite lost myself—when a middle-aged woman emerged breathless from the crowd as if she'd spent the last several hours looking for me, thrust a scribbled address under my nose, and asked, in French, if I could help.

What do they see? I'd like to believe, of course, that I possess a certain quality that instantly identifies me, to any passerby, as a man who knows how to get around—a confident and purposeful strut, perhaps, or a radiance that advertises intelligence, like the lightbulb of cartoons. In fact, I do seem to have a good sense of direction. I also admit to an obsession with maps; I've been accused of spending too many vacation evenings hunched over them, plotting the quickest subway route for the next day's visit to the art museum (and then, once inside, studying the museum's diagram of rooms like an archeologist). There is, for me, great satisfaction in understanding the geographic complexity of a city, and where I stand within it; seeing how the blocks and roads and rails all fit together in an unfamiliar place is like a revelatory moment of learning, when the basics of calculus, for example, become suddenly clear. The knowledge, too, helps soften that nagging sense of urban insignificance.

The strength of my interest certainly came from my father. He had an uncanny memory for geography (layers and layers of maps must have existed in his head), and when he told his stories, he'd often digress into formidably precise descriptions of routes or locations, even those he hadn't seen for thirty years or more. And if you happened to confess to him some apprehension about finding your way from one place to another, he'd express disbelief. "Look, it's easy," he'd tell you, and your departure would be delayed until you heard about every landmark on the way. He often expressed admiration for the rich man who spends months planning a round-the-world excursion, buying tickets, making reservations, only to decide at the last minute not to go. The study of the route, my father explained, was often better than the trip.

His influence didn't stop with his death. Recently, for the first time in a few years, I visited the sprawling cemetery where he's buried, but with great frustration I couldn't remember the location of his stone. Carrying a map I retrieved from the funeral home, I came across a man searching for another grave; he asked me where he could get a map, too, and I explained, with sudden confidence, the quickest route to the office.

What attracts the lost, I suspect, is this: I look like someone they know. At parties or bars, a stranger will scrutinize me after a while, then turn to a friend and suggest with a knowing grin, "Doesn't he remind you of so-and-so?" Or I'll hear, "Haven't I seen you somewhere?"—always from people I've never met. On one occasion, while I waited to check in at a hotel, a man happily approached me, waved, and asked, "What are you doing here, Rich?" Not wanting to annoy a possible lunatic, I replied that I was merely waiting in line. He squinted and moved closer: "You're Rich, aren't you?" No, I said, but he persisted. "You don't have a little boy named Stewart and a daughter who's two?" I shook my head, warily smiling, and he finally went off, looking unconvinced.

Despite my apparently ubiquitous looks, I can't deny the pleasure of being an impromptu guide. It gives that shiver of instant authority. The lost, who have already admitted weakness, are at your mercy. You hold the power of healing—with a few words, you can improve someone's evening, you can prevent potential despair. The anxious brow relaxes with relief, and you feel the way a doctor must when prescribing a patient's cure. One afternoon in Seattle, an embarrassed cabbie pulled up beside me to ask where to find a particular downtown restaurant requested by his passengers. When I told him, he exuberantly nodded over and over, as if he'd just been bequeathed a great secret truth.

Giving directions can be addicting, too, much like answering correctly in a game of Trivial Pursuit. Immediately you want another question. Step right up, I want to say to the crowd after

I've guided another couple on their merry way—I'll tell anyone how to get anywhere.

Not that I've always been accurate. On a few occasions, I have confidently gestured and smiled, only to realize, moments after the car has disappeared into traffic, that I meant left, not right. Or I'd confused 24 with 42, the number of the bus that goes to the other side of town. Walking away, I can imagine only disaster ensuing, my error having sent them into some unforeseen maelstrom.

But in the end, when all is said and found, getting lost may not be so bad. It keeps us social and a little humble, two qualities that seem worth promoting in an age of increasing devotion to faceless communication and public boorishness. So if the world keeps asking, I'll keep answering, trying to point it toward a tiny part of its future, that essential but elusive destination—just four blocks south and a left at the light. You can't miss it.

—Robert Shuster
WINTER 2007

If you wanted to pick the number whose very sound best and most comically captures middle age in all its dust-bunny grayness, it would be hard to top the number of years I have been alive as of this writing: forty-three. Yes, forty-eight and fifty-six are older than forty-three, but somehow they just *sound* cooler. And I am living proof that forty-three is old enough for some of the less savory trappings of middle age: once-bionic eyes that now strain to make out what's on the nearest street sign; prescriptions for three—three!—different kinds of medication; and the nine-to-five schedule of the working stiff ("stiff" being an allusion to the state of my lower back). There are compensations, though. My wife and children come to mind. There is also a certain indifference to mass opinion, one that lets me, for example, do a couple of things casually that I wouldn't have dared do at all as a teenager: (1) dance and (2) wear shorts or swimming trunks that reveal the skinniest legs anyone has ever seen. And there is one benefit I couldn't have foreseen twenty years ago.

For the past few years, I have kept a succession of notebooks in my right hip pocket. The notebook is there from the time I get dressed in the morning until I get undressed at night, whether I am sitting or standing, at work, at a funeral, or at the local flea market. (The notebook is usually a three-by-five-inch, forty-eight-sheet Clairefontaine; I tried a Moleskine someone gave me, but the wear and tear reduced it to shreds within five months, and the Clairefontaines hold up for the twelve to fifteen months it takes me to fill them.) The notebooks are repositories for the titles of books, records, and films that I read or hear about and want to investigate. The notebooks are less important in themselves than for what they signify, which is curiosity—a feverish desire to learn, particularly about the arts. When I'm feeling "plugged in," as I like to call it, I can forget that I am not a twenty-year-old, newly minted adult waking up to the wonders of the world.

Of course, the world, even the world of the arts, is an awfully big place. One person, even if that person's name is Harold Bloom, Susan Sontag, or Cornel West, can learn only so much, and only so much at a time—and if you open yourself to everything, the sheer amount of *stuff* out there can lead you beyond exhilaration into bewilderment.

As for the solution, I came across an eloquent expression of it in my job. I am the editor of a magazine of biographical articles which appears eleven times a year; the biographees are living people in a wide variety of fields. Most months, reading over the proofs of the articles, I am struck by connections between and among people who would seem to have little in common. One of the issues, for example, included articles on the theologian Stanley Hauerwas and the nonfiction writer Susan Orlean, two people whose ideas, you might think, wouldn't necessarily intersect much. But here is the surprisingly salty-tongued Hauerwas talking in an online interview about religion: "Being a Christian gives you something to do. It means your life is not just one goddamned thing after another." And here is Orlean writing in her book *The Orchid Thief*: "The reason it matters to care passionately about something is that it whittles the world down to a more manageable size. It makes the world seem not huge and empty but full of possibility."

My own tools for "whittling the world down" have been my passions for learning about (in no special order) books, jazz, and film. Living in a world where I can immerse myself in these things is like being at an ongoing party, to which all trumpeters, novelists, cinematographers, directors, essayists, and saxophonists, great and minor, have been invited. Some of the guests turn out to be more interesting than others, but that's a party for you. The notebook helps here. Several years ago I read an article about the writer Andrea Lee, which quoted her as saying that her "favorite book of all time" is Mikhail Bulgakov's *The Master and Margarita*. Into the notebook it went. As sometimes happens, I transferred that information from notebook to notebook until, having written it down two or three times without reading the book, I concluded that I never would, and stopped the transfers. Then—three weeks before this writing—I was in the Strand Bookstore, at Twelfth Street and Broadway in New York, when I overheard two men talking. "I was on the subway and saw a guy reading

The Master and Margarita," one of them said. "So I checked it out. I couldn't put it down." The Strand didn't have a copy that day, but back in the notebook it went . . .

A month or so ago I bought a jazz CD called *Boss Tenor*, a 1960 recording by the saxophonist Gene Ammons. The writer of the liner notes, LeRoi Jones (who was not yet Amiri Baraka), listed some of the saxmen who were influenced by either Coleman Hawkins or Lester Young (whereas Ammons had synthesized the influences of both, in Jones's view). Among the names mentioned were Ike Quebec and Wardell Gray. Now, I prided myself on being able to recognize, blindfolded, sax solos by Hawkins or Young, or Benny Carter or Ben Webster or Charlie Parker or Johnny Hodges, or even such slightly lesser lights as Charlie Rouse or Don Byas—but Ike Quebec? Wardell Gray? *Who?* Into the notebook went their names, and off I went, to the Virgin Megastore at Union Square . . .

Last winter I picked up Phillip Lopate's *Totally, Tenderly, Tragically*, practically a one-book course on great films—one that I almost couldn't read for writing down movie titles in my notebook, many of them works by Japanese directors I didn't know: Yasujiro Ozu, Mikio Naruse, Kenji Mizoguchi . . .

I enjoy each book, film, and record for itself, but what truly fascinates me, and what I hope for with everything I read, watch, or put on my stereo, is a work's connection to something else. It occurred to me as I listened to the music of the bassist-composer Charles Mingus, for example, that it bears similarities to the films of Robert Altman: that the films, with their many characters crowded into a single shot and their simultaneous conversations, might be mere exercises in cacophony but are instead works of power and beauty—pulling off a feat similar to that accomplished by Mingus's polyphonous compositions. In another example, it seemed to me that New Journalism, as practiced by Tom Wolfe, had features in common with a musical movement that came along at roughly the same time: Free Jazz, as ushered in by the saxophonist Ornette Coleman. The decidedly eccentric Coleman, instead of playing melodies based on chord progressions, as had the groundbreaking Charlie Parker before him, based his melodies on his individual response to the totality of a piece of music—lending even more freedom to an art form already characterized by improvisation. Similarly, Wolfe, in his essays and nonfiction books, is not bound by point of view, shifting between his own and that of his subjects to marvelous overall effect. These connections make the party of art feel smaller, more intimate to me, while adding new dimensions to the things in it.

Recently I've tried to expand my focus, just a little. On the same day as the overheard conversation in the Strand, I went to the Guggenheim to see an exhibit of Jackson Pollock's drawings. That visit's entry in my notebook, made as I stood in front of Pollock's *Untitled, 1943*, refers to the "simultaneity" the drawing has in common with Charlie Parker's music. I can't, at the moment, remember what I meant by that. Maybe, though, there is a link to be found between the works of those two self-destructive artists, who both died in the mid-1950s. Maybe I will find it. I have time. I'm only forty-three.

—CLIFFORD THOMPSON
SPRING 2007

I'm not much of a TV viewer. My wife, on the other hand, is in the habit of switching on the box in the evening, when she's finally done working. Her tastes definitely lean toward escapist entertainment, although—thank God for small mercies—they don't include *Sex and the City*. They do, however, include those ubiquitous Dick Wolf police procedurals and their many clones, and so I've acquired a glancing familiarity with the genre. She doesn't so much watch these shows as let them wash over her while she goes about her nightly business, brushing her teeth, changing her clothes, glancing through personal correspondence. For me, however—perhaps because I wrote for television when I was younger—the medium is just too intrusive to ignore that way. The ability to read a book, or even think, while Mariska Hargitay and Dann Florek (my cast list is probably several seasons out of date, but it's the re-runs that are inescapable) discuss police strategy is beyond me.

Over the past couple of years, I had heard a lot of buzz about the HBO series *The Wire*, but I resisted checking it out. I wasn't enthusiastic about attaching myself to an established series *in medias res*, for one thing. Too much catch-up required. And in any case, the investment involved in watching a complex, multi-episode series seemed daunting. Next thing you know, you find yourself adjusting your schedule around air-times, and worrying about fictional relationships when you ought to be attending to real ones. But this last Christmas, my son, who, after a couple of decades of uncomfortably close observation, has some inkling of my tastes, brought home the first three seasons of *The Wire* on DVD, and all but insisted that I give it a try. Within an hour or two, I was hooked. We spent much of the holiday in front of the TV. Plans to watch "just one episode" would quickly expand to several hours of viewing.

In its essence, *The Wire* is another police procedural, and not, superficially, so very different from the precursor it most resembles, the excellent *Homicide: Life on the Street* (with which it shares both its Baltimore setting and a not insignificant portion of its cast). The show follows a unit within the Baltimore Police Department that employs electronic monitoring devices to pursue its investigations (hence the title). This aspect of the show is handled superbly—the writing and acting are exemplary—but would not by itself be enough to elevate *The Wire* to the astonishing level it achieves. We've seen these sorts of components before, although rarely quite so skillfully executed: a unit of mismatched misfits who coalesce into a superb team, revealing unsuspected talents along the way; the individual dysfunctions (bad marriages, excessive drinking, a history of corruption) that interfere with and occasionally enable the various team-members' ability to do their job; the conflicts and turf-battles with higher-ups in the department, in other law-enforcement agencies, and in city government; the rule-breaking and hot-dogging. All these are handled artfully, more than artfully, but they hardly make the series unique.

Where it differs, and where it starts to assume the complexity one is more inclined to associate with nineteenth-century fiction than with a TV cop show, is in its treatment of the law-breakers, the bad guys the cops are pursuing. In seasons one and three, the police are after drug dealers in the housing projects on Baltimore's west side; in season two, crooked union executives on the Baltimore docks. In both cases, but especially when dealing with the drug dealers, the writers bring a level of specificity, intricacy, and human sympathy to the ostensible villains that is almost disconcertingly absorbing.

Not that there is anything sentimental in these portrayals. There is no facile, Sixties-style softening of rough edges, no liberal redemption. Violence is a necessary tool of the drug dealers' trade, and it is seen to be employed without compunction and frequently with distressing glee. The unmitigated brutality on display is often startling in its ugliness, without the quasi-pornographic glamour one finds in a series like *24*. And the web of personal betrayals, betrayals of family and friends as well as business associates, is an essential element of the plotting. That customers' lives are being blighted on a daily basis is an integral, unexceptionable part of the dealers' enterprise, and occasions no perceptible qualms.

But despite all this, the enterprise itself is rational, and the way it is conducted—even the violence with which it is conducted—is rational as well. It is not for nothing that one of the two drug lords is portrayed taking an advanced business course at a local community college (and getting an A on one of the papers he submits). The product being sold may be contraband, but enlightened marketing praxis still prevails. In one scene, aiming perhaps a bit too broadly for comedy but effective (and very funny) all the same, he presides over a council of his underlings as if they are a board of directors, even insisting on following Robert's Rules of Order.

And the personal relationships among the drug dealers and those in their ambit are beautifully evoked. The extraordinary cast makes a huge contribution here, of course, but a lot of the credit has to go to the first-rate writing. Not one character, nor one relationship, is generic. The two drug lords, for example, best friends since childhood, are menacing and yet eerily vulnerable, young men walking a precarious tightrope; when their individual ambitions begin to diverge and conflict, the inevitable showdown, suspenseful and very slow in coming, is full of authentic sorrow, deeply felt regret, as well as rage. (It's a regret we share, despite all the brutality we've seen both commit.) And the strung-out police informant, a lost soul, a hopeless derelict, acquires a certain quirky, comic nobility as the series proceeds. Then there's the homosexual freebooter who makes his living by ripping off drug dealers through a combination of guile and ruthlessness; he emerges with the dash and idiosyncratic sense of honor of an urban Robin Hood. These are all star turns in a series that abounds with star turns provided by unknown actors rather than stars.

HBO has been responsible for the best—not just some of the best, but all of the best—dramatic programming in the history of American television. With *The Wire*, it has established a new standard.

—Erik Tarloff
SUMMER 2007

~

"Humans are clouds; wherever they turn up, the sky darkens." This is one of those aphorisms I remember from my youth, possibly from *Reader's Digest*. Or is it a shade too bleak for that sunny magazine?

The idea that we are shady types, and that this situation came about because somewhere someone made a tragic mistake, is deeply embedded in our thinking and feeling. In Genesis, we are shown the actual moment when this occurrence took place, and I don't know of any more convincing tale about this feeling of having been thrown out somewhere, with the extra barb of having brought it all down on ourselves.

There's an amusing illustration of this feeling—this time looked at from underneath, as it were—in a tale told by E. B. Tylor in his *Primitive Culture*. People on Borneo apparently thought that orangutans were pretending they couldn't speak in order to avoid being drawn into the human race, since if they were human they would have to work. There's wisdom for you: one look at humanity, and they've already decided not to travel down that road.

In contrast to this attractive fancy, there are lots of real people who, though they are already under way as humans, would like to quit the enterprise. No, they don't want to die; they want to rid themselves of certain aspects of humanity. It's not just the corrupt bunch of planet-wasting, warring morons they want to leave behind. Exactly which layers they would like to shed I find it hard to pin down. "Corrupt, planet-wasting, warring, moronic" are too easy. Who wouldn't want to get rid of those? No, they want to leave more than that behind.

Recently, here in Holland, I came across a man who tried to enumerate these items. His name is Henk de Velde, and he was talking on television about his plans. He is about to leave Holland on a never-ending sea voyage which he thinks may last from four to forty years. He has no goal in view other than the effort to cut himself loose from all kinds of things, in the hope that once he is free he will succeed in melting into the surroundings.

As the son of a modest artisan, I cannot help wondering who is going to pay for all this detaching, and as a thinking being, I wonder what it is that this Sailor wants to achieve.

As for this commingling with his surroundings, which he experiences as infinitely relieving, it has happened to him once already. He describes an experience which is quite common in the region of uncommon experiences: "In the wild landscape of Siberia I had the feeling of walking into nothingness. I knew nothing and I was nothing. I had the feeling of standing near God, even the feeling that I *was* God. I felt like a speck in the universe, a tiny part in a greater whole . . . ”

A tiny part that is God and knows nothing—a very apt description of a situation that beggars description. But it’s not just knowledge he wants to get away from. He would also love to escape from the clutches of his fellow-beings. “What I would really like to achieve is a situation where I need nobody and nobody needs me. Not even my son Stefan. I hope to achieve this within three years. By that time I want to have severed all ties.”

There is a disarming artlessness in the way this Sailor clearly describes the faultline in his position. The question is, after all, whether Stefan (to mention only him) will embark on a similar escape route during those three years, arriving at a comparable position of indifference, so that in the end these two men will achieve a situation of balanced mutual neglect. Can you imagine a sadder result? It probably won’t work out that way, which is sadder still: behold the Sailor, impervious wanderer, past all need of human company, and look at his son struggling with the pain of being abandoned by his father. Or the Hollywood version: Sailor and son in desperate search of each other, scouring the seven seas and finally collapsing into each other’s arms on a desolate beach in Brazil.

Back to his basic motive. We are talking here about an effort to blast a passage through the Original Curse in the hope of ending up back in the Garden of Eden. I don’t think this itinerary exists, but we all share the longing for it; that’s why his sailing away has gotten so much attention.

Wouldn’t it be wonderful to get away from us? Didn’t we dream up God precisely to assuage this longing? God is a way out of us which leads Upwards, but you can also head the other way, trying to slip away Underneath humanity.

Biologically speaking, this longing for a situation in which you don't feel or know or want anything is like an invitation to jump down the evolutionary ladder. How far down, though? Among the higher primates, too, "no ape is an island"; one ape is no ape. Being always implies connecting with others, and if you really wanted to break loose from everything and render yourself truly inviolable, you'd have to give up on living things. Lifelessness, that's the ticket—you cannot get more stoic than a rock.

We shall close the meeting with Beckett's gentle admonition: "You're human, there's no cure for that."

—BERT KEIZER
SUMMER 2007

For the past few months, I have been living two lives, mine and Frank Bascombe's. This is a very odd sensation, because in many ways Frank and I couldn't be more different. He is a former sportswriter who now sells real estate; I hate sports and try as much as possible not to think about home prices. He has had two marriages and three children; I've had only one of each. He went to military school and served, briefly, in the Marines; I am pretty much a pacifist. He hails from Mississippi but has ended up deeply rooted in New Jersey; I, a Californian, pop back and forth between the two coasts. He often drives his car in an inebriated state, tends to think in terms of instantaneous, vicious, if sometimes amusing ethnic slurs, and sizes up every woman he meets as a potential bed-partner, including the current girlfriends of his adult son and daughter. I do none of these things. Perhaps most importantly, he is a fictional character and I (presumably) am not.

Frank is not exactly a likable guy—in some ways he is a complete monster—but I have grown attached to him over these months, and I'm extremely sorry to have parted company with him now that I've finished *The Lay of the Land*, Richard Ford's third Frank Bascombe novel. The first, *The Sportswriter*, appeared to great acclaim in 1986; the second, *Independence Day*, won the Pulitzer Prize in 1996. I paid no attention to either book at the time, mainly because I couldn't overcome my sports aversion sufficiently to read a book with "sportswriter" in the title, so I could never get started on the series. This, however, has turned out to be a lucky thing, because when *The Lay of the Land* came out in late 2006, I finally decided to bite the bullet and begin at the beginning, and as a result I have experienced the whole sweep of the project at once—not only the sense of fast-forwarding through life with Frank, from age thirty-eight to age fifty-five, but also the unusually condensed perspective on American history, from the middle of the Reagan era through the aftermath of the first Iraq War to the gloomy November when Bush and Gore tussled over the 2000 elections. (One of the few things Frank and I heartily agree on is politics: most of his nicknames for the candidate who became our current president could not be printed in a family newspaper.) The effect of this acute perception of the passage of time has been to evoke in me the kinds of tremulous emotions that are aroused by the greatest of multi-generational movies, like Orson Welles's *The Magnificent Ambersons*, say, or Marco Tullio Giordana's *The Best of Youth*. And in reading the Bascombe trilogy in this way—all at once, but with plenty of time to savor the delicious particularity of its style and the old-fashioned pleasures of its character-driven narrative—I have come to think that it is one of the great unsung achievements of contemporary American literature, better even than John Updike's Rabbit books or Philip Roth's American trilogy.

Part of the reason it is better is that Frank himself is such a problematic character. Among other things, he is deeply, irredeemably self-engrossed. At certain points in his progress through middle age, I wondered if he had the emotional wherewithal to forge *any* kind of permanent connection with another human being. This became especially clear toward the end of *Independence Day*, when, having taken a road trip with his (admittedly horrible) teenage son, he essentially stood by while his son suffered a violent accident. And then his first thoughts, right after the accident occurred, were about himself. Typical Frank.

But that is the good news as well as the bad, for Frank Bascombe is extremely skilled at thinking about himself. In fact, he may be one of the most persuasively and fascinatingly self-analytic figures of his era, inside or outside of fiction. It is not that Frank is always right about himself, or even close to omniscient; he often fails to see what even we can see about his condition. But he is always interesting to listen to on subjects that concern us all (aging, divorce, work, friendship, memory, death, to name but a few). He is filled with theories about his own life and Life in general, so that every experience he undergoes gets commented on and categorized and compared to other experiences. He has even devised phrases to describe the periods he is going through (the Existence Period in *Independence Day*, the Permanent Period in *The Lay of the Land*), and though these labels are somewhat self-mocking, they are also serious. He is that rare being, a character who fills his entire novel—his entire *three* novels—and yet leaves us room to see around him.

Immersed in Richard Ford's Bascombe trilogy, we readers are simultaneously steeped in Frank and critical of him, just as we are both participants in the recent events of American history and observers of them after the fact. It is a unique, deeply satisfying perspective, filled with dark humor (some of Frank's meanest comments about women and ethnic minorities made me snort with involuntary laughter) as well as with unsentimental sadness. I resisted the immersion for years, but now that the experience is over, I miss it terribly—in part, I am sure, because I resisted it and was then won over. I wouldn't have suspected I'd want to spend so much time with someone like Frank, but now I can't quite imagine what to do without him.

—WENDY LESSER
FALL 2007

"There are no wholes here below," wrote Emily Dickinson, and it is the neatest summing-up of Plato's philosophy I ever came across. We lumber along through life with an all-pervading sense of imperfection, untidiness, incompletion, clumsiness, awkwardness; and we have a use for these concepts because we know, or seem to know, of a world where marriages, haircuts, cars, trees, and even human characters are truly beautiful.

The most annoying of our many imperfections is the moral one. If only people could be truly good. But they are not, and the question is: what keeps us from goodness? Clearly something seems to hinder us from really getting hold of it. That something has been identified, in various folk sayings and idiomatic terms, as the animal part of our nature. People can behave like "mad dogs," causing "beastly" events. Lawyers are sharks, politicians rats, policemen pigs. You know this zoo. It contains a few especially choice denizens, amongst whom I would single out Bernard von Bülow, the man who succeeded Bismarck as chancellor. Of him it was said that "*Gegen Bülow ist ein Aal ein Igel*"—meaning "Next to Bülow, an eel is a hedgehog."

Being human, in this view, is something that rests like a thin layer on top of the brute mass underneath. In *Primates and Philosophers*, Frans de Waal describes it as the "veneer theory." The theory only deals with humans in the role of angels or creeps—that is to say, our moral sphere. Veneer theory has nothing to say about humans as thinkers, writers, composers, etc. It would appear that we regard ourselves as way out of animal reach while we are writing a sonnet, calculating a rocket-propelling device, or composing an opera. But in the domain of ethics there is always a threatening animal in us, which might burst through the veneer. For centuries we have regarded animals as creatures consisting of urges they blindly acted on. Hunger, aggression, sex—all animals did with these impulses was to run away unthinkingly from unpleasantness, and their pursuit of pleasure was just as mindless.

Quite unlike people. We ponder our course of action; we wonder what our doings entail for others; we can even suppress our hunger, aggression, and sexual urges. People can postpone or even altogether abjure satisfaction. They enter into a debate with themselves, or with others, or with others within themselves, before they decide to help someone or let him perish.

According to this view, you can see people doing remarkably good things which you will never see animals perform. Thus this inclination was considered to be nonterrestrial, unbiological, non-animal; it did not stem from nature but from God, who superimposed it on our animal essence.

This account has now been brushed aside, because nothing supports it. We find no hints in the world which point in this direction. We wouldn't even know what such a hint would be like. Morality stems from nature. Anyone suspecting a different origin has some showing to do.

Not everyone feels at ease with this vision. People who are religiously minded, for instance, like to hang on to God as the provider of the veneer. No surprise there. But de Waal comes across a more startling perspective. Some people wish for, or discover, a layer on top of the human genome where it is possible to put up a defense against the ferocious twins, Genome and Environment, who otherwise would be running the entire show according to their whims. For instance, at the end of his celebrated *The Selfish Gene*, Richard Dawkins writes: "We are built as gene machines and cultured as meme machines, but we have the power to turn against our creators. We, alone on earth, can rebel against the tyranny of the selfish replicators."

Frans de Waal reads this as a perfect example of veneer theory. Dawkins points at a potential capacity in humans to wriggle themselves loose from the bondage of Genome & Environment. He even adds that we are the only animals blessed with this capacity. This is a very odd statement, which initially I read without any misgiving. I merely thought, "Why shouldn't Dawkins be just a little bit optimistic about the whole dreadful business?"

To appreciate the oddity of Dawkins's remark, imagine someone delivering a detailed lecture on the nature and history of combustion engines. He goes into Benz, Diesel, and even Wankel, and then concludes with the astonishing announcement that he himself is the lucky possessor of a car engine which runs without the input of any energy at all. This contradicts everything he has just been saying about engines.

Dawkins's remark may also be seen as a present-day version

of Descartes's notion that all animals are mindless robots whose doings are completely explicable by the laws of mechanics (Genome & Environment determine everything), whereas only humans have a soul (which can transcend or overrule Genome & Environment). Dawkins cites an example of such an overruling in our use of contraceptives. But I think that G&E might well be capable of assessing our pressing population problem and coming up with this suggestion about how to solve it.

And now we're stumbling into a thrilling confusion.

Because at this point we get stuck in trying to obtain a clear view of the activity which consists in the weighing of these questions. Here we are, clearly strutting about outside the reign of Genome and Environment. Veneer theory is a mistaken effort at drawing a boundary between man and animal; as far as our moral nature is concerned, de Waal sends us back to the woods. But when it comes to art and science, we definitely seem to hold our own. Are these activities veneer again, albeit of a different sort? And will this veneer turn out to be as illusory as the moral layer?

Awaiting further developments, we'll have to settle for Nietzsche's characterization of man as the animal hitherto defying classification.

—BERT KEIZER
SPRING 2008

~

I had looked forward to seeing Adrianne Krstansky's all-woman production of *Macbeth*, by the Actors' Shakespeare Project in Boston. I was intrigued by the girl concept, especially for a brutal play that presses so hard on questions of manliness and womanliness. But, in spite of my ready sympathy and their good acting, the production lost me. It needed men. Or, at least, I did. And perhaps, paradoxically, its most successful dimension was the way it made me feel their absence. My wish may not have been Krstansky's intention, but, by the last act, all I wanted was for some six-foot-tall testosteroned dude to grab back the scepter and the speeches from the attractive Amazon with shoulder-length blond hair who called herself Macbeth. And this from a feminist who enjoys seeing the classics shaken and stirred as well as straight up.

The Actors' Shakespeare Project finds its spaces where it can, and last year you could have scraped me off the low cement ceiling of the former parking garage where they mounted an intensely disturbing all-male production of *Titus Andronicus*. It was the first time I'd seen that play, and it will be the last. It's too grotesque; I'm too old. *Titus* is so appalling, so over the top in its violence, that the transgendering of female into male seemed like a singular act of mercy calculated in some small way to spare the audience (in this case, me) from the direct impact of the rape and mutilation of Lavinia. We were seated around the stage, and there was nowhere to hide. Gaining enough emotional distance to stay present was, in fact, an extreme sport. The cross-dressing nudged my horror off balance just enough to keep me in my seat. I could slightly distract myself by looking to the man in the woman. Still, at moments the actor's delicate portrayal of violated femininity broke my heart. Why does a shaved-headed, mute man in a sleeveless, long, silky dress wrench me apart as he suggests a raped woman who's had her hands cut off and her tongue cut out? By acting, certainly, yet there's something more to it. I'm not sure, but even as his maleness created breathing distance, it simultaneously accentuated, through a slightly askew mimesis, a sympathy with the female that a female probably could not have successfully granted herself.

For *Macbeth*, the stage was a high-ceilinged, pillared, cinder-blocked room at Boston University, with seats on each side arranged to create a narrow, long, oblong space in the middle. From where I sat, I could look left toward a small primary stage, or right and slightly behind me toward a tiny secondary one (about the size of the desk that filled it). I had only partial vision of the second. In this case, the unconventional arrangement felt like an impediment. Sanctioned by a more formal stage, the women might have had a chance. Granted physical distance, I might have spent less time laboring to reconcile male characters with female faces, hair, height, and breasts.

But beyond the staging, why didn't it work? It wasn't the acting, which was certainly good enough, though it might be argued that great acting could have tipped the balance. It puzzled me. Why could I suspend disbelief enough to tolerate male as female in *Titus*, but not the reverse in *Macbeth*? My husband, who has taught his share of Shakespeare, suggested that all-male productions are traditional. The plays were written for them; the maleness is artistically intended, anticipated, historically apt, so the fit is better, and it's easier to accept. His observation was helpful, but it didn't completely settle me. I recalled that a friend's daughter last year received plaudits as Prospero in a small-town production of *The Tempest*. So I wondered if it was partly the fact of a tragedy. Maybe an all-female production of *The Taming of the Shrew* would have worked. Or maybe it was a question of mix. I suspect I could have more easily borne a woman as Macbeth had Banquo, Duncan, *et al.* been "in gender."

Still pondering, I found myself thinking about opera. The

crossover part of Cherubino in *The Marriage of Figaro* works brilliantly, partly because of the enchanting arias, but also because the masculinity it attempts to capture in the figure of Cherubino is adolescent and emergent, soft, hormonally overwhelmed, bisexual. And the woman-on-woman love pursuit becomes mildly yet delightfully homoerotic; the viewer's reward for partially suspending disbelief is playful sexual pleasure.

But what psychological return might one garner from the Macbeth switch? If there's novelty, even perverse feminist satisfaction, to be had in witnessing female-on-female political violence, it would have to be found in the femaleness itself, not in the mock maleness. Elizabeth II, Catherine the Great, Margaret Thatcher—one can summon half a dozen women who wielded large political power. Not enough. The stunted image we collectively possess of violence perpetrated by female leaders is inadequate to bear the competition from so many millennia of manly rulers, and their firm association with war and death. ("No," Virginia Woolf once wrote, "I don't see what's to be done about war. It's manliness; and manliness breeds womanliness—both so hateful.") The difference between the unisex *Titus* and the unisex *Macbeth*, finally, is an ironic one between private and public. Sexuality and sexual violence bend better on stage than public power. We know that gender moves all over the bed in sex, that women wreak their share of private havoc. But before we can have a successful female Macbeth, we will have to have collectively witnessed many more vile and violent female leaders about whom tales can be told. We'll have to possess a credible image where now there is but a void. I could think about Krstansky's *Macbeth*, but if I started to feel myself transported, it was to the wrong place. Instead of witnessing a power grab run amok in a dank old Scottish castle, I felt I was back in the 1950s watching talented teenagers at Miss Hall's School for Girls trying to do pants parts.

—Janna Malamud Smith
spring 2008

~

In 1977 I was living in Ann Arbor, sharing an apartment with my then-girlfriend Pam, a third-story space shaded by tall trees, with an old-style wooden fire escape that came right up to our large kitchen window to create what was almost a deck. We used it for that, keeping the window open all summer, moving in and out to sit on the edge of the platform, having our coffee in the morning, beers at night. The summer, I remember, was long and hot and we were always around that window, staying near it to catch whatever breezes we could, and enjoying the light like two Icelanders, because the rest of the place was dark and attic-like. I was working at Charing Cross Book Shop then, dealing used and rare books all day long with my partner George, and resolutions about restraint notwithstanding, I came home every night with more books. They filled the far wall of our little bedroom, spilling over into stacks in every corner. I could see that it was becoming a problem, but I didn't stop coming home with bags. Truth is, I like the feel of a place that is overrun with books. I remember how I used to lie on my back in bed and let my gaze bump slowly and methodically from spine to spine, looking away every so often to renew my contract with what I believed was my true vocation—writing. The idea then was that I was dealing books just to make money. I was building up steam to make a break. Soon enough I knew I would explode into a new life, making good on my promises, typing like a man possessed, filling pages, sending to magazines. But not just yet. I wasn't quite ready to give up the life I had going. I still enjoyed getting my tall cup of coffee at Kresge's and then crossing the street to unlock the store; I liked planning the day's buys, and sorting through new purchases with George, and joking with all the regulars who came in every day without fail. And if one of them asked me how my writing was going, I found a way to deflect, managing to suggest that great things were in the works without ever saying what they were. And so the season went on, the long summer, window open to the light, the air, Pam and I pursuing our own jobs and friends through the day, connecting up at night to cook and drink beer on the fire escape. Sometimes—pretty often, it seems now when I look back—I was by myself in the apartment, sitting on the edge of the bed in that little bedroom near my bookshelves, scheming my life while I moved my head slowly back and forth.

I was in that posture when I first saw it. Something. A large yellow blur in my peripheral vision. When I creaked on the bedsprings there was a rush, a fast reverse scuttle. I got to the kitchen just in time to see the swerve of a thick tail and then hear a light thud as it landed on the fire escape. When I got to the window it had vanished. A cat, obviously one of the toms we always heard yowling at night down by the garbage cans.

I don't like cats, I never have. I think of them as cold and sneaky, two attributes that my wife, Lynn, a therapist, insists are pure projections on my part. I know without being told that this doesn't reflect well on me, but there it is. My response to seeing the yellow tom in our apartment was to become hyper-vigilant. I didn't, as someone else might have, just close the fire-escape window. Not only was it too hot, but that would have been a gesture of defeat; I would be allowing an alley cat to dictate to me. No, I left the window open and went back to my place. But from that time on I stayed alert. I had no choice. I didn't want to think about the cat, but I couldn't stop myself. In fact, the more I tried to forget that image, the more it cut into my focus.

After that there were other episodes, bolder visits. Once I came out of the bathroom and found the thing standing at full attention in the middle of the living room. He looked at me and he read my mind. With a bunching of the back and then a few quick muscular leaps he was up onto our breakfast table and out. I realized I was breathing heavily, as if I had just climbed the stairs. Then a few days later I walked in the room and found him hovering right in the window, tilted forward, right at the point of jumping in. He scurried and was gone.

He seemed to be coming daily. And still I couldn't make myself close the window, not when I was home, even though he was taking up more and more of my attention. Then I got my idea. It was beautifully simple—and obvious. First I got a long piece of string and tied it to the window latch so that I could yank it shut from the other room with a single pull. Next I filled a wash-basin with cold water and put it near the kitchen door. And then I waited. And waited, and waited. Like a fool. Aware of myself as a fool. But I didn't care. I kept on with it, that day, and then the next.

Looking back, I'm struck by the fact that Pam had no part in any of this drama. Where was she? Was she working or studying? I can't remember. Nor can I say why I was there so often. What was going on with my job? Where was I getting these free afternoons? Work didn't usually end until after six. How was it that I sat there all those days in that little bedroom space, waiting? But I did, in memory anyway. And the waiting paid off. Because right in the dead center of a hot summer afternoon I looked up and saw him there. Just like that. Tense, rigid, only a few feet away, staring at me, me staring back, as if we'd been staring at one another all our lives, the tom not moving so long as I stayed still, every muscle on alert, staying like that even as I edged my hand a few inches over, leaping only in the same wild instant that I yanked the line, but not quickly or powerfully enough, for as I then got to my feet I saw he was there, bunched up next to the stove, slightly bigger suddenly, as if he'd grown in those few seconds, watching me again, poised as I made my way toward the basin, but then blurring into fast motion as soon as I ducked, so he was now in the living room, beside the couch, in the corner, with nowhere to go but up and over. I carried the bucket in both hands, my breath tied in big hard knots in my throat, more awake than I had been for months. And then—well, I see it now like the famous surrealist photo, the one with Salvador Dalí and the flying cats, the water fanned out flat in a quicksilver shape, clear to the least stray droplet, pure chaos immobilized. Here were the two of us, the tom and I, in the slow time of assassination and calamity, the whole bucket of water hitting him broadside, his raspy primal screech like nothing I've heard, his incredible leap free of the couch and room and gravity-bound frame of one of his lives a sure world record, followed in the very same second by the crash of his big body against the window-frame, and then the giving creak of the hinge and the multiple thumps of his amazing getaway. There is nothing more to be said. The wall and carpet were soaked, but they would dry. I knew that the yellow cat would never come back. I stood still and glowed for a while with the satisfying shame of my violence. It wasn't really until this morning, when I remembered the whole business, that I saw how it was another story, too, a minor sort of literary story, though I would have to think about how to tell it so that the cat in that corner was not too obviously me in my life, my every muscle flexed for flight.

—Sven Birkerts
summer 2008

~

What happens if you are born in the latter part of the twentieth century in America and find your most personal reflection, the mirror of your inner self, in music created on another continent more than a century or two before your birth? You become a musician as a child. You learn desire in music before you know it as a woman; you know the sorrow of loss before you have mourned. You feel all this as you translate the black dots and lines on the score into sound and try to make sense of them. What does this do to your relationship to your own present, the physical present which surrounds you? Where are you when you lift your head from the keyboard and look at the world?

The differences between a child musician and an adult musician are minor. I perform today works of music that I first performed when I was eleven years old. When I play these works today—say, Chopin's mournful E minor Prelude—my entire life is there. The living room again becomes suburban, the piano sits under a stairwell, my father reads the newspaper in the armchair, my mother is in the kitchen talking on the phone, my brother is in his room behind a closed door. The Chopin Prelude, when I was eleven, became a place, a place which I could enter that was entirely my own. With no walls around me, I could move far into an interior space that was untouched by the activity and the tension around me, the often palpable potential for explosion underlying the domestic scene. The Prelude was a haven: perhaps one could say a haven from the present, but it *was* the present, as I put my foot on the pedal, lifting it and then pushing it down again with each changing harmony, and listened to the resonant sounds float upward around me.

The music was also a code. Here was a magical universe where I could confide my deepest secrets, make my most personal anguishes and unknown desires public, without revealing a single name or betraying any confidence. No one knew what I was saying, yet here was a limitless repository for feeling. And so I discovered early on the importance of living in a world beyond words. Years later, as a student in Paris, I read Malraux: "He who so fiercely seeks the absolute will find it only in sensation." Malraux was writing about a terrorist, but I thought it was about myself.

I played my first concert after 9/11 in early October of 2001. A concert of chamber music by Mozart: the Kegelstatt Trio for clarinet, viola, and piano, and then the dramatic G minor Piano Quartet. In the second half, I sat backstage and listened as Richard Stoltzman led the transcendent quintet for clarinet and strings. The audience was rapt. In those strange days, any large assembly of people felt oddly defiant, tinged with danger but also with a deep need to congregate. As this was, for almost everyone present, the first concert post-9/11, there was an added intensity of both playing and listening. The music of Mozart, with its uncanny ability to communicate the full range of human emotions with disarming simplicity, spoke with new urgency. How many times in the last two centuries, after horrific acts of inhumanity and violence, had Mozart's music reaffirmed for us the possibility of beauty, of life? Now it had for me a new fragility, a new vulnerability. These works were not inevitable; they did not have to exist and they may not always exist. What had previously been unthinkable to me came as an obvious thought. Music became a cultural artifact that could disappear like anything else.

The music that I love relies on memory. The musical forms cannot be seen, the plots cannot be summarized. The landscape of music is followed by our ear blindly, and it is only the ability to remember, the unconscious absorption of material so that its variations and returns are recognized, that allows us to perceive a cohesive shape that gives pleasure. The narrative is without subject—it is about nothing. But it is about nothing in the same sense that life itself is about nothing. In this sense, it is about everything. Defined by time, it is time itself.

Since Aristotle, time has been viewed as a succession of nows. Kant warned us that "time yields no shape." Yet within the confines of a time period that begins and ends in silence, a great piece of music carves meaning in the air. It establishes a grammar of tension and resolution. Out of nothing, a structure emerges, an invisible landscape of place, with home, conflicts, and wanderings, crises, doubts, and climaxes, and, finally, return. Because this is done wordlessly, the ability to engage with music is sensorial; in the moment of listening, the music is experienced rather than understood. Sensorial but, unlike the primal sensual pleasures of food or sex, in need of the filter of the mind. The listener's engagement is a complex mix of attentiveness and distracted daydreaming, only moments of which can be translated into words; and with complex forms of music, it is only upon repeated listening that our engagement deepens. "In music . . . there is always a gap, a lacuna, bridged by the imagination of the listener," wrote Baudelaire. How can we recognize the return without memory? We don't know we remember until we hear the return.

Take the final ballade of Chopin, the magnificent F minor Ballade, opus 52. It welcomes us gently, enfolds us between the bell-like repeated octaves of the treble, adds a quickening middle voice and leads us downward to the resonant bass, searchingly repeats itself, and then finds a still center and waits. Waits for a memory of a theme to arrive: a memory of something we do not yet know. The theme emerges haltingly, searching for itself, coming from a distant past and moving gradually into our present. The unfolding of this haunting melody is one of the most exquisite sequences in all of Chopin's music. But for each of us who listens, what is the memory of? It is the searching for that which cannot be held. The music is always in flight, can only be recognized in motion.

What do you do when the present is so strange that you need to dissect and analyze the world around you on a daily basis, as though you had arrived from another planet? The hours at the piano need no explanation. But the outside world hovers precariously, nervously, alien.

Immortality is not about living into the future; it is about having access to the unending past. This is the magic of great art, this time capsule that comes to us breathing life. It is an error to view immortality as a forward trajectory. When I sit at the piano, the music is of a culture and the culture is of a time and when I live in it, which is often, I live elsewhere. We could call it reverse immortality.

—SARAH ROTHENBERG
WINTER 2009

~

Early one morning in August, 1974, the people of Lower Manhattan looked up. What they craned their necks to see wasn't quite believable. At the top of the Twin Towers, 1350 feet above the ground, a man was walking in the air. Or, no, he was walking across a thin cable strung between the buildings. And he wasn't just walking. He was kneeling, sitting, stretching out on his back. He was running, bouncing, balancing on one leg. For forty-five minutes, the man looked at home in that unlikely place, until police officers, who considered what he was doing illegal, arrested him, put him in handcuffs, and brought him before a psychiatrist and a judge. At a press conference afterwards, one of the officers, a caricature of a guy you'd expect to see at the donut shop, explained that what he had seen couldn't be described as walking. It was dancing.

Man on Wire, James Marsh's recently released documentary about the event, treats it as both art and a crime, and the wire-walker, the French *funambule* Philippe Petit, as both an artist and a criminal. The film—a mixture of present-day interviews, reenactments, and some footage from the time—is constructed as a heist movie. We meet The Team and follow their preparations for *le coup*, from designing the rigging to casing the joint and creating fake IDs. We sit in suspense through the reversals and defections and near-misses. Though the subsequent history of the buildings (not mentioned) gives these activities some unsettling associations, the form glamorizes Petit and his compatriots as wily outlaws, rebels, guerrillas. Aspects of Petit's personality reinforce that impression. Very much alive in the fifty-something-year-old man is the schoolboy fond of elaborate pranks.

At the same time, Petit is presented, and sincerely presents himself, as an obsessive artist. He speaks of his calling, his destiny. He has a vision. Even before the towers were built, he had imagined his feat, coming across a rendering of the proposed design in a magazine and drawing a line between the two buildings. When he says the buildings were made for him, he sounds a little like George Mallory explaining his motivation to climb Mt. Everest. But to the question he mocks as very American—"Why?"—he responds that there is no why, which sounds more like art-for-art's-sake (and very French). It is apparent that for him the act is a performance, the wire a stage. He recalls feeling attached to the crowd so far below him. The possibility of failure he describes as "a beautiful death."

The wire-walking, like the idea itself, is beautiful. The balancing is beautiful, the weight shifting through his body, the plumb lines, the kneeling like a courtly bow. He's a Harlequin of the Skyscrapers, scraping the sky. What moved the cop to call it dancing was Petit's taunting of the authorities, his you-can't-catch-me gamboling. He smiles up there. That joy is beautiful—the audacity of lying down!—and after all of the suspense, all of the obstacles, it's beautiful to see him execute the simple superhuman skill he's trained himself to master, beautiful to watch him conquer fear and gravity and good sense. It's the ultimate site-specific dance, with the space around the moving figure giving it meaning and the moving figure forever changing the meaning of the space. Except, unlike most site-specific dance, this one has stakes as high as they can possibly be.

The psychiatrist judged Petit sane, and the judge sentenced him only to public service, a wire-walk across Central Park's Belvedere Lake. (At that lower height, he did more tricks, somersaults and such.) Petit characterizes his use of the World Trade Center as "illegal but not harmful." Yet the most affecting part of the film comes in the last few minutes, when it becomes suddenly clear that there was a cost after all. Petit's girlfriend and his male best friend, both intimately involved in the project from the beginning, reveal that the completion of *le coup* was the end of the love affair, the end of the friendship. This isn't explained, though it's suggested that Petit's newfound fame was to blame. Equally significant, it seems to me, is how the project took over their lives and left a hole when it, the unsurpassable feat, was done. This was another way that Petit pushed a common feature of art-making to an extreme. "The important thing is that we did it," the best friend bravely asserts. "They can't take away what happened." But he chokes up as he says it, and it's not at all clear that he means it. Coming so late in the film, the revelation leaves you feeling almost as if Petit *had* fallen; it hits the same place in your stomach. It colors the final images of the present-day Petit walking a wire at his home, still at play, as he espouses his carpe diem philosophy of living life on a tight rope. There's always a cost.

—BRIAN SEIBERT
SPRING 2009

When I first moved to New York, in my twenties, I encountered clotheslines. This was in Brooklyn thirty years ago. Apartments on both sides of the alley, by very old neighborly agreements, had strung pulley-style lines across the open air—and I was dismayed by the spectacle because I thought that these, here where I'd arrived, were the flags of poverty. Where I'd come from, in the suburban Midwest, everyone had dryers. It would have been unthinkable not to have a dryer. This was my first exposure to the mysteries of social class outside the Midwest, and I guess I supposed ignorance and bad luck and general low standards would go along with the stiffened blue jeans, the roughened nap of terrycloth bath towels.

These days where I live, far away in the boondocks, I sense myself at the brunt of an American avant garde when I wield a handful of wooden clothespins in the corner of a meadow off my mudroom. My dryer is idle. The propane jets aren't rumbling, nor is the big drum rolling. The stainless-steel vent outside doesn't discharge clouds of visceral moisture. During the thirty years between Brooklyn and now, it has been possible to watch environmental collapse looming up on all sides in various forms. Economists last summer were reviving the word "stagflation" to describe the present consequences of our improvident treatment of the earth. But mainstream economists aren't making the point that the dollar isn't the basic economic unit. It's sunlight. It's all sunlight: we're made of sunlight: every dollar paid across for steak and broccoli, and every mile traveled in an SUV, is translatable from calories of incident solar radiation on the planet, origin of wealth, origin of economic goods, stored as petroleum, stored as sugar.

I suppose when I was a child, clotheslines were for a lower or a surpassed social class; and today here, too, in my rural area, we've got newly arrived suburbanites who have argued for "Covenants and Restrictions" that would forbid clotheslines, along with other rustic eyesores like trailers. Clotheslines will be associated with an older culture superseded as hillbilly whose particular dignities and felicities aren't evident to the newcomer. Personally I wonder, hopefully, whether one day clotheslines could become fashionable, and could start appearing, along with organic vegetable gardens, on the lawns of Winnetka, the redwood decks of Sausalito, every clever hostess's badge of fashion: the rough bath towel in the guest cottage.

Such simple measures may be the only real anti-war actions available to us that aren't ineffectual or merely histrionic. We all like to say, "I didn't vote for Bush," "I didn't vote for McCain," but we do keep gassing up our cars and buying—you name it—bottled water? So we *are* voting for war and global warming and the whole mad bonfire, voting actively and consistently and with true effective force. Folks of the leftward persuasion will say the war's motives were venal to begin with; those on the right will answer that the war was a necessary, if nasty, duty in a real world. That's an open debate. However, both sides will agree in principle on one thing: our affluence is a determinant of our foreign policy.

Our sense of our own American superiority has always been our favorite, and our most cloying, scandal. The reality is, we're now emerging as a third-world nation, in the sense of having a classic "dual economy" unsupportive of a middle class, having exported our middle-class opportunities overseas. I, through a combination of accident and choice, have ended up in the clothes-line class—and I must say it feels pretty buoyant, this particular liberation from privilege. The whole chore is an interruption in my usual hectic trance, requiring an abrupt shift to solitude and quiet, outdoors, far even from the incessant NPR in our kitchen. The meadow ground is hummocky and treacherously soft underfoot from gophers' work. The drudging physical activity itself, of pinning up laundry, if nowhere near strenuous, involves a lot of lifting and reaching and is slightly swimming-like. And then all day, until at sundown the whole line-up is stiff and toasty, I find the sight of a line of laundry actually jubilating. To a book-absorbed fellow's eye it bespeaks the old levitation metaphor of immortality and incarnation and the mystery of personality and even futurity. My two boys, eight and seventeen, are absent all day at school (as, all too soon, they will be more permanently absent at colleges), but they are also present, these afternoons, their distinctive personalities pinned up in a choir in the breeze along with ours, arms upraised among the bedsheets' great flying badges on the tilt of the meadow.

—Louis B. Jones
SPRING 2009

~

Every Saturday afternoon we went to the movies, a double feature at the Carroll Theater on the corner of Utica Avenue and Crown Street in Brooklyn. Carroll Street was one block farther up the avenue, so why the theater was called the Carroll rather than the Crown I never understood.

We went some time after lunch, whenever the mood struck and regardless of what was playing—comedy, drama, mystery, horror. Indeed, we had no idea what would be playing, unless we'd passed the Carroll a day or two before and noticed the colorful placards in their glass cases, with photos of the stars. It never occurred to us to look up the times either movie would begin: the notion of theaters making their schedules available to the viewing public was quite beyond us at the age of ten, or eleven, or twelve. Going to the movies meant drifting in somewhere in the middle of the first feature, then suspending its scenes in memory during the rest of the show—two hours or more—until the afternoon came full circle as the images began looking familiar.

We were herded into the Carroll's shadowy depths by the matron, a stocky, tubular woman dressed in a white uniform like a nurse, who seated us in the children's section, off to the side, so we wouldn't disturb the adults, of whom there were very few on a Saturday afternoon. Nonetheless the matron kept strict watch, striding up and down the aisles, hushing whisperers with stern warnings. Though we mocked her among ourselves, the matron was an object of fear because she could get us thrown out of the movie and then what would we do with the rest of our Saturday afternoon?

Our nonchalant readiness to accept whatever was in progress on the screen might sound like sweet bygone naïveté, evoking nostalgia for the simple life: no checking the time, reserving tickets, waiting in line . . . I tended to regard it as such, until I discussed it with my astute friend Alice, also from Brooklyn, who pointed out that on the contrary, starting the movie in the middle had a distinctly postmodern cast, an omen of hypertext, even: we were dealing with the given information in fragments with no context, or only a slowly clarifying context.

I thought this over and saw that Alice was right. Not only did we have to locate ourselves mid-plot, seeking a foothold in a zone of utter ignorance. We had to invent, by intuition, who the characters were and surmise their histories. We didn't know if the figures on the screen were friends or foes, lovers or married, and we didn't know who was bad and who was good. If someone was murdered, we didn't know if he deserved to be murdered and we should be happy, or if he was an innocent victim and we should be sorry. If characters kissed, we didn't know if it was their first kiss or their last. We didn't even know if we were close to the beginning, or in the middle, or near the end.

Far from producing unease, the condition of not knowing was thrilling. Before we gained some inkling of the goings-on, the plot was wide open, a vast expanse of potentiality, gradually narrowing as the possibilities sorted themselves out, some evaporating, others looming large, until an intentional pattern emerged.

When the movie was over, so many tantalizing questions remained: how did the whole imbroglio evolve, who was the sinister old man who turned up near the end, what treachery had taken place in that august mansion? Why was everyone bent on keeping the lovers apart? Who was the dead man everyone kept talking about? Was there anyone else we had not yet met?

It was a long time before our curiosity could be appeased. In the interval came the Disney cartoons, then a new installment of *Superman*—resuming whatever peril we'd left him in last week—and *Movietone News*, with its perennial opening footage of skiers executing stupendous leaps down the Alps, followed by highlights of current events. After the coming attractions, which we promptly forgot, we watched the second movie in the ordinary way, from beginning to end. At last, the original movie, to be summoned from memory. Now we had to reshape all the premises we'd worked so hard to formulate. So those two were not really friends at all, but rivals for the estate, pretending good will. So the murder we'd seen was the ultimate in a string of gruesome murders. So that man was the renegade father, that woman the long-lost daughter.

As we reassembled the plot, superimposing the actual story against the one we'd constructed from insufficient data, things began fitting together reassuringly. The movies of my childhood, a more stable, trusting era, were linear, their plots meant to be comprehended. A reliable directorial hand would guide us through the landscape. And yet the effort of reassembly, I see now, was very much like watching today's movies, so many of which are built of fragments scattered in a jumbled time frame. Arriving in the middle transformed those simple movies of the past into postmodern films, the kind that set us down in the center of a labyrinthine design and abandon us. We were, in a sense, being prepared for the future, for movies that replicate, unwittingly, our experience of arriving in the middle.

Predictably, on those Saturday afternoons, a sense of déjà vu would insinuate itself. A scene would look familiar, then another and another. We shifted restlessly in our seats, nudging each other, provoking the matron's fierce glance. Someone would murmur, I think this is where we came in.

Now and then one of us wasn't quite sure, couldn't quite recall, so we'd wait a bit until she said: Oh, right, I remember. Okay, I guess this is where we came in. Or someone else might urge: Let's just stay till the cops find him hiding in the bushes, or till the mother realizes it's her long-lost child—I want to see that again. And so we waited until everyone was satisfied and ready to leave—unless the movie was so entrancing that we stayed, by consensus, to see the second half all over again.

—LYNNE SHARON SCHWARTZ
SUMMER 2009

Recently I went to purchase a high-tech computer backpack at the new electronics mega-store called PUBLIC, located, appropriately enough, in the heart of Athens, Constitution Square. At the entrance of the large, refurbished nineteenth-century structure, where people sip coffee at a bar perched strategically in front of the store, stands a big bronze plaque:

From this building, on October 18, 1944,
George Papandreou, Prime Minister of Greece,
gave the Speech of Liberation that marked the end
of the German occupation.

At the time he gave that speech—and in fact up until the end of his life—my grandfather lived in a house located in the area of Kastri, a suburb north of Athens. Not being a rich man (for he had been born into poverty), he built his home far from Athens, where in the 1930s real estate was dirt cheap. Back then, there were practically no other homes around. Today it is my sister's home: my grandfather left it to her, his only granddaughter, as a dowry in his will. The neighborhood is now considered extremely upscale, and builders covet the only remaining pre-war home, with its two acres of untouched pine forest.

Each Saturday of my childhood—once we had returned to Greece from Berkeley, where I was born—our family would have lunch at the house in Kastri. The family seemed fully united, and this particular constellation, consisting of father married to mother, grandfather divorced from grandmother, and us four kids, felt engraved in granite. We were usually served chicken with rice and a béchamel sauce, while my grandfather and my father, who had decided to enter Greek politics and abandon his academic career in Berkeley, discussed the issues of the day. Some time was allotted to us kids, but the high point for me was when lunch was over. That's when the old man would give us an allowance of a hundred drachmas, worth three dollars and thirty-three cents. With this injection, on the return trip I would stop in Kifissia, at a kiosk that still exists forty years later, to buy American comic books. They went for a dollar each, which meant I could and did buy three each Saturday, saving the change for three weeks to buy yet a fourth. I amassed quite a collection in those years, but was not able to bring it with me the night we fled the country in 1968, with my father's life in danger from the military dictatorship that had just released him from jail. We left with only a small suitcase each: comic-book collections were deemed inessential, and on the scale of things, they certainly were.

At those lunches, my grandfather never failed to act the perfect gentleman, and would always offer my mother and sister a rose. He would say with some pride that he himself had planted the rosebush when he first moved in. Some days, he would walk us into the garden so that he could show us the most recent bloom; he'd bend and say, "Smell. This is life." Here was a man, I later realized, who was in touch with his senses, was always well dressed, always aware of his image, always polishing his voice and his rhetoric, a man who even in exile found ways of loving the places where he found himself.

On the night of the 1967 coup, when most of the politicians were dragged to prison in their underwear, my father included, my grandfather asked the soldiers to do him a favor and give him a moment. If he was going to be arrested, it was going to be in style. As reported to us much later by my father, the old man arrived at the political holding ground (a way-station for the prisons) fully shaved and nicely cologned, and wearing his three-piece suit to boot. Not only that. In full display was the *pièce de résistance*: a rose from his very own rosebush pinned to his lapel.

When he was finally released from prison, my grandfather spent his final days in that Kastri home, under house arrest, before his demise at the age of eighty. Each day, he wore his suit and tie, without fail. He could barely bend down to shine his shoes, but he wanted to look completely unruffled each morning, as if being under house arrest was a temporary condition.

In the spring of 1968, the last spring he would ever enjoy, Kastri dripped with life: the rosebush, the pine trees, the small olive grove. My grandfather wanted to smuggle out a speech to the BBC, which was broadcasting into the country, but he was being watched. He had a recording machine, which the guards had failed to notice, but how was he to use it without being discovered? He decided to play the palaverous, cranky old man recalling his past. In front of the soldiers, out in the garden, he would take his walk but now he would talk to himself, sometimes quoting himself from his old speeches, other times coming up with completely new ones. At first they listened in: after all, he was considered a danger. To impress upon them his imbalance, he purposely exaggerated the old flourishes, the intonations, the pauses. Here, in the garden, surrounded by scurrilous but also some respectful soldiers and sergeants who sat beneath the tall pine trees, it didn't take much to act as if senility had finally come to collect one more soul.

He read the actual speech into a carefully placed microphone in his office. (By then, the soldiers had given up listening in.) As the son of a village priest, he often injected religious anniversaries with political purpose, and the Easter of 1968 coincided conveniently with the first anniversary of the coup. His speeches always had a certain biblical style to them, a pithiness and a tendency to aphorism which gave them a unique voice. *Greece of Christian Greeks*, this speech began, mocking the dictator's penchant for beginning his own speeches with those very same words. *Today, the Greece of Christian Greeks is catholically protestant. Today, though we celebrate the resurrection of Christ, we mourn for the crucifixion of the Greek people.*

I recently had occasion to listen to the unedited recording—apparently the BBC filtered out the extraneous sounds when it finally aired the speech. I swear I can hear bits of my own childhood in the background: the sounds of the street, a car in the distance, a lone motorcycle racing up the hills of Kastri, its single lung sputtering with intent. Perhaps it's only my imagination, but I think I can also distinguish the hoarse cry of the *paliatzis*, a man who would drive through the neighborhoods on a horse-drawn cart, selling old items collected from abandoned homes.

—Nick Papandreou
SUMMER 2009

~

It is well-known that the standing of the mind as regards the brain is immensely contentious. (Do we even need both terms, we have to ask ourselves?) But it is worth pointing out that there is an extra awkwardness, philosophically speaking, in the fact that there is no word in French or German exactly corresponding to the English word "mind." Descartes, in the Latin version of his *Meditations*, uses the word *mens*, which comes nearest; but in the French version he tends to speak of *esprit*, which has a subtly different meaning, often being rendered in translation as "intelligence." Moreover, in English poetry, as distinct from English philosophy, "mind" has had an especially glorious career. Let me quote:

The mind, that ocean where each kind
Does straight its own resemblance find,
Yet it creates, transcending these,
Far other worlds, and other seas.
(Marvell)

Yes, I will be thy priest, and build a fane
In some untrodden region of my mind,
Where branchèd thoughts, new grown with pleasant pain,

Instead of pines shall murmur in the wind.
(Keats)

High and mighty forms that do not live
Like living men, moved slowly through the mind
By day, and were a trouble to my dreams.
(Wordsworth)

O the mind, mind has mountains, cliffs of fall,
Frightful, sheer, no-man-fathomed.
(Hopkins)

This high valuation of the word "mind" strikes one, if not very logically, as somehow confirming Gilbert Ryle's insistence in *The Concept of Mind* that the mind is not a place, or a tool, or—really—a "thing" at all. We are talking, however, of a specifically English, or English-language, affair. The titles of books by the French brain-scientist J.-P. Changeux tend irresistibly, in English translation, to have the word *Mind* wished on them: the title of his *L'Homme neuronal* becomes *Neuronal Man: The Biology of Mind*, and his *Matière á pensée*, a collaboration with Alain Connes, is transformed into *Conversations on Mind, Matter and Mathematics*. A general article about Changeux in *The New York Review of Books* for 26 June 2008 was headed "How the Mind Works: Revelations." Much the same happened to Claude Lévi-Strauss, whose *La Pensée sauvage* became in English *The Savage Mind*. (Thus—though this is not relevant—its title also lost a charming pun; for another meaning of "la pensée sauvage" is "the wild pansy.")

This vocabulary is really very significant. John Locke, in his *Essay on the Human Understanding*, most often speaks of the "mind"—though on occasion he speaks of the "soul," without making it altogether clear what he regards as the difference. He writes that "He that considers how hardly sensation is, in our thoughts, reconcilable to extended matter, or existence to anything that has no extension at all, will confess that he is very far from certainly knowing what his soul 'is.'" Could the soul, in some sense, be material? He does not think it impossible. Can matter think? He does not know what to answer. This is dangerous territory, onto which he wants to stray as little as possible.

The truth is, any and every attempt to define the mind is dogged by failure, as indeed is the case with the soul. Kant is very explicit in the *Critique of Judgment* that it is logically impossible to prove the existence of a deity or an immortal soul, since any proof would have, inappropriately, to draw material from "the world of sense"; and this being so, it is also impossible to *define* them. This, or something similar, seems equally true of the mind. The *Shorter Oxford English Dictionary* defines "mind" as "The seat of consciousness, thoughts, volitions, and feelings." But this is to beg the question; for how could joys, sorrows, etc. have a (physical) "seat"? It could only be meant metaphorically, and, if you are speaking in metaphors, you might well prefer to make their "seat" the heart. The *Oxford Companion to Philosophy*, for its part, neatly, if a trifle churlishly, sidesteps any obligation to define the mind, saying, "You have a mind if you think, perceive, or feel. Your mind is like your life or your weight."

Philosophers are fond of discussing what they call the "mind-body problem," but it has proved desperately slippery—and this is partly because, to some extent at least, it is not a universal or even a pan-European problem but one about the semantics of the English language. But at least it can be agreed that to call it a "problem" is to be resuscitating, perhaps perpetuating, Cartesian dualism. The question, often posed in the eighteenth century, whether "matter" can "think," never seems to carry much plausibility, but—so one feels—to bring in the brain ought to sharpen up "materialist" discussion greatly. In practice, however, it proves not to. For—the mind remaining so obstinately indefinable—no opposing of the terms "mind" and "body" turns out to be possible: it is as if there were not room enough in the world for both of them. Mark Solms and Oliver Trumbull, in their *The Brain and the Inner World*, write (rather on the lines of the *Shorter Oxford English Dictionary*):

> Nerve cells are of roughly the same type and employ roughly the same sort of metabolic and other processes as other cells in the body. And yet the brain has a special mysterious property that distinguishes it from all other organs. It is the seat of the mind, somehow producing our feeling of *being* in the world right now. Trying to understand how this happens—how matter becomes mind—is the *mind-body problem*.

It is pleasantly phrased but, one is bound to feel, no more than a bedtime story, with nothing of a scientific or philosophical nature to be learnt from it. The neuroscientist Steven Rose, on the other hand, in his *The Conscious Brain*, distinctly offers—what we were beginning to think impossible—a definition of the mind. He argues in this way. Descriptions of the behavior of the brain will be of different kinds according to which particular "level" is under scrutiny. The levels, ascending from the quantum structure of the brain's atoms, via the chemical, the anatomical, the physiological, the psychological, and the social-psychological levels to the sociological at the pinnacle, form a hierarchy or pyramid; and for the purposes of his book, he explains, he defines the mind as "the sum total of brain activity" at a level *above* physiology and *below* social analysis. (At these levels, the mind, he implies, is identical with, it simply *is*, the brain under another name.) But the trouble with this is, it is not really a definition. The so-called mind-body problem is, plainly, a question about that hallowed enigma, the relationship of the mind to the body. But to be *identical* with something else is not to have a relationship with it; identity is not a relation at all.

Thus the "mind" eludes capture. Certainly it is a marvelous, and marvelously untameable, word.

—P. N. FURBANK
SPRING 2010

~

Some years ago, in my parents' house in Menlo Park, I saw a family photograph I'd never noticed before. I was struck by the balance of the composition—the way there was an undeniable center to the picture, yet with an element that pulled away. It was familiar: the center was my grandmother, Helen Hyman, born in Portland in 1892, then in her early thirties, and her oldest daughter, Elizabeth, my aunt, born in San Francisco in 1920, then about five; the part of the picture that was pulling away was my mother, Eleanore, born in San Francisco in 1923, then about two. My mother was no longer talking when I found the picture, but I took it to her and asked her if she knew when it was made and if she knew who took it. She smiled and pointed to a light pencil signature in the bottom right corner: Dorothea Lange, 1925.

As a young photographer in San Francisco, Lange made her living taking pictures like these—except that they weren't like the family pictures you usually paid a photographer catering to professional families in a sophisticated city to make. You expect the smiling mother and her daughter perched comfortably on her mother's lap, her arm on her shoulder; you don't expect a second, younger daughter, turned away, looking at a toy in her hands, in her own world, or in any case not in the world of the family the picture is supposed to represent, but didn't.

A lot is going on here. The shock of recognition I had when I first saw the picture was two-fold. First, I saw in my mother, when she was barely a child, the person she would become: "fragile," as she was described when she was twenty and first married, pursued by her own depression through the next decades, finally suicidal. Growing up, I assumed all kids got home from school to find their mothers lying in bed in a darkened room. All of that was present, like a flashbulb going off eighty years after the fact, in Lange's picture—but also present was Lange's most famous photograph, *Migrant Mother*, taken in 1936, at a migrant worker's camp in San Luis Obispo County. It would become the most famous photograph of the Depression: a mother at the center, two children burying their faces behind either of her shoulders, and a baby in her lap—sleeping. But with the dirt on its face and the loll of the head, your first impression might be that the baby is dead. Gone. She is already somewhere else.

What was at work in both photographs was Lange's eye. Her first eye—what in blues would be called her first mind—looked for and constructed a center of gravity. But her second eye—her second mind—looked for discontinuity, displacement, a gravitational pull away from ordinary symmetry, which pulls the picture itself away from what would appear to be its subject.

The first subject in *Migrant Mother* is Florence Henderson's handsome, worried face, her eyes gazing into a near-future that refuses to come into focus. The first subject in the picture of my grandmother's family is the proud mother and her safe, protected daughter. The second subject, in both pictures, is that of the youngest child, who seems part of another story altogether—a child who cannot be protected, or who doesn't want to be.

Plainly, my grandmother did not look over the photographs and say, "Miss Lange, this is not the sort of picture I was hoping to receive; we are a happy family." My grandmother was a grandiose and spectacular woman, but she flinched from very little. She must have known that in whatever way, for whatever reason, Lange had seen and told the truth.

—Greil Marcus
summer 2010

~

It was after Obama's election, as the economy teetered then devolved, that I first noticed the landline had stopped ringing. Oh, it would ring but it'd only be that same Robo-calling lady, saying, *Wait! Don't hang up, I'm calling with a courtesy reminder that your auto warranty is about to expire . . . !*

As with any edging-toward-antiquity technology, The Telephone—as my grandparents formally referred to it—now seems slightly haunted to me, which is why, when it rings, I softly close the door of the room where its main console sits on my desk and tiptoe away. I want not to know who it is or if they've left a message. It could be in there now, half-hidden behind a row of books, blinking *guilty, guilty, guilty*, telling me I'm further behind than I've ever been. Spooked, I now flinch at the sound of the ringer.

Which is odd, since I do tend to talk and talk. I have so little trouble talking that when I worked in publishing in the early 1980s—before deregulation, 900 numbers, and actual true-to-life Phone Sex—my jaunty, informative chattiness was called Giving Good Phone.

Before, back when we would actually *talk* to our friends, as we now, evidently, would rather not.

Each of my grandparents was born in the West in the last decade of the nineteenth century; each viscerally remembered how long it took for news to get to you, coming overland via letter or, more succinctly, by telegraph. These were people who traveled by train, who listened to the radio. The automobile and aeroplane were the major technological advancements into lives only briefly intruded upon by television.

People respected the telephone, a phone call being an event that brought grave news from afar, from Montana, where the bachelor uncle still kept the family ranch, or from Back East, where most Californians did not go. When the phone rang, a house was startled into a sense of urgency. Someone went to answer it, everyone else grew silent. My maternal grandparents had immaculate posture, standing stock still in the central hall of their house in the hills of Glendale. Their desk phone was black, made of heavy Bakelite plastic, and sat on the Telephone Table, built into the hallway for this specific purpose, where the Phone Book, published by the Phone Company, fit perfectly into its slot.

People stood to take a call because it never lasted more than a minute or two. Cost was assessed in three-minute intervals, so nobody ever got on the phone to carelessly chat. A local call cost a dime, Long Distance was breathtakingly expensive. My grandparents had a private line but imagined that the Operator might be listening in, people remembering the party line. (This resembled Facebook in that two people might carry on a back-and-forth conversation that everyone else on that line would be able to overhear.)

My grandparents were from a generation that believed that when one achieved an education, one then demonstrated this in every linguistic nuance, full stop. None of them approved of the person who might say, *I'm gonna go call so-and-so up,* as this sounded lower-class to them, dangling its preposition out there like the shirt that had come untucked. Good at identifying their linguistic inferiors, my grandparents drilled into us the difference in the usage between *I* and *me.* Me and so-and-so going off together to call somebody *up* caused them unimaginable psychic and auditory pain.

I, however, loved the American idiom, all its carefree, rounded-off syllables, the way vernacular moved always in the direction of speed, and idiom was what I used back when I was always rushing off impulsively to call somebody *up*, something I now almost never do.

I will now do almost anything to avoid speaking on the phone or having to listen to any living person talking to me on it. I will text you or email or speak to you into the air of the car, having asked Bluetooth to "find" my cell phone. Your voice comes out of the car's speakers, surrounds me so immediately I can pretend you're there riding in the car with me.

I dial out now only with an agenda and by appointment. I try to get the computer voice named Julie at Amtrak, who honestly *can* help me, and prefer the electronic system at the pharmacy, which will patch the syllables of my name together out of its data sort with the emphasis off, so the person the electronic woman calls JANE van den BURGH feels both simultaneously recognized and anonymous.

Phone rings after dinner. My husband and I are watching *24*, or *Glee*, or *American Idol*. Let it ring, he says. It's only the symphony, we already gave to the symphony. But the name that rides the crawl on the bottom of the TV screen tells us it's not the symphony. Instead, it's one of the several dead people who call here regularly: Chas Vetter, who died in 2006, B. Christensen, who's been dead for almost nine years, W. M. Williamson. Never knew Mr. Williamson, but he's been gone for literally decades.

I know enough about my own superstitions to get that an actual *dead person* isn't calling me; still, a dead person's name showing up on a fairly regular basis will cast a funereal pall into the otherwise pleasant day. It's their widows who are actually calling, so I get up and hurry down the hall to pick up the handset, as I will for any widow over the age of eighty. Not one of this clutch of widows still has her husband's voice on her answering machine, as happens with a recent demise. Her kids will always engineer the upgrade after their own disquieting experience of calling their mother's house and getting the booming voice of their dad, now dead. But no one thinks to change a listing.

If you call the home of B. Christensen and no one's there, you'll get Anita in her teeny little old lady voice, saying, "This is A-nit-a Chris-ten-sen." She is speaking distinctly, as if she's talking to people in too much of a hurry. "I can't come to the phone right now," she says, "but you *may* leave a message." Her message promises nothing, simply ends with a little crackle of impatience. I can imagine Anita reading the script that her son Steven, who set up the machine, wrote out for her.

Anita lives next door to me. She and I hardly ever talk on the phone. Instead, she'll call to say that she's left a piece of cake on a plate on the white wicker table on my front porch, saying she didn't want to disturb me by knocking on my front door. She doesn't want to disturb me because she thinks I'm in here doing this quiet thing that is my secret work, so secret she all but whispers the word *writing*.

And she's told me not to call her to say I'll be dropping by. Instead I am to open her kitchen door and let myself in, as people always do. The window over my sink looks directly at this door—I watch people come and go all day. When we first moved here, Anita said she thought we might guess she was dealing drugs. Not drugs, she said, then lowered her voice to whisper what she *really* does, which is *cut hair.*

Just don't ever leave me a message on that thing, Anita told me, waving in the direction of wherever her answering machine is kept, adding: *I pay it no attention.*

Anita can't use an answering machine because its technology came along too late to do anything but accuse her of manual stupidity. Though I'm thirty years younger and can text like a wizard on my iPhone, my attitude toward the answering machine is not all that different from hers. On my cell phone I can at least delete a voice-mail message unheard, but the electronic system of the landline requires that I hear the message in its entirety, that I come to its end or it will mark it Skipped and put it back in the queue. If I really cannot bear it and hang up, the system knows and will immediately call me back, the message starting in exactly where I left it.

I'll put the handset on Speaker, set it on the desk, close the door, and move down the hall away from it, listening not for the words but for the change in timbre that means its cheerful mechanical voice is about to tell me I may now Press 7 to Delete. Listening to a message from way down the hall is the only way I've figured out to get rid of one.

Anita and I recently discussed these worthless machines of ours, which were actually expensive. We could donate them to the Methodists, she said, for their Junktique. At least *you* could, she said. Steven would never let me get away with that. He'd come and put me in a *home.*

—JANE VANDENBURGH
SUMMER 2010

~

Despite the fact that I've written four books that are, in whole or part, biographies, I have long intended to write a piece called "Against Biography." In it, I would lament the poor state of the practice: those paint-by-the-numbers books that mechanically color in the biological blueprint (birth, childhood, adult anecdotes, death) to the exclusion of form, fantasy, or reflection. I would sniff at the loose baggy biographies that record for posterity every sneeze and cough, every hairpin turn, every vision and revision, in lieu of the small, inscrutable, and telling moments in life, which are generally the poet's rather than the biographer's quarry. "No one is too great a fool, too complete an amateur, or too thoroughly ignorant of craft to undertake the writing of biography," said Edmund Gosse, whom I would quote. Or Oscar Wilde, who put the matter more directly: biography adds new terror to death.

Wilde's remark alludes to the prurient nature of biography, its habit of lifting up the bedclothes or rifling through dead people's pockets. "Poets don't have biographies; their work is their biography," said Octavio Paz, whom John Updike quoted when Updike tried, unsuccessfully, to head off at the pass any of the would-be biographers circling his aging body. *Can't we trust the tale, not the teller?* he seemed to be saying, as he fortified the position sometimes known as formalism, which more or less discards biography as being irrelevant to the intricate workings of art. And when this position was reiterated by Roland Barthes in his essay "The Death of the Author," and then amplified by Michel Foucault, many anti-biographers could further bolster their formalist suspicions: the author is dead, only the text lives. As usual, Gertrude Stein—with more zing and less pretension—got right to the point: "The lives of great men all remind us we should leave no sons behind us."

As I'm suggesting, biography creates a great deal of anxiety, much of which has sought shelter in one or another well-wrought disavowal. To give an example: some years ago, when I ran into an academic film critic whom I hadn't seen in a long time and told him I was writing a biography, he condescendingly swirled the sherry in his plastic cup and asked how it felt to work on something so "theoretically regressive." A few weeks ago, while standing in line for a movie, I asked the poet Richard Howard (eminent translator of Roland Barthes, by the way) if he had once believed that, when it comes to art or even history, persons don't matter—that only aesthetics or grand narratives do. Yes, he said, he had once supposed so, but no longer did. If he hadn't changed his mind, it would have been a great irony, since one of Richard Howard's keenest contributions to poetry is *his* voice, giving voice to other people: to Milton's daughters and Isadora Duncan and Willa Cather and H. G. Wells, to Robert Browning and Edith Wharton and a person named Richard. As the poet James Longenbach once said, Richard Howard's is a poetry of recovery.

If biography is also an act of recovery, what does it bring back? Does it bring back the subject? Not really; that can't be done. Biography first convinces us of the fleeing of the Biographied, said Emily Dickinson. Acknowledging their limits, the best biographies pursue what we have lost and are always in the process of losing: people. Buildings and trees last much longer. Our words vanish as soon as we've spoken them, or if they don't vanish, they reappear, not ours but as something else, somewhere else, always receding before us, puzzling, human, maddeningly reconstituted and just out of reach. Henry James put it this way: "recovering the lost" is "at all events . . . much like entering the enemy's lines to get back one's dead for burial."

This doesn't necessarily mean that biography is a mortician applying makeup to a corpse. What is being recovered is not the life *per se* or the works *per se*, but the way the subject thought about those works and that life, whether he or she was artist, scientist, writer, banker, tinker, baker. The works produced, whatever they are, may be composites, fragments, borrowings that shift and change, but we concern ourselves with the someone who worried and wept and succeeded and failed and pulled those things (those works of art, or books, or professions, or domestic lives) together. These are people who lived and, as Descartes implied, to live is to think. Or, to quote James again, this time from his own biography of the sculptor William Wetmore Story: "To live over people's lives is nothing unless we live over their perceptions, live over the growth, the change, the varying intensity of the same—since it was *by* these things they themselves lived."

If biography is anything, it is not a chronological litany or an encyclopedic archive or a documentation of who, what, and where. Nor is it divorced from what used to be called the history of ideas. We may talk about evolutionary theory (an idea) or creationism (another idea) or racism (a stupid idea) or health care reform (an idea whose time has come) or formalism (sometimes a useful idea) or agnosticism (an idea about an idea); but we need, it seems to me, to remind ourselves over and over that ideas do not exist in vacuums, which is to say without the people who perceived or created or constructed or even debunked them. Biography then recovers, or tries impossibly to recover, the conflicts of existence that render the person *behind* the idea both human and unique. We invent the form in which we house those lives, which is the shape of the biography. For biography is a crafted story, an invention of form, which reveals the meaning of the "unbearable sequence of sheer happenings." (I quote Hannah Arendt.) But like all revelations, like all good writing, it's neither fixed nor final. There are as many biographies as there are subjects and writers.

When I finished my biography of Janet Flanner, who wrote the Paris Letter for *The New Yorker* for fifty years, I agonized lest some of her friends—and especially our mutual friend, the incomparable writer Sybille Bedford—might not like or even recognize Flanner in my portrait of her. Sybille said something to me I never forgot: "I have my Janet Flanner, you have yours, and Janet had her own."

—BRENDA WINEAPPLE
FALL 2010

~

Like all the other apartments I've ever lived in, the apartment in which I spent my childhood was full of books. However, the word "full" doesn't really come near the truth; neither do the words "crammed" or "crowded," because not only was every wall covered with shelves (each of which was packed with volumes from every imaginable century), but the books also sometimes served as rugs, tables, sofas, chairs, and even, almost, beds. I don't mean that there was no furniture in the apartment and that we sat on piles of books or ate from other still taller piles—with a consequent disquieting sensation of constant instability—but that the rugs, tables, sofas, seats, and even beds were often buried beneath vast tomes: for example, the complete and very abundant works of the late-Renaissance philosopher Francisco Suárez. I remember those in particular because, on one occasion, I had to wrestle for hours with the philosophers Suárez and Condillac in order to make a large enough space on the floor to play with my toy soldiers. Bear in mind that my size at the time (I was seven or eight) didn't really equip me for the easy removal of those large seventeenth- or eighteenth-century volumes obstructing my innocent games.

In fact, for myself and my three brothers, the house was one long obstacle course, almost two hundred yards long, the obstacles always taking the form of books. That is why, from an early age, I became used to negotiating the words of the great philosophers and writers, with the inevitable result that I have a deep-rooted lack of respect for anyone who writes, myself included. It still surprises me when I see how other people (especially politicians and commentators) kowtow to writers or else fight to appear in photos accompanied by some scribe or other, or when the state rushes to give succor to ailing, ruined poets, privileging them with a treatment that only heaps humiliation on equally ruined or ailing street cleaners, businessmen, waiters, lawyers, and cobblers. My scant respect for the trade to which I belong (from the most ancient of academicians to the most youthful of libelists) derives from a childhood home in which, as I have said, I grew used to mistreating and misusing almost all the seminal texts from the history of culture. Having too much respect for the kind of individuals who partially soured my childhood and invaded the territory occupied by my thrilling games of bottle-top soccer would seem to me masochistic in the extreme.

But to return to the description of my childhood home: things did not stop there. I mean that my parents, not content with that overweening love of books, felt exactly the same about paintings. It's hard to understand how those two loves could be compatible, especially when you consider that there wasn't a blank or empty wall to be seen in my childhood home. The absurd habit of hanging pictures in the bathroom and even the kitchen had not yet arrived, and given that it was the custom then to have two servants (a cook and a maid, who were always at daggers drawn), there was no way that one could set aside a room for paintings (as dentists and notaries do), a kind of mini-museum; the only room that could have been used for this purpose, and the only one in which there were no books, was occupied by the terrible rows between cook and maid, from which, according to some mysterious preordained law of subjugation, the latter almost always emerged the loser. Although, having said that there were no books, I realize now that the room, in fact, contained the two hundred Simenon books carefully and devotedly collected by my father. They were in French, of course, but I suppose it was a case of what later came to be called subliminal warnings, so that the servants wouldn't overstep the mark in their quarrels or be tempted to steal any non-literary objects when it came to their inevitable dismissal. Inspector Maigret was watching.

Anyway, my parents' pictorial enthusiasm led to a method of placing the paintings they acquired on top of the books, using a crazy mechanism that converted the canvases into small hanging doors. The pictures were hung only by their left side, so that they could be easily "opened" to reveal the volumes they normally covered. An excellent copy of Fra Angelico's *Annunciation* by Daniel Canellada, numerous landscapes by the nineteenth-century artist Ricardo Arredondo, an equally large number by the painter and friend of the family, Alfredo Ramón, some miniatures by Vicente López, a few portraits by Vázquez Díaz, a few works by Benjamín Palencia, and the occasional Eduardo Vicente, all hung absurdly from the highest shelves, thus eliminating from the rooms still more lateral space. I thus became accustomed to seeing paintings hung not against a smooth, white, plain backdrop, but surrounded by the spines and edges of bound volumes, which may be why I have equally scant respect for painters. Indeed, whenever I see a painting in an exhibition or museum, I have to repress an initial impulse to "open" it and "take out" a book by Kierkegaard or Aristotle, as if the pictures were just strongbox doors behind which were to be found the greatest bibliographic treasures. Only after that first impression, which converts any masterpiece into a small decorated door, only then can I concentrate and see what there is to see.

The truth is that, despite all these inconveniences, I still cannot conceive of any comfortable abode whose walls are not carpeted with the brightly colored spines and edges of books and built-in paintings; and although the various apartments in which I've lived in various countries have always been very temporary and not, of course, mine, I have never been able to feel even minimally at ease in them until I have acquired a few books and placed them on the shelves, a pale reflection of that childhood bounty. Only then have I begun to think of the place in question, be it in England, the United States, or Italy, as habitable. An apartment is made up of floors, ceilings, and walls, and although I prefer the first two to remain uncluttered or, at most, adorned with a rug or lamp, the walls need to be totally covered so that the books can speak to me through their closed mouths, their motley, multi-colored, and very silent spines.

—JAVIER MARÍAS
(TRANSLATED BY MARGARET JULL COSTA)
WINTER 2011

~

After hours at Klavierhaus, in a room behind the gallery of showpiece Steinways, Sophia Rosoff is teaching class. Nine of her students are here, amateurs and professionals alike, ranging in age from twenty to eighty. Rosoff sits quietly while they play, head cocked, eyes huge, seeming to receive the music with her whole body. She never interrupts nor offers corrections. Technical perfection is of little interest to her; like her mentor Abby Whiteside, Rosoff deals in rhythm.

"Show Barry how we are learning fugues now," she tells her student Fiona, who has just played a Bach Prelude.

Fiona closes the cover over the keys. "This is soprano, alto, tenor, and bass," she explains, showing us her hands and her feet. She taps out the rhythm of the first two voices with her hands. When the third voice enters, she stomps it out on the floor.

Like all Rosoff's set-ups, this way of learning a fugue puts rhythm first, drawing focus away from peripheral concerns of fingers and notes. At age ninety, Rosoff still sees about fifteen students a week. Pianists who walk into her book-filled Upper East Side apartment expecting a traditional lesson are in for a surprise. Depending on the day, she may have them balance eggs on a china plate, walk across the room like Groucho Marx, or dance and sing their Chopin mazurka.

"I don't teach," says Rosoff. "I explore. I clear the tracks so the feeling the student has for the music can emerge."

After Fiona, the elder statesman Barry Harris takes the piano. He settles down onto the bench, which Rosoff adjusts to encourage connection to the instrument and balance on the sitting bones. The room fills with the sweet sound of his waltz "To Duke With Love." Widely considered one of the greatest living bebop players, Harris is one of a long list of successful jazz pianists to have studied with Rosoff, including Fred Hersch, Walter Bishop, Jr., Michael Kanan, and my husband, Ethan Iverson, who first introduced her to me as "the marvelous Sophia, my white witch."

"No fingers!" Harris announces at the end of the waltz. "I am a firm believer in Abby Whiteside, and I know you don't play with your fingers. You play with your butt, your feet, your toes." He shows us his forearms. "You know how sometimes you get pain here? Since I've been doing this, no pain. Believe it."

Michael Kanan is another believer. The jazz pianist and vocal accompanist for singers Jane Monheit and Jimmy Scott came to Rosoff with an excruciating, twenty-year case of tendonitis. "When I walked in the door the first time," he recalls, "Sophia didn't say hello. She just looked at my arms and said, 'It's worse on the left side, isn't it?'" After the first lesson, sixty percent of his pain was gone. His eyes fill with tears as he says, "My musical life can be divided into two parts: before Sophia and after. It's like, come for the pain reduction, stay for the enlightenment."

Classical pianist and educator Robert Hallquist came to Rosoff in 1982 with a right thumb so extended that by the end of a recital he could barely play an octave. "She didn't even look at the thumb," he says. "She went straight to being connected to what I was doing, in a way I'd never been taught before in ten years of conservatory and doctoral training. She had me do very simple things with the keyboard, tracing out patterns, and soon I was doing things I had never been able to do before. Then she looked down and said, 'So what's this problem with the thumb?' It was simply remarkable. Sophia works with the way you perceive things, the way you see patterns, the way all of you works together to create a musical statement. It took me by storm."

Abby Whiteside's way of finding the music was to outline first. She had students play only selected notes of a piece, following the musical and rhythmic highlights. "Outlining creates a musical statement that the composer heard," Rosoff explains. "It gives you shape and direction, a sense of the whole, which is greater than the sum of its parts."

In order to coordinate breath with music, Rosoff expanded upon outlining by adding "rhythm talk," in which the player speaks a repeated word such as "little."

"It changed the way I feel rhythm in jazz," says Michael Kanan. "For years I was struggling with trying to get a propulsive sense of swing. When I started doing rhythm talk, suddenly it felt much easier to play anything I wanted. She also had me dance, putting my feet on the first and third beat and my hands on the second and fourth. That has to do with big bands, because in early swing bands the bass would play on one and three and the piano, guitar and high hat would play on two and four. So you are representing the whole rhythm section. Then I would just hear the harmony in my head and sing the melody. I was representing the whole piece of music in my body, just by singing and dancing."

The prominent jazz pianist and composer Fred Hersch has studied with Rosoff for thirty years. When asked to explain why Rosoff attracts so much jazz talent, Hersch says, "It's the emphasis on rhythm. The classical players love her, but she is so different from what they've been trained in—fingers, strength, power. Also, Sophia has never been a self-promoter, never affiliated herself with a conservatory. She always stresses that it's not a technique or a method. It's all about connection."

Hersch finds outlining particularly relevant to the jazz player, and he teaches it to his own students at the Juilliard School and the New England Conservatory of Music. "Jazz is outlining," he says. "The chord changes are your outline. I tell my students that the changes are like a glass bowl—transparent yet solid—and you can put rocks or water or goldfish in the bowl. Sophia's been an influence in terms of letting the student make a mess, letting them hang out in uncertainty for a while. There's not one right way to outline, just as there's not one right way to play 'Autumn Leaves.'"

It is getting late. All the students at Klavierhaus have had a turn, but Rosoff doesn't want class to end. As great jazz musicians tend to do, Barry Harris showed up late, so he missed hearing her youngest student play.

"Would you like to play again, Jeremy?" she asks. "Let Barry hear you."

"The Debussy?"

"The jazz."

Jeremy goes back to the piano and reprises his deconstructed version of "Take Five." Rosoff looks back and forth from her young protégé to her old friend, twinkling. At the end of the song, she asks Harris to play again, too.

"What should I play?"

"Play anything."

Harris walks to the big Steinway and plays a haunting ballad that no one knows. When we ask what it is called, he changes the subject: "I just bought a new piano. A Petrof. It sits way up high. I can hardly see the keys."

"You don't need your eyes," Rosoff says. "Use your ears."

"It really has a spring to it. You know how the keys come back naturally and you're supposed to let them do that on their own? Well, this one really does that."

"It has an accelerated action," she says.

Then class is over, and I help her gather up the dark chocolate and homegrown cucumbers her students have brought her—everyone always gives Rosoff gifts; the Maharani of Baroda gave her 107 saris—and she lets me hold her hand as we walk into the night.

—SARAH DEMING
SPRING 2011

~

At a dinner party in London, Edmund de Waal tells some academics what he knows of the story of his netsuke. He has inherited 264 hard and small "playthings," passed down in his family from a Parisian to a Viennese to a Japanese to him, a half-Dutch Englishman. He feels the story "isn't getting smoother, it is getting thinner." Soon he'll still possess the netsuke but their stories, the "pulse of their making," will be lost. It's there, at the dinner table, probably rubbing into the patina of a fork or the mahogany table, that Edmund de Waal, a potter by profession and by choice, decides he can no longer go on sharing these anecdotes that have become flat, cliché, a stamp, so unlike the intricate, surprising carvings he rolls in his hand. "I can either anecdotalize it for the rest of my life," de Waal tells us, "or go and find out what it means."

The patina of a story can either be rubbed away to reveal the real, or added to, layer by layer of dust. In *The Hare with Amber Eyes*, his account of the history of these objects and of the family members who possessed them, de Waal pushes deep into the archives and photographs and letters and mansions, and what rises to the surface is not only the cultures in which his family grew into opulence and then was stripped of nearly all its objects and stories, but the secret history of touch. We see the Jewish, Odessa-born Charles Ephrussi struggle to belong in Paris's Rue de Monceau; we see Charles finely situating his collection of netsuke front and center in his filled salon, made at home with Degas pastels and Moreau's gilded heroes and his yellow armchair. Like a netsuke, like a "thing" poem by Rilke, a story should be defined and hard and alive. No sentimentality, no excuses, no melancholy. "Melancholy," de Waal tells us, "is a sort of default vagueness, a get-out clause, a smothering lack of focus. And this netsuke is a small, tough explosion of exactitude. It deserves this kind of exactitude in return."

His aim, in this book, is to understand how Charles Ephrussi and his nephew Viktor and his grand-niece Elisabeth and his grand-nephew Ignat (Edmund's beloved Uncle Iggie, through whom he inherited the netsuke) thought about their lives and their work and these little pieces of boxwood and ivory that somehow stayed with the family when all else was lost. In pursuit of this, de Waal journeyed to see what their eyes saw, went to touch what their fingers stroked or shattered or neglected altogether. De Waal looks, literally, from his grandmother Elisabeth's childhood bedroom window to see if she could see into the lecture hall at the university across the street—the same university where she would eventually become the first woman to graduate with a law degree. Elsewhere, in a museum, he "surreptitiously [reaches] a hand over a velvet rope to stroke the arm of an Empire fauteuil . . . for research." It's the type of chair Viktor Ephrussi chose for his Palais in Vienna; it's cold to the touch.

"How objects are handed on is all about storytelling," de Waal writes, and if he wants those stories to come alive, for the dust to collect into lineaments and into lives, he has to find out how his family handled, then handed on, these netsuke. Like all of the Ephrussi family members that owned them, the netsuke were exiled from their homeland, sent into foreign lands where they had to be either kept private or daringly made public. The collection was, like the family banking business, a large and sometimes unbearable inheritance, even if these small objects could be hidden in a mattress or collected in a leather attaché case. If de Waal could know how these netsuke were handled, he could recover what his family thought. "Touch tells you what you need to know: it tells you about yourself," he insists.

So off we go with de Waal into the "resting places" of the netsuke. We start in Paris on a golden hill, where Charles, spared the weight of the banking business and left to his art-writing and salons and married lover, begins collecting netsuke during the wave of *japonisme* that flooded Paris. When Charles begins collecting "Jew Art," losing many of his Impressionist friends, the netsuke are displaced from his life and he gives the entire collection, vitrine included, to his newly married cousin Viktor in Vienna. And as we see this collection within a collection crated up and shipped to the family's other business headquarters in Vienna, to the dusty, reinvented intersection of the Ringstrasse and Schottengasse, we're there with Edmund de Waal reflecting on the story within the story. "Why this gift? Of all the paintings and plasters and gold, why give your cousin Viktor, the budding scholar, this playful set with its rats on fishbones and naked woman tangled with the octopus? What are you trying to say, Charles, that 'under the grey-glass roof, the whole house is like a vitrine that you cannot escape?' Is that what you feel?"

This thinking about another's thinking is attributable to de Waal's constant obsession with touch. We're given colored photographs—something to handle and roll and push into to inspect, the fruit of de Waal's two years of forced research. (What must it feel like to read SPEKULANT next to your family member's name in a book and then to keep reading, to see the red stamp and ISRAEL written over the given name, and to question whether you should open any more of these doors?) And when de Waal has walked us through all those resting places—and you must walk as a flâneur does, vagabonding but with purpose, touching this "dangerous buoyancy" to see how these people think—he goes to the starting place of the family, in the dust of Odessa, the birthplace of his great-grandfather. "And perhaps if I stand in the house . . . I will understand. I am not sure what I will understand. Why they left? What it means to leave?" What it means, at any rate, for the netsuke to have come as far as they have, having come to rest, for the moment, with him.

—Tim Carr

SPRING 2011

First large hole in the ground, Southeast Kansas: As you approach West Mineral, Kansas, you already see the form of Big Brutus, but the size of this form is deceptive, for Big Brutus is situated in a wide shallow depression of his own making, and so his bulk is hidden to someone driving along at the level of the surrounding land. Big Brutus is the world's second- largest electric mining shovel, which readers of the children's book *Mike Mulligan and His Steam Shovel* will wish to call a steam shovel, though no steam was involved. Big Brutus, one hundred and sixty feet tall, was employed in the mining of the shallow deposits of coal and other ores that are dispersed throughout Cherokee County and neighboring areas. When my father was a child in nearby Galena, he saw Big Brutus at the height of his powers, lurching about the coal field. It is possible that Big Brutus provided both the coal that fired the town lead smelter and the lead sulfide upon which the coal worked, and from which the town of Galena took its name.

I visited Big Brutus in the company of my wife, also a native of the so-called Tri-State mining district, and whose several and puzzling health problems may owe something to the fact that the serpentine lake immediately behind her childhood home is, in fact, a rained-in coal pit or, less technically, a large hole in the ground. I am as much a Kansan as she, and so I bought a Big Brutus hat as a show of my state pride, but I never had the courage to wear it, for fear that it would be taken ironically. I fear additionally that it is wrong to commemorate a machine that was, most basically, a giant bucket responsible for digging large holes and making people sick.

Second large hole in the ground, Southwest Kansas: Greensburg is dubiously honored by the presence of the world's largest hand-dug well, which is altogether larger than one might expect. Known colloquially as the Big Well, it is over a hundred feet deep and some ten yards across. For a small fee, one buys the privilege of descending a rickety, open-tread staircase to the bottom, certifying that one is approximately as stupid as the original inhabitants of the town, who after all dug the entire well by hand.

One is permitted to ascend the staircase free of charge. Merely climbing out of this damp abyss is a chore; the brute labor of creating the hole without mechanical tractive power, in the Kansas heat, is simply beyond contemplation.

I visited the well in 2004 on a weekend trip with my father. In May of 2007 Greensburg was erased by a tornado. My father traveled there again the following month, and he assured me that, although every structure was obliterated and every tree reduced to a suckering ring, the well remained.

Third large hole in the ground, South Central Kansas: Off US-77 in Cowley County, in or near Rock, there is a decommissioned Titan II ICBM complex. This Titan was condemned to serve in the bowels of the earth from the 1960s until the 1980s, when it was pardoned in a gesture of detente.

The Strategic Air Command has posted a sign warning trespassers that deadly force is authorized to protect the installation, which looks very much like a small section of fallow field. A man of my height and build climbs over the three-strand barbed-wire fence with some scrotal peril. Grasshoppers explode in all directions as I tromp around the field in search of the cement blast ports, where flames would have shot out in the final hour of the world.

In 1978, several years before I was born, a man like myself died here when propellant was inadvertently spilled from the missile. But walking about, one would not know that a man died; one would scarcely know that anything ever happened here at all.

It is traditional to hold one's breath while driving through Rock, and some say that this custom dates to the 1978 propellant spill, which enveloped the town in a large, toxic cloud. However, we Kansans also hold our breath while crossing many other small towns, as a show of strength.

—Ben Merriman

SUMMER 2011

~

Now you're slipping toward the plan. You arrive at the river. There you light a cigarette. At the end of the road, on the corner, there's a telephone booth and that's the only light at the end of the road. You call Barcelona. The stranger picks up the phone. She says she won't go. After a few seconds, during which you say "okay," and she echoes, "okay," you ask why. She says that Sunday she's going to Alella and you say you'll call her next time you're in Barcelona. You hang up, and a cold air enters the booth, out of nowhere, when you think the following: "it's like an autobiography." Now you're slipping through the winding streets. Gerona can be so bright at night, you think, just two sweepers chatting outside a closed bar and at the end of the road the lights of a car disappearing. I shouldn't drink, you think, I shouldn't sleep, I shouldn't do anything that might disturb my focus. Now you're stopped near the river, on the bridge built by Eiffel, hidden in the iron framework. You touch your face. On the other bridge, the bridge called *de los labios*, you hear footsteps, but when you look for the person there's no one there, just the rustle of someone descending the stairs. You think: "therefore the stranger was like this and that and, therefore, the only unstable one is me, therefore I've had a magnificent dream." The dream to which you're referring just crossed in front of you, in the subtle instant when you were acknowledging a truce—and so became transparent briefly, like the Lawyer of Glass—and it consisted of the apparition, on the other end of the bridge, of a crowd of eunuchs, merchants, professors, housewives, naked and holding their testicles and sliced-off vaginas in the palms of their hands. What a strange dream, you say. No doubt you want to cheer yourself up.

REALITY. I'd returned to Gerona, alone, after three months of work. I had no chance of getting another job and I didn't really want to anyway. The house, in my absence, had filled with cobwebs and things seemed to be covered by a green film. I felt empty, no desire to write and, when I tried, unable to sit still for more than an hour in front of a blank sheet of paper. The first few days I didn't even bathe and soon enough I got used to the spiders. My activities were reduced to going down to the post office, where on rare occasion I found a letter from my sister, from Mexico, and going to the store to buy scraps of meat for the dog.

REALITY. In a way I couldn't explain, the house seemed touched by something it didn't have when I left. Things seemed clearer, for example, my armchair seemed clear, shining, and the kitchen, though full of dust stuck in scabs of grease, gave the impression of whiteness, as if you could see through it. (See what? Nothing: more whiteness.) In the same way, things were more distinguishable. The kitchen was the kitchen and the table just the table. Some day I'll try to explain it, but then, two days after returning, if I set my hands or elbows on the table I experienced a sharp pain, as if I were *biting* something beyond repair.

—ROBERTO BOLAÑO
(TRANSLATED BY LAURA HEALY)
FALL 2011

The old family memories exist on tapes and disks, Betamax and VHS cassettes, 8mm tapes, digital hi8 tapes, minidisks and floppy disks and disembodied hard drives—every manner of recordable consumer media released in the last forty years, all stacked in a closet of my parents' apartment in Fort Lauderdale. Next to the tapes and disks are the machines themselves, the old beasts, growing increasingly farcical in their advancing age. We have three old video cameras, each one smaller than the one before, each still in its carrying case with all the extra straps, the batteries, the unused remote controls, all the orphan cables with their twist ties intact, still emanating that smell of new Sony that would discharge from the box as you opened it, evoking a factory somewhere in Japan, sterile conditions, precision and quality—all of these associations part of their consumer appeal.

A chunk of my past from one particular period is preserved in Sony 8cm DVD-RW Rewritable DVD Camcorder Media (1.4 GB). There are probably thirty of these DVDs. I've tried to organize them many times and always failed, underestimating how much time and patience it takes to look through hours of meaningless footage. You really need to set aside an entire day, which I will never do. Meanwhile—and this is an unexpected twist—the media itself is degrading. Those tapes are silently eroding in that closet. Even a DVD has a lifespan, it turns out. Our agents in the battle against forgetting are abandoning their posts.

I found an old cassette marked "Grandmother." I vaguely remember the day it was recorded, in 1980, when she came to visit from Turkey. We recorded it on a black Sony cassette recorder with built-in microphone and handle, about the size of a shoebox. My grandmother spoke into the machine with the ceremonial finality of someone preserving her voice for posterity. As long as I had known her she was aware of her imminent mortality, which lent her a comic air to a ten-year-old. "I'll be dead one day and you'll listen to my voice," she says, and in the background my brother and I are laughing at her gravity. Listening to it now, I hear bravery in her voice, which is shaky with age. Yet the recording itself is now of poor quality. There is a high-pitched tone that comes and goes and makes it difficult to hear what she is saying. There are points when her voice warps and fades and then returns, points at which she is unintelligible. It's as if she is slipping away, the last material traces of her are disintegrating. The past has taken flight and soon it will be out of reach.

I can only wade through two Betamax cassettes of random television shows and commercials from the Eighties, Walt Lazar Chevrolet, a trip to the Renaissance Center in downtown Detroit, footage of a forgotten park in the summer. Soon I lose interest. There may be a priceless moment in there somewhere, some message from the past that will inform my adult life, but I do not have the patience to find it. Yet you cannot bring yourself to erase any of this. How can you throw away something unique and irreplaceable? My brother is six and has managed to turn the camera on and is delivering a monologue about birds. If we are accustomed to valuations based on scarcity, then what could be more valuable than images from a youth that will never be recaptured? Today's childhoods are photographed and videotaped in an uninterrupted fashion. Everyone carries a camera phone with video, and footage of every experience is immediately uploaded to Facebook to punctuate its relevance. Is this a compulsion to hoard? A desire to hang on to something? Who will have the time to review all this content?

This past Thanksgiving, after our turkey dinner, I attached the old VCR to a Sony flat-screen television and started watching some family friends who have since died and whose memories had sunk underneath, except at the points where fastened to the present by photos. How curious to see and hear them again in scenes I didn't remember. I felt for a moment as if they had come to life and had become individuals with agency again, not destined to be those people repeating forever the same scenes in the photographs. And then the camera focused on my parents. They were on a boat laughing, looking young and happy. How come I had never seen this scene before? The image had already started to decay a bit and there was a scratchy quality to the video. It's only a matter of time now, I thought, and made my way to the living room to find them sitting on the couch. They were softer around the edges than the people I had just seen in the video. I sat on the couch and put my arms around them, holding them both for a long time until the dog wandered in from the kitchen and climbed onto my lap. We sat like this for some time, as if posing for a portrait.

—Mert Erogul
FALL 2011

~

My car has Louisiana plates, but when I am back in New York, visiting at my mother's, I drive like a New Yorker. I know the lights. I know the good avenues. I enter the topographical flow. There is, at any given moment, a precise number of cars with Louisiana plates moving through the streets of New York. I have no idea if the number is ten, or a hundred, or a thousand, but I am sure that among them all, I am the driver most at home on these streets.

This extends to the logistics of parking. Alternate side of the street parking is a circadian rhythm that enters the marrow of your soul. To have a good spot becomes a source of well-being, inducing feelings of rootedness. To be adrift without a spot, when the music has stopped and everyone else has found a place, is to be a refugee cast adrift in the Diaspora, fated to circle like a mythological character. If the ancient Greeks had cars, there would have been a tragedy about parking.

Alternate side of the street regulations are suspended for religious holidays. The regulations themselves have the qualities of a religious observance. After the street sweeper has passed, drivers appear, like some molting species dropping from the trees. The cars move to the right side of the street, settling in like congregants getting comfortable in a pew.

Now comes the spiritual aspect of alternate side of the street parking: you have a spot, but you must wait in the car until the no-parking window is over.

My mom is not quite up for the frantic moving of the car, but she is willing to sit. She brings a book, or a newspaper. She brings a scarf and a coat.

"Mom, it's warm, you don't need all that," I say.

"Just in case," she says.

I am briefly furious at this unnecessary expenditure of effort. I see in this excessive bringing the excessive holding onto of things which makes her apartment so magical and also maddening. She is a documentary film maker. So her house is a production company, too. It is filled with boxes, papers, accumulations. But does that mean her purse has to have three pairs of glasses, and their cases, and four little packets of tissues, along with cough drops, in the box and also loose, and various little purses, one for change and one for credit cards, and tiny papers, obscure receipts whose print has faded? My daughter and my mother play a game at her house: they go on a "mission," roving the house searching for "clues." It is a house full of them. The Lindt chocolate in the cupboard. A clue to my mother's desire that life have sweetness. (Which lately has provoked from me a lecture on the perils of sugar.)

I open the car door to let her in. She is doing me a favor, after all. She is ready to sit here for an hour while I rush off on errands. She sits in the driver's seat, key in the ignition, even though she doesn't really drive. It's a legality—you can't be just near your car or in the passenger seat if you want to avoid a ticket. You must be in the car, prepared to move it.

Invariably what happens is that once I get her installed in the driver's seat, when I'm free to go, I instead go sit in the passenger seat. We talk there, in that curiously private space of a parked car. Sometimes we talk all the way until the no-parking window is closed and we are free to go. Sometimes even beyond. With a wife, and a kid, and now a baby, I don't really get this kind of sustained private time with my mom, unless we are sitting in a car together that is going nowhere. It's the odd fact of our life: from the distance of New Orleans we have long phone conversations, exchange emails that bear a strong resemblance, in length and style of greeting, to letters. While I'm living in her apartment, though, we tend to wave as though passing on the street, albeit with her in slippers and me in underwear.

—Thomas Beller
WINTER 2012

~

My uncle is dying. I come back from sitting with him to find novels, essays, plays, biographies strangely unsatisfying. This is one of the few spaces left in our lives still reserved for poems. Two have been sustaining me over the past few weeks. They face the subject head-on and are both rigorously formal, but where they end up, and the men who wrote them, couldn't be more different.

The first is Philip Larkin's "Aubade." As with all of Larkin's longer poems, what fascinates me is its narrative quality, five stanzas containing the movement and mystery of an entire novel. Yet in no sense is the verse subordinated to mere telling. It's not one of those hybrid novels-in-verse. How Larkin does this is a mystery, and one of the reasons I return to his work again and again. The "story," to adopt this approach, concerns the poet coming home from work, getting drunk, and waking in the middle of the night to face what he has been averting his gaze from all evening: "unresting death, a whole day nearer now." This fear is not argued away but heightened and reinforced as he methodically disputes the traditional consolations offered by Western thought. Religion ("That vast moth-eaten musical brocade"), philosophy, stoicism are considered and dismissed. There's a beautiful music born of the tension between the complex, masterfully handled form—rhymes of *ababcceffe*, with never a stumble or awkwardness—and the poet's deliberately unheroic stance, that of a child in the dark scaring himself senseless.

> Most things may never happen: this one will,
> And realisation of it rages out
> In furnace-fear when we are caught without
> People or drink. Courage is no good:
> It means not scaring others. Being brave
> Lets no one off the grave.

The novelistic "turn" comes in the last stanza. Night has passed. We have *felt* it pass. (How? No clue. I still haven't pried loose Larkin's secret.) With dawn, the plainness of objects reasserts itself. He sees the day, next in a series of unchanging trials, taking shape before him. What lukewarm comfort he finds is in the very physicality of the world, to which his physical being—visible now along with the "wardrobe" and "telephones" and other materially verifiable facts—still belongs. It's hardly a trumpet blare of victory but rather a deeply human and moving recognition that he is still, in some sense, supposed to be here. Then, in the poem's strange, lingering, final image, "Postmen like doctors go from house to house." The postmen, Larkin explained elsewhere, are delivering letters, evidence of tenuous human connection, somewhat assuaging our isolation. But the picture of an army of doctors fanning out, tending to the doomed as if this were a song written in plague-time, undercuts whatever comforts the benign thought of a mailman may bring.

While "Aubade" is irresistibly quotable, an obvious keeper in the canon, if ever there was one, it is hardly delivered from on-high by some priest-like Augustan poet. The gloomy, at times almost whining voice is all too uncomfortably familiar to most readers. It's us at four AM, bleary, petulant, and so very afraid, a part of ourselves rarely shown in art yet one we instantly acknowledge and respond to. I suppose the deeper consolation the poem offers is its own existence, that our degrading fears and selfish despair can provide a fit subject for art.

The second poem is by Thom Gunn, whom Larkin detested. He "privately mocked" him and managed to accidentally omit a big chunk of Gunn's "The Byrnies" when compiling *The Oxford Book of Twentieth-Century Verse*. One can see why there would be little sympathy between the two. While the Hermit of Hull wrote of sexual frustration and an inability to rid himself of guilt and terror, Gunn left England and moved to San Francisco, where he dropped acid, celebrated hedonism, and seemed to live in a pan-sexual bubble. But that's a very superficial reading of his work. "Lament," written at the height of the AIDS epidemic, performs the same utilitarian function as "Aubade." It takes us *through* death, keeping our eyes wide open, though setting us down in a very different place.

Composed in couplets, "Lament" follows with remorseless detachment a friend's decline as he is taken by disease.

> Your dying was a difficult enterprise.
> First, petty things took up your energies,
> The small but clustering duties of the sick,
> Irritant as the cough's dry rhetoric.

This "dry rhetoric" extends to the poem as well, with its insistent half- and off-rhymes. Their not-quite-chiming creates an atmosphere, a voice, as distinct as Larkin's but one far less public, less plangent and crowd-pleasing.

Just as Larkin dispenses with the clichés of consolation, so Gunn stubbornly refuses to sentimentalize his friend's disintegration. Rather, he is a reporter, forcing us to confront the mundane process of dying with no gorgeous music or distancing metaphor. Details, which only appear at the end of "Aubade," are what this poem largely consists of. Hospital equipment, symptoms, nurses, drugs. Why? Supposedly he's talking to his friend, who is dead now and when alive knew all this far better than he. I suspect it was to dispel the mystery and taboo surrounding a largely unacknowledged slaughter. Rather than join the hysteria, Gunn adopts a tone of unbearable quiet. It's poetry delivered through gritted teeth. He has been summoned, unwillingly, to perform an act of duty, of witness.

Such scrupulous lack of emotion is necessary, not just in self-defense, the way we instinctively recoil from the sick, but to achieve the artistic synthesis he is aiming for. The more wrenching the encounter, the cooler its depiction, as if an imbalance must be corrected. Gunn seems to address this when summarizing why his friend never achieved great recognition in life:

> You lacked the necessary ruthlessness,
> The soaring meanness that pinpoints success.

Here, the ruthlessness art demands is in full evidence, so much so that the end, when it finally comes, is almost an aside, a foregone conclusion no longer capable of bearing dramatic weight. A lesser writer would have felt compelled to adorn it with all sorts of hyped-up significance, but here the friend slips away, unnoticed. Instead, we are left with the poet in his garden, "delivered into time again," reviewing this "difficult, tedious, painful enterprise." Tedious! Again, as in Larkin's admission of fear, we glimpse an aspect of our nature too often ignored or denied, that it is tedious to die, that death is more often wearing, even boring, than momentous. There's a great deal of pain in this admission. This is grief, but grief restrained and minutely observed, the tragedy being that life, so brilliantly paid homage to earlier, has been rendered colorless, leaving the poet with nothing in return except, once again, a poem. While Larkin permits himself a note of fragile, dawn-thin hope as reward for making it through another night, Gunn's assessment of our predicament is more grim. Surviving another's passing, he seems to say, only brings into question exactly *what* it is one has survived. Death, once truly encountered, is never truly left behind.

I come home and make dinner for my family. During the evening, I jot down notes of possible topics to bring up with my uncle when I see him next, so the conversation will not lag and the silences yawn. I think how unbridgeable the gap is between any two people, particularly people who care for each other. I read these and other poems obsessively, compulsively. Perhaps what they offer is proof that attempting to bridge the gap, to try and communicate, however doomed to failure such an attempt may ultimately be, is important, is paramount, if we are to remain emotionally alive. Perhaps. For whatever reason, they provide comfort, when nothing else does. Then I go to bed.

—THOMAS RAYFIEL
WINTER 2012

~

I owe the discovery of László Földenyi to Cees Nooteboom, who, in one of his epistolary assaults, insisted that I should read him and sent me a Spanish translation of one of his essays, *Dostoyevsky reads Hegel in Siberia and bursts into tears*. Among the many paths that lead us to read a book (all of which have something mysterious about them) is that of the title. We may not be immediately attracted to a book called *The Divine Comedy* or *Les contemplations*, but only a soul of stone can resist *Dostoyevsky reads Hegel in Siberia and bursts into tears*. I read it immediately, in one sitting, and then again, and then once again, for luck. The contents amply justified the magnificent title. My ignorance of Hungarian is word-perfect: my reading was therefore limited to only a few of Földenyi's works in Spanish and German, and yet it was enough to judge him, in my view, a brilliant, original, clear-cut thinker whose illuminations I gladly followed through philosophical, historical, and aesthetic considerations. His books on melancholia, art, and criticism are masterworks.

Long ago, Copernicus's discoveries shifted the self-centered vision of our world to a corner that has since constantly shifted further and further towards the margins of the universe. The realization that we human beings are aleatory, minimal, a casual convenience for self-reproducing molecules is not conducive to high hopes or great ambitions. And yet, what Nicolà Chiaromonte called "the worm of consciousness" is also part of our being, so that, however ephemeral and distant, we, these particles of stardust, are also a mirror in which all things, ourselves included, are reflected. This modest glory should suffice us. Our passing (and, on a tiny scale, the passing of the universe with us) is ours to record: a patient and bootless effort begun when we first started to read the world. What we call history is that ongoing story which we pretend to decipher as we make it up. This Dostoyevsky fully understood when he said that, if our belief in immortality were destroyed, "everything would be permissible." Like history, immortality need not be true for us to believe in it.

From the beginning, history is the story told by its witness, true or false. In the Book VIII of the *Odyssey*, Odysseus praises the bard who sings the misfortunes of the Greek "as if he had been there or heard it from the lips of another." The "as if" is of the essence. History then is the story of what *we say* has happened, even though the justifications we give for our testimony cannot, however hard we try, be justified. Centuries later, in a dusty German classroom, Hegel would divide this "invention of what took place" into three categories: first, history written by its assumed direct witnesses (*ursprüngliche Geschichte*); second, history as a meditation upon itself (*reflektierende Geschichte*); third, history as philosophy (*philosophische Geschichte*), which eventually results in what we agree to call world history (*Welt-Geschichte*), the never-ending story that includes itself in the telling. Immanuel Kant had earlier imagined two different concepts of our collective evolution: *Historie* to define the mere recounting of facts and *Geschichte*, a reasoning of those facts—even *a priori Geschichte*, the chronicle of an announced course of events to come. For Hegel, what mattered was the understanding (or the illusion of understanding) of the entire flow of events as a whole, including the river bed and its coastal observers, and in order to better concentrate on the main, from this torrent he excluded the margins, the lateral pools and the estuaries.

Földenyi imaginatively suggests that this is the horror Dostoyevsky discovers: that history, whose victim he knows he is, ignores his existence, that his suffering goes on unnoticed or, worse, serves no purpose in the general flow of humankind. What Hegel proposes, in Dostoyevsky's eyes (and in Földenyi's), is what Kafka would later say to Max Brod: "There is hope, but not for us." Hegel's *caveat* is even more terrible than the illusory existence proposed by the idealists: we are perceived but we are not seen.

Such an assumption is, for Földenyi (as it must have seemed to Dostoyevsky), inadmissible. It's not just that history cannot dismiss anyone from its course; the reverse is also true—the acknowledgement of everyone is necessary for history to be. My existence, any man's existence, is contingent on your being, on any other man's being, and both of us must exist for Hegel, Dostoyevsky, Földenyi to exist, since we (the anonymous others) are their proof and their ballast, bringing them to life in our reading. This is what is meant by the ancient intuition that we are all part of an ineffable whole in which every singular death and every particular suffering affects the entire human collective, a whole that is not limited by each material self. The worm of consciousness mines but also proves our existence; it is no use denying it, even as an act of faith. "The myth that denies itself," says Földenyi wisely, "the faith that pretends to know: this is the grey hell, this is the universal schizophrenia with which Dostoyevsky stumbled on his way."

Our imagination allows us always one hope more, beyond the one shattered or fulfilled, one as yet seemingly unattainable frontier that we'll eventually reach only to propose another lying further away. To forget this limitlessness (as Hegel tried to do by trimming down his notion of what counts as history) may grant us the pretty illusion that what takes place in the world and in our life is fully understandable. But this reduces the questioning of the universe to catechism and that of our existence to dogma. As Földenyi argues, what we want is not the consolation of that which seems reasonable and probable, but the unexplored Siberian regions of the impossible.

—ALBERTO MANGUEL
SPRING 2012

~

Toward the end of last summer, less than a week after Hurricane Irene thrashed her way through the New York City area, 217 little stars were born, one by one, in the Hudson River. Well, not exactly *in* the river—on top of river-sloshed pilings, which used to constitute a pier: Pier 49, to be exact. A litter of brand-new stars, one to a piling, twinkling now white now royal blue, now as individuals and now as clusters, now lighting up by happenstance and now blazing in geometrical patterns. You don't see that every day. In fact, in New York City, thanks to the ambient light that is shed 24/7 from manmade sources and a bit of air pollution, you rarely see stars of the astronomical persuasion day or night, in the water or even in the sky.

And that is precisely the point, as I learned from the father of these stars, Jon Morris, Creative Director of The Windmill Factory, an organization based in Williamsburg, Brooklyn, whose motto is "Manufacturing the Sublime" and which, according to its website, "partners with responsible corporations, not-for-profits, [and] arts organizations to creatively address social or environmental causes." In this case, the cause is that the night sky in New York is disappearing. The *real*, the *original* night sky, that is—disappearing as a focus of perception and of meditation on mankind's pitifully small place in the universe. The mission of Morris and his team of engineers, designers, and volunteers was for this art installation on the pilings of Pier 49, called *Reflecting the Stars*, to do more than lead the casual viewer to ponder the beauty of the work and the harbor. It was their fervent hope that those of us who studied it would be led to think hard about the way the city squanders its artificial light—think sufficiently hard to turn off all but the most necessary lights at home, request that office buildings put their lights on timers, and lobby our legislators for stricter zoning of the way our city is illuminated.

The fact that Morris's constellations were, one might say, upside-down through their placement in the Hudson is in keeping with New York's paradoxes. Outside of *Reflecting the Stars*, the most spectacular astronomical constellations in the city can be found on the ceiling of the main concourse in Grand Central Terminal, where the symbolic images of the constellations (Orion, etc.), painted in gold outlines on a green firmament, are punctuated by "stars" embodied by LED lights peeking through the green. A number of Grand Central travelers who have paused to look up over the decades have noticed that the sky on the ceiling is reversed from the way Nature has it, and that the winking stars are somewhat out of place. According to Wikipedia, two explanations have been offered for these discrepancies: the first is that the ceiling represents the night sky as God, looking down on the stars from somewhere even higher, would see it; the second is that the ceiling's designers made a few mistakes. So, to put constellations in the Hudson rather than somewhere overhead is as New York, one might say, as the beloved egg cream, which contains neither eggs nor cream.

The night I spent time with Morris's outdoor wonder, the weather was idyllic: a temperature of seventy-five degrees, soothing breezes from the water, and the new moon hanging in the west while holding the old moon in its arms. The sunset, a sailor's delight of pink and blue with a long horizontal streak of crimson, could have been signed by Monet. Sailboats skidded here and there; a dinner-cruise ship, flaunting a gaudy string of brilliant lights across its ample deck, sliced through the water. On the Hudson's far shore, Hoboken's historic and exquisite Erie Lackawanna Terminal (the stained-glass skylight in the waiting room was constructed by Tiffany) announced itself in fiery neon as "Eri Lackawanna," having sacrificed its final "e," perhaps, to the cause of environmentalism; and other spectacular lighting seductively competed for attention with the LED twinklings turning on, one by one, as the sun finally checked out. Even so, after about ten minutes, the surrounding eye-candy began to seem a little vulgar in comparison with the more austere and understated yet delightfully unpredictable chance-operated choreography of Morris's installation, each of whose luminaries contained a teeny burst of solar power, connected in a way I don't pretend to understand to some kind of computer that randomly turned them on and off. A kind of accompaniment, as inaudible to human ears as the ancient Music of the Spheres, was provided by sound waves initiated for the purpose of protecting the fisheries that are sited at the bottom of each pier post from the ill effects of solar LEDs. I don't understand how this was achieved, either. But, then, I didn't understand much of the electronic music that John Cage and his composer-colleagues provided for the dances of Merce Cunningham, and it didn't prevent me from appreciating most of Cunningham's art—even, on occasion, the art of the musicians.

Cage and Cunningham ineluctably came to mind in the hour I spent with *Reflecting the Stars*, owing to the chance operations of the light movements, to the sound that quixotically was silent, to the hymn to the natural world the installation is intended to be, and to the coincidence that Pier 49 is almost directly across the West Side Highway from Westbeth, the building where the Cunningham company, foundation, and school were housed for many decades. In June of 2009, a month before Cunningham died, he announced to the *The New York Times* that, following one last world tour, his company would close up shop forever following its last performance at the Park Avenue Armory on the last night of 2011. Dance companies fold all the time, of course—usually for financial reasons. What I don't believe we've ever seen before, though, is a company that gracefully rolls to a full stop after a long, planned farewell.

Reflecting the Stars had a more nebulous ending date, but it was no less final than the ending of the Cunningham company. Each of the LED lights was encased in a steel pipe cap, which was designed to rust within days of its installation. The rusting is part of the art work: it is intended to be understood as an analogue for (as the website for The Windmill Factory puts it) "the natural decay of the once-bustling transportation pier." Once the caps rusted so much that the lights were compromised to the point of invisibility (which happened sometime in the late fall), volunteers went out into the Hudson and collected the 217 LEDs. Could anything more closely approach a realization of John Cage's faith in spontaneous coincidence or the floating worlds of Merce Cunningham's pristine dances?

After I wrote the preceding paragraph, I stepped outside my house and looked up at the sky, where I saw a star. I stared at it for a full five minutes to be sure it wasn't a plane; it stayed steady. And the air was so clear that its apparition didn't even twinkle and darkle. It was a real star, a drop of radiance pouring from a point in time and space I can't begin to imagine. However, the hour was so late and I am so untutored in the heavens that I don't know if it was the evening or the morning star, or if the ball of energy that originated the light itself still exists. Only that the light endures.

—MINDY ALOFF
SPRING 2012

~

Most people who learn capoeira—an Afro-Brazilian martial art form—don't begin by studying Portuguese, but that's what brought me to it. One morning, as my Portuguese instructor spoke about capoeira, I remembered passing by the Capoeira Arts Café in downtown Berkeley in 2007. One of the world's renowned capoeira masters, Mestre Acordeon, founded the academy; he was the student of Mestre Bimba, the legendary master who opened the first legal school of capoeira in Brazil and helped establish the art as the global phenomenon it is today. Back then, I thought to myself, "I'd love to try that, but I don't have time right now."

But as my Portuguese class progressed, and I got beyond the past tense and started the subjunctive mood, I decided to stop attending the academic course and put my energy into learning capoeira instead. I figured I'd be sure to hear Brazilian Portuguese spoken on a regular basis, plus I'd get to try the martial art I had thought about doing "one day." It's been less than a year since my journey began, and capoeira has already taught me intense physical and rhythmic lessons.

Running and cycling, my main athletic activities for the last ten years, are focused on forward movement and are fairly individual. In the end, it's you versus the road. When I trained as a cyclist, I usually went out in the blistering cold at six AM and rode with my friend Corinne for twenty-eight miles around the Berkeley hills, sneaking these training rides in before our graduate seminars would start. During most of our rides, I deferred to her experience and let her lead, which meant that I spent most of our rides looking at her back. In cycling, the eyes need to be focused forward, and preferably on the road.

Capoeira is anything but forward, and an entire social ecosystem prevents one from training in isolation. The group dynamic of the ritual combat forces players to confront each other while being observed by a surrounding circle of musicians and other players. This circle, called a roda (which means "wheel" in Portuguese), is where the game actually happens. Whereas the cyclical motion in cycling is confined to the wheels propelling riders in the same direction, in capoeira the cyclical motions begin with the circulation of the players facing each other around the roda. The two players engaged in a game also rotate around each other, with their blend of fighting and rhythmic dance moves, and around themselves, as they wind up to throw circular kicks or escape them. In capoeira, you hardly ever see your opponent's back—and if so, only for the briefest of seconds, while he spins to kick you, or to escape your kick coming his way.

After being so used to the linearity of cycling, I found that capoeira challenged my sense of direction and my ability to know where my body is in space. One of the more outstanding moments in my early training happened when we were practicing how to do a move called the macaco, which means monkey. The idea is to crouch on the floor like a ball, place one hand behind the body, and swing the other hand diagonally across, up, and over the head. The feet should follow together above the head as the body flips, much in the manner of a chimpanzee—hence the name of the move. I'd never tried anything like this before, and my legs flailed all over the place, not going anywhere close to where they should be going. A fellow with more experience came up to me and told me to "jump with both feet" as I swung my arm up and over. Those simple words clicked, and the next time I swung my arm, both my feet lifted off the ground and headed, together, in the right direction. I felt elated.

However, the biggest challenge so far hasn't been physical, but musical. At one informal barbeque I attended with some members of the academy, the group sat around playing traditional capoeira songs. Someone handed me a tambourine-like drum, and I discovered something unexpected about myself: my fear of playing a consistent beat. The roda depends on the music, and a skipped or erratic drumbeat may cause a significant shift in the energy of the game. While playing the drum, I suddenly perceived—with both my body and my mind at once—how my physical performance would improve once I confronted this fear. The music and songs are an essential part of the art form, and in order to progress and earn higher belts, one must master playing and singing the songs as well as the physical movements. Hence Mestre Acordeon's famous summation of capoeira as "a dance like a fight, a fight like a dance, a song . . . a way of life."

Just as all the new Portuguese words I've been learning have transformed my sonic perceptions of the world around me, capoeira has begun to transform my physical perceptions. I find myself moving through the world attempting to make my trajectories from point A to point B more rhythmic, dynamic, and graceful. And this is true even when I'm all alone.

—JENNIFER ZAHRT
SUMMER 2012

~

My buddy David Ruenzel and I, driving along on a trip that took us through California's Central Valley, were crowing about Hemingway (his penniless characters were always supping and drinking proper stuff—how did they manage it?) when, in the agricultural fields ten miles east of Mendota, my car lurched to the right. My hands instinctively gripped the steering wheel. At first, I thought my tires had slid on tomatoes fallen off a truck, but the glowing gauge on my instrument panel showed a tire.

Punctured tire in the boondocks. I slowed the car with light pressure to the brakes. As I pulled to the shoulder, gravel ticked against the fenders. In the field to the right idled a large tractor with metal wings on both sides, wings that were conveyor belts rolling cantaloupes into a bin. Workers grabbed, boxed, and stacked the cantaloupes—a swift process. I had seen the machine many times. It's efficient, like a great monster walking toward you, the inescapable thing in your nightmares.

The August dust was rolling over the car when David and I got out. Right away, I understood the back right tire was the culprit. Bending down, I frisked the tire and located a nail. I stood up, mildly upset that our trip was altered by this roadside emergency. I looked at the monster machine and its crew of ten at lunch. They huddled in the shade of the great umbrella over the driver's seat and sat against the tires that were as tall as they.

We were a novelty. The workers stared at us, their lunchtime entertainment. Then a very boyish boy got up. He hurried over, his hand to his straw hat when the wind of his hustle nearly knocked it off. He turned and, in Spanish, shouted to his *jefe* that he was going to help us. He continued high stepping over the cantaloupes, like a football workout.

"Where is it?" he asked as he approached the trunk. He was breathless. His chest was heaving. By "it" he meant the spare.

I was glad for the eagerness of this young man. He was like me when I was nineteen, thin as shadow. He pulled back the carpet in the trunk and brought out the tire, small as a Cheerio compared to the others. He located the jack, tire iron, and lug wrench. Soon the car's right side was rising with each *click-click* of the jack.

David and I, neither of us handy, just watched the youth, now wrenching off the lug nuts, with a grimace from the strain. We assessed our limitations. We can't change an electrical outlet or a fan belt, lay bricks, or clear a drain without awful chemicals. (I have, however, climbed my roof and poked an untwisted clothes hanger into the downspouts.)

We joke that our one ability is that we can *taste*. We can taste enchiladas, lasagna, and chicken grilled Spanish-style with legs in the air and sizzling immodestly on a spit. We can judge fruit—two bites of an organic Fuji apple and we'll have something to say. We can assess salsa and might even chime in with a thought or two about the texture of meatloaf. We taste drink—"That beer is like, really cold and good. I'll have another."

Actually, I'm untruthful when I say I'm not handy. Tires I can do. Once I worked in a tire factory, at a machine where I buffed the white walls white again.

That warm August afternoon, dressed in a clean linen outfit, I could have struggled with this emergency, but the wonderful young man had come to my rescue. We left him to his work, David now talking about Steinbeck, whose characters were often as poor as Hemingway's characters but seldom ate or drank. What was this about Hemingway's oral fixation?

Tired of literary talk, I hovered over the young man, still on his knees. I learned that he came from a large family—six boys—and that he had just graduated from Mendota High School. I told him I was a poet and he said, lowering the jack, "Oh, I know who you are. You're Gary Soto."

David and I looked at each other.

The young man said that he had heard me at a school assembly. He recalled the story of my first girlfriend, Lupita, and my bicycle date with her, how I didn't have enough leg strength to propel the bike so we had to change places. I got on the crossbar and Lupita, a soccer player with muscled calves, pedaled me. The bike did wheelies from the strength of her pedaling. I was amazed that he remembered my little jokes.

When he finished the job, I gave him forty dollars. We shook hands, an oily grime pressing onto my palm, grime that might suggest that I had changed the tire. I waved to the *jefe*, who had allowed the young man to help us, even though lunch was over and the workers were moving at a quick pace alongside the great monster tractor. Black plumes coughed from a tall exhaust pipe. The Mexican flag waved in the wind.

From Mendota to Fresno, David and I talked about Steinbeck, novelist of farm workers, specters we see from the road. Up close, we see people better.

—Gary Soto

SUMMER 2012

~

So I have been making a list of words. If I give you a few can you figure out the governing principle? Here's three: Rhythm, Zone, Police. No? Cemetery, Story, Planet. Okay. It's "Greek words in English."

How much are these worth? Are they worth the three hundred and fifty billion euros that is Greece's debt? That is one argument made today in IMF-land by some nationalists who shout: "We gave Europe their language! They owe us!"

Quotes from unknown poets, inspired by the 1821 War of Liberation against the Turks, are back in popularity. Key phrases are yellowed in and circulated over the blogosphere—old soldier to a wealthy man: "My blood gave you your crown . . ."

In fact, of that massive debt, doubtless an onerous burden (all Latin in that phrase, since the Romans one-upped the Greeks for terms used in finance), a hundred billion is actually financial borrowings of Greeks from Greeks—think pension funds that bought Greek bonds (now worth nearly zilch, a very non-Greek word). So let's reduce that burden of debt a wee bit, since it is not owed to the foreigners but to the Greeks themselves. This Greek-to-Greek debt surely cancels out the linguistic borrowing element.

Tally now stands reduced.

Is there a word-for-word price? What about Greek origin words that are extremely common in English, like "butter" or "zoo"? Does price vary according to frequency of use?

There are words and there are words.

Some have a deeper importance and provide greater meaning to us all, words like philosophy and plot and theater. Can you imagine Marx without the dialectic? Literary critics without synchronicity and antithesis? The medical profession without pediatricians and podiatrists, endocrinologists and gynecologists? Shrinks without therapy?

Is there a money-back guarantee if the word doesn't work for us? What if it gets us into trouble? I recall a very long discussion about philanthropy with my friend Henry Roncali when I was fifteen that lasted for weeks and ended up with my giving away twenty dollars to a homeless man on Yonge Street. Do I get a refund? I recall being accused of being an egoist by a girlfriend—the beginning of the end. My written reply was rather Latinate, however. "You are not at all magnanimous, you are officious . . ."

What about extremely rare words like hypogynous or apotheosis? A zero price? Who keeps the lexic meter running? Who are the protagonists in this endeavor?

But hold on there. Do English speakers not owe the Italians some sort of linguistic fee? Do we not owe the Germans for the achtungs and verbotens in all those Captain America comic books? And what would we really do without Yiddish, you putz? Mugwump and moose, papoose and moccasin? And the Irish, also buckling under the hard boot of the IMF—with their brogues and their leprechauns . . .

The Nordics, relatively debt-free, have a say in the debt buyback scheme as well. I would say Wednesday is worth much to me. Squat in the middle of the week, it's when I have time to think, pause, and write. I think we owe the Vikings about twenty-five billion for that. Although Thursday is a close second, come to think of it, predisposing me to the upcoming weekend as it does.

And the French did their part in bolstering up the English language. They gave us petty and pettiness, art nouveau and la vie française and joie de vivre and vin blanc and le jogging, though I think Italian Prime Minister Monti should tax the French every time they try to monopolize the dictionary of love. (Oh, but the Ancients, they pretty much own the House of Eros, no?)

One psycho-linguistic explanation that I was given to explain Merkel's stance towards Greece runs as follows: in German the word "debt" (Schuld) also means "guilt." Thus, indebted Greeks are automatically guilty Greeks.

I could go on. So could you. At the end of the day I think we would all find that the debt of one language to another is pretty much squared away.

Or maybe not.

Maybe when all is said and done, and the linguistic DNA deciphered, the West still owes Greece about fifty billion for use of its language.

But can't this be balanced out by going the other way around? Do not the Greeks owe a drachma or two for use of their words?

Take ouzo, Henry Miller's drink of choice. One urban myth (Latin and Greek in that term) claims it derives from an accident: the grappa-like liquid mixed with anise was sent regularly abroad. On the crates were written the words: *Per l'uso di . . .* For the use of . . . .

There is also another list: Greek words invented by non-Greeks in English. I don't know how to price that one. Example: Utopia (for No-Place) was in fact invented by Thomas More, a man well-steeped in the classics. Do the Greeks now owe the Right Honorable Lord Chancellor's descendants some serious payback?

Another such oddity is the word *Disaster*—a bad alignment of the stars—from "dis" (negation) and "aster" (star). This word exists in neither ancient nor modern Greek, though it is solidly Greek.

"Don't dis me" might be worth quite a lot, if the meter runs on degrees of cool. Don't dis me is what the Greeks are saying right now. Because when it comes down to it, even more than getting rid of that despicable debt, even more than claiming that the world cannot abandon the place where it all began (albeit before any of us were alive), today's Athenians want back one thing: respect.

We are all, American-Greek mongrels like me and pure-bloods of Turkish-Vlach-Ancient origin, grasping for straws, right now, to create the new narrative. Will it be "indebted country wags its hand at the rascally foreigners and absconds"? Will it be "indebted country works hard, shoulders its past and stands tall"?

I prefer the latter. My one-line narrative goes like this: first comes the epic heroism, then the democratic dialogue, and finally we arrive where we must—therapeutic catharsis.

—Nick Papandreou

FALL 2012

~

My grandmother opens the door for me, taking tentative steps in her embroidered Chinese slippers.

"My Don Quixote," she says, her voice already quivering, "he's lost an arm."

"When did he last have it?"

"Before the move." My grandmother has moved many times, but when she refers to "the move," she means her emigration from Odessa to Toronto, over twenty years ago.

A cast iron statuette of the great knight of Spanish literature used to populate all Soviet apartments, where he stood in the company of a diminutive, crawling, four-legged devil, made of the same material. When I ask why Don Quixote, my grandmother gives me the look that says I haven't lived long enough to understand the things that really matter in life. "Your aunt Rena has a fake metal Don Quixote," she tells me, "but I bought the real thing—from the cast iron factory in Kasli—when I went to the Urals on a business trip."

When I meet her, my grandmother is an old woman who wears prickly wool sweaters over dresses made of rough silk, which she calls *crepe de chine*. Her past as a respected mechanical engineer lies dormant under layers of Soviet fabrics, but occasionally she lets memories trickle out: a young cab driver in Yerevan who offered her a *night of passion*; a tour of Tbilisi; a business trip to Krasnoyarsk, where she stood on the banks of the Yenisei river, shivering and unprepared for Siberian spring, and survived two weeks on a diet of bread, jam, and canned sprats in tomato sauce.

Apart from her piano, my grandmother managed to import the staples of her Soviet apartment to Canada. She transferred the embroidered lace from the upright piano to her armoire, where it forms a base for a collection of plastic white elephants displayed in order from smallest to largest. Don Quixote stands with a sword—tucked under his right arm—resting on his foot; he is nose deep in a book he grips with the only arm he has left. He and the devil adorn her nine-volume Pushkin set, just as they had in Odessa. Only now Pushkin resides next to Nabokov—the *pedophile* writer, as she calls him—an unthinkable combination in her former life.

We sift through the objects of her past, and I begin to feel like Don Quixote running around Spain tilting at windmills, mistaking them for real giants. I find a box with Russian jewels tucked away in an underwear drawer: garnet pendants, earrings made of red gold with clasps in the back, a few lacquered brooches, one with Princess Vasilissa and the other with an orange and pink floral bouquet on a black background.

"What are you saving these for?"

"For you and your sister." We already have three pairs of Bulgarian sandals, Yugoslavian tan-colored wool dresses, crocheted sweaters, turquoise Soviet wool underwear that goes down to your knees, a one-piece bathing suit made of terrycloth with breast cups so hard they feel like yoghurt containers, navy blue frilly polyester slips, and now, more brooches and earrings.

I take a break from the quest and sit with my back resting against a dusty Uzbek rug that hangs just above her bed.

"Did this carpet hang in your Odessa apartment?"

"No. We never put it up. Your grandfather kept it rolled up in the corner of our living room. We were saving it." They bought the carpet two years after my parents and I emigrated; in 1978, my grandparents refused to follow us to Canada, convinced that we were headed for capitalist decadence, wouldn't have money for food and clothes, and would be longing for Soviet Russia. A year later, they changed their mind, but the borders to the West had already closed. They lost their jobs, applied for visas to Canada, packed their apartment into boxes, and waited. It turned into an eight-year-long move, the end of which my grandfather never lived to see. For the last years of his life, my grandfather stared at a rolled-up carpet.

In the end, we find Don Quixote's arm in a miniature Sicilian ceramic pitcher I had brought back from one of my trips to Europe. There it is, wrapped in a starched handkerchief. The legendary knight's arm could have easily been mistaken for a metal toothpick.

"Should I glue it back on?"

"And it would change what?" My grandmother runs her chipped nails through the lines of her bedspread, examining the remains of her own life, and wraps the appendage back in the handkerchief.

—JULIA ZARANKIN
WINTER 2013

~

I like the way Rousseau declares in the first sentence of his autobiography that he is about to do something that has never been done before and that will never be done again.

The problem with any first sentence, says Joan Didion, is that you're stuck with it. Everything else is going to flow out of that sentence. And by the time you've laid down the first *two* sentences, your options are all gone.

Before beginning, too many options. Then, in the next breath, none.

When you can't sleep, goes an old cure for insomnia, start telling yourself the story of your life. For some reason, writer's block has always felt to me like a kind of insomnia.

I like that Norman Mailer said there's a touch of writer's block in a writer's work every day.

I don't remember who said, Insomnia is the inability to forget.

When you're having trouble writing, get up, go out, take a walk in the street. You will discover that certain streets exist precisely for this purpose. Once, I saw a man—homeless by the look of him—digging through the trash. He pulled out a couple of sheets of newspaper, examined them, and threw them back. Fishing deeper, he hauled up a magazine, squinted at the cover, and threw it back. Shit, he said, walking away. There ain't nothing to read in these fucking cans anymore.

Rousseau goes on to say that he has embellished the story of his life only to fill a void when his memory failed. But, of course, he never gives you the head's up.

Never write I don't remember, Editor says; it undermines your authority.

But write as if you remember everything and Reader will smell a rat.

I like the student in my graduate fiction writing class who said, I've read your novels and there's one thing I have to ask: Do you make some of that stuff up?

I like that Allen Ginsberg told a teenager who wanted to know what he should write about that he should write about his love for his friends.

I once made the mistake of writing about a love too soon after it was over. Forgetting Chekhov's advice that you should sit down to write only when you feel as cold as ice.

How can a man who knows nothing about love be a great novelist? a character in a novel by J. M. Coetzee says about a character named J. M. Coetzee.

I like that Virginia Woolf said, Everything I read these days, including my own work, seems to me too long.

That Borges said, Unlike the novel, a short story may be, for all purposes, essential.

But not that Jeanette Winterson said, I think long books are rude.

Not that Céline said, Novels are something like lace, an art that went out with the convent.

More and more, I like the idea of a pen name.

Sugared Nouns was the computer's suggestion after spell-checking my name.

Some writers use pen names so that they can be more truthful; others, so that they can tell more lies.

I like how Lily Tomlin used to introduce one part of her act: The following skit is about my parents. I have changed their names to protect their identities.

I like the sliver of ice in the heart that Graham Greene thought every writer must have. I have it.

And the grain of stupidity Flannery O'Connor said the writer of fiction can't do without. I have that too.

I like that Alan Bennett said, For a writer, nothing is ever quite as bad as it is for other people, because, however dreadful, it may be of use.

Oncologist says, That doesn't sound like any writer I know.

I like John Banville's paraphrase of Bennett: Writers don't suffer as much as other people.

There is always a sheet of paper. There is always a pen. There is always a way out, wrote H. L. Mencken. Who nevertheless hoped that his life would not last too long.

Write . . . paper . . . pencil are said to have been the last words of the poet Heine.

I like that, at the end of his life, Darwin said he wished that he had read more poetry.

That Keynes said he wished that he had drunk more champagne.

That Chekhov said, It's a long time since I drank champagne, then drained his glass and died.

I like last words. Beethoven: I shall hear in Heaven. Käthe Kollwitz: Good luck, everyone.

And nutty epitaphs: I know not everyone is unhappy about this.

I wanted to write a comic novel, then realized I had my own life to hand.

Once you start on the road to autobiography, fretted Calvino, where do you stop?

I can tell the story of my life in just four words. Good times, bad times.

There will always be lacemakers. There will always be convents.

But about you, my love, I will never feel as cold as ice.

—Sigrid Nunez
SPRING 2013

~

I composed my first poems in the dark. In fact in the "double dark"—that is, at night in a small woods that only the moon lit, and also totally without the guidance or knowledge or light, if you will, that great or good or even mediocre poetry might have given me. In truth I never thought of these early compositions as poems; I never thought of them as anything but what they were: secret little speeches addressed to the moon when the moon was visible, and when the moon was not visible, to all those parts of creation that crowded around and above me as well as those parts that eluded me, the parts I had no name for, no notion of except for the fact they were listening.

I was fourteen years old and living for the first time on the outskirts of my city, Detroit, in an almost completely undeveloped area that still contained the trees and untended undergrowth a boy could transform in his imagination to an untamed wilderness. If you stood in the crotch of a copper beech and inhaled the thick atmosphere after rain or just before rain and closed your eyes, you might come to believe you were in that fabled garden we were given and later lost, and you might want to speak to all the wonders that are our human inheritance; you might even want to say thanks for being a creation in a world of other creations. You might want no longer to be alone and misunderstood, and for that you needed poetry.

Sadly enough I did not have poetry, although it was on hand. Had I gone to the bookshelf in our tiny study at home, I could have taken down a volume of Robert Service and read in galloping, rhymed lines how a plucky boy no older than I had killed his Prussian tormenter, a sadistic major; or I could have turned to my mother's favorite poet, Francis Thompson, whose "The Hound of Heaven" she would declaim on nights the phone didn't ring or she had no gentlemen callers. How she loved those lines:

> I fled Him, down the nights and down the days;
> I fled Him, down the arches of the years;
> I fled Him, down the labyrinthine ways
> Of my own mind, and in the midst of tears
> I hid from Him, and under running laughter.

The flight goes on—"Adown Titanic glooms of chasmèd fears"—for a couple hundred more lines and ends in an embrace. I'd been hearing the poem since I was seven or eight and it wasn't getting better. Boys that age are tough critics and savage when it comes to the taste of their parents. If that was poetry I didn't need it.

What were my models for my dark-time psalms? Let me describe my compositions: they were Whitmanian without the benefit of Whitman. That good, gray, gay poet was not taught in the Detroit public schools, at least not in those I attended. And no living poet was taught, not even the Poet Laureate of Michigan; I refer to our newspaper poet Edgar A. Guest who gave us the immortal, oft-quoted "It takes a heap o' livin' in a house t' make it home." (Somehow "The People's Poet," as he was then called, never made the snooty anthologies, though his work still appears in the *Reader's Digest.*) Who was taught in my schools? We memorized a sixty-line passage from the prologue to the *Canterbury Tales* and also stunning passages from *Macbeth*, but you had to have the genius of John Keats to accept such giants as an influence, and even at fourteen I knew I was not a genius.

Let me be clear. I had no idea that I was writing poetry—and of course I wasn't, so let me put it another way: I had no notion that I was trying to write poetry. I began this solitary in-the-dark process, which would last some years, without its ever occurring to me that I was attempting poetry. I simply had no name for what I was doing, but even without a category to place these experiments in I found them incredibly satisfying. At the time I knew exactly why they thrilled me. I had discovered a voice within the self I'd had no idea had been there, a voice that could speak of all the things I would never have dared share with anyone, a voice that tried to consider the value of being alive, the sense of what it was to be alive, not so much as Philip Levine or any other Levine or any other Philip, just to be alive. Everything I composed was joyous, as though there were not a skeptical thought in my mind. Yet in my daily dealings with the world I was a teenager, a skeptical and at times even cynical teenager, just as most of you were all those years ago. I did not then know that the work ahead—the writing of poetry—would take years, that what I had begun almost by chance in the crotch of a copper beech would become the work of my lifetime, what I would labor to perfect for seventy years and always fail to reach a perfection. Nor did I know that in order to bring that work to any satisfactory level I would need help from sources I did not know existed.

—PHILIP LEVINE
SUMMER 2013

~

In Arezzo, where you go to see frescos by Piero della Francesca, there hangs a large, startling, magnificent crucifixion painted on wood by somebody unknown. The effect is disturbing. You expect to see a great name, and you're confronted by this crucifixion, impertinently and outrageously beautiful, by nobody. Mr Anonymuzzioso. The frescos are only a few feet away, but the crucifixion holds you.

I'm glad I saw it. I've come to love Anonymuzzioso and his innumerable works; it is appropriate that his magnificent crucifixion hangs in the shadowy and somber vault of a church and not in a museum. It would be no less magnificent in a museum, but the atmosphere of mystery would be lacking. The light would be too good. There would be irrelevant noises, no secure feeling of privacy, and there could never be the right sort of silence. For that you need stone, high massive stone walls.

Anonymuzzioso always surprises me with the same strange sensation. I am reluctant to describe this strange sensation because it might seem like an idea, and it has nothing to do with an idea. It is more like a reminder of something known but forgotten or repressed. Something congenital, original, and useless. Apparently there is a vestigial organ that once served a purpose in the evolution of the species, but no longer does anything necessary to survival.

Maybe I was born with a susceptibility to useless sensations; not only useless but so impractical as to cause anxiety, make me feel weak, unmanly, like susceptibility to love, or a drug, or what you feel when reading a book that you want never to end, which is to say, anxious and incoherent happiness. You know, after all, that it will end, so it's luxurious anxiety, a wallowing in the spirit.

I want to be plain.

In the church in Arezzo, the large and startling crucifixion gave me the sensation of great art unfiltered through a great name, and it overwhelmed me with a simple conviction—there is great art. To put it differently: there is a thing that is greater than me. In an extremely narcissistic era, it isn't easy to confess to this sensation. But there you have it. Great art made me happy, albeit anxious. Nothing could be simpler than what I felt in the church in Arezzo. I thought maybe it was too simple, too child-like, a kind of unbecoming innocence. This giddiness, this delicious fear, demands resistance, self-criticism, doubt. I must think, think, think until I understand it, master it, and it is dead. But I couldn't and there was no use trying.

—LEONARD MICHAELS
FALL 1996